WALES
A 2000 PIECE JIG-SAW

Wales
a 2000 piece jig-saw
An A-Z guide of fresh and forgotten facts

Gareth and Paul Shaw

GWASG CARREG GWALCH

ISBN: 0-86381-596-0

Cover design: Smala, Caernarfon

First published in 2000 by
Gwasg Carreg Gwalch, 12 Iard yr Orsaf, Llanrwst, Wales LL26 0EH
☎ 01492 642031   📠 01492 641502
✆ books@carreg-gwalch.co.uk   Website: www.carreg-gwalch.co.uk

The authors welcome additions for use in subsequent editions.
These can be forwarded to Shaw's Holidays, Y Maes, Pwllheli, Gwynedd LL53 5HA.
Faxed to 01758 613835 or sent via email to all@shaws-holidays.co.uk

About the authors:

Gareth Willis Shaw was born in Holyhead in 1938 and attended various North Wales secondary schools including Holyhead Comprehensive, John Bright Grammar School, Llandudno and Ysgol Ramadeg Pwllheli. After graduating with honours in History at Bangor he taught in Liverpool before becoming Head of History at Blaenau Ffestiniog and then Porthmadog. In 1971 he and his wife, Yvonne, started Shaw's Holidays (then and still now one of the largest holiday cottage letting agencies in Wales). Gareth enjoys travel, music, theatre and golf.

Paul Shaw was born in Pwllheli in 1964 and was educated at Ysgol Glan-y-Môr Pwllheli. He studied journalism at Sheffield and worked for the Bailey Newspaper Group in Gloucestershire in the mid 1980s. He is currently manager of Shaw's Holidays letting agency, compiles quiz league questions and spends leisure hours practising at the bar. Paul is married to Mandy and is father of Amelia.

'Wales: A 2000 Piece Jig-Saw' is Gareth and Paul Shaw's first collaborative foray into publishing.

Ä is to Norway what Y is to France. No, this is not the opening of a Mensa-style brain-teaser. Ä and Y are among the shortest place names, whereas Llanfair Pwllgwyngyll on Anglesey, when it is written in its entirety of Llanfairpwllgwyngyllgogerychwyrndrobwllllantysiliogogogoch, has twenty-two vowels and twenty-nine consonants (Welsh alphabet in which *ll* and *ch* are counted as single letters) and is the longest place name in Britain.

A.A. . . . Boduan near Pwllheli in Gwynedd boasts a rare telephone box. Erected by the Automobile Association in 1911 it is now a grade II listed building and is just one of four throughout Wales. It is strangely sited adjacent to Lord Newborough's (of Boduan Hall) main gate as was another one at Glynllifon (outside Dinas Dinlle, Gwynedd). Did this save his Lordship paying extra for *home-start* if servants could push the Bentley to the box and make a free telephone call?

A40 – Trunk road from Shepherds Bush to Atlantic Ocean via South Wales.

A5 – the London to Holyhead road which starts at Marble Arch and ends at the Pelham Gates in the Anglesey port. Much of it was constructed by engineer Thomas Telford who was commissioned by the government to build this 268 mile (430 km) road to cater for the traffic to and from Ireland, which followed the Anglo-Irish Union of 1801. Even in Snowdonia the maximum gradient allowed was only 5% according to his brief.

A55 – the North Wales Expressway which is a dual carriageway between Bangor and England, and incorporates a tunnel under the sea at Conwy.

AB (also Ap) Before the Act of Union of England and Wales in 1536, surnames were unknown in Wales. The Welsh system ran along the following lines. Rhys, son of Gruffudd, was known as Rhys ap Gruffudd. Ab and ap were abbreviated forms of *mab* (son). In turn Rhys ap Gruffudd's son, named Llywelyn, was known as Llywelyn ap Rhys. Anglicisation following the 1536 Act of Union meant that the Welsh had to adopt the English system of fixed family surnames that were passed on to all descendants. Sion ap Rhys became John ap Rhys or John Prys or John Price. Sion ap Henry became John Penry, John Parry or even John Harrison. Not until the late 19th Century's rekindling of Welsh national consciousness was there any marked reversion to the old patronymic system, when Owen M Edwards named his son Ifan ab Owen Edwards. Nowadays family surnames are being axed by some 'thinking' Welshmen, who simply drop the Jones or Evans and give their offspring two forenames – entertainer *Dafydd Iwan dropped the Jones as did his actor brother Huw Ceredig. The equivalents in other countries would be Mc or Mac (Scotland/Ireland) O (as in O' Hare) (Ireland/Scotland) von (Germany/Austria) and van (as in famous singing Cockney chimneysweep Dick van Dyke). However, the Austro-German version is disappearing von by von.

ABBEYS . . . religious houses proliferated in Wales in the Middle Ages. Some are very well-known because of their ruinous beauty or their romantic-sounding names, such as Valle Crucis, Strata Marcella or Tintern. Wishing to justify his mass axing of the religious houses in 1536, Henry Vlll ordered a report on their condition. Some rather predictable 'findings' emerged, as did some of a more alarming nature such as the abbot of Valle Crucis' arrest for highway robbery – not on his own patch but in distant Oxfordshire (see Highwayman). Meanwhile, one of the monks of Strata Florida was found counterfeiting in his monastic cell, and even the monastic 'inspectors' were not all that saintly. One Dr Ellis Price, a flamboyant Cambridge graduate, wore his red doctoral gown (he was known as *y Doctor Coch* (The Red Doctor) to overawe the clergy, and had the audacity to be accompanied by his mistress during his inspections – dirty habits all round.

ABBOT & SON . . . In 1536 the Abbot of Basingwerk Abbey was Nicholas Pennant – son of the previous incumbent whose watchword was 'keep it in the family'.

ABER . . . a common prefix for place names in Wales. The Welsh word means 'mouth of the river' or 'confluence of two rivers'. Examples include Abertawe (Swansea), Abersoch and Abertillery. The name might seem like a misnomer in the case of Aberglaslyn in Gwynedd as it is now around six miles inland, due to a vast drainage and reclamation scheme engineered by William Alexander Madocks in the early 19th Century.

ABERAERON . . . in Dyfed. A 19th Century planned town, the brainchild of Alban and Susannah Thomas who inherited a vast fortune and built the town and harbour.

ABERAFON: The first Labour Prime Minister, Scots-born Ramsay MacDonald died at Aberavon.

ABERCARN: In 1878 at the Prince of Wales Colliery there were no fewer than 268 fatalities as the result of an explosion.

ABERDYFI . . . In Southern Snowdonia this was the birthplace of the Outward Bound Movement in 1941. A Survey of Merionnydd in 1565 refers to Aberdyfi as a haven with only three houses. (*Bells of Aberdyfi)

ABERFAN . . . former coal-mining centre in the valleys of southern Wales. Tragically remembered as the site of a disaster in 1966 when heavy rain caused a coal tip to slide down onto the village, including the primary school, killing 144 people of whom 116 were children.

ABERGAVENNY (Y Fenni) . . . Town in Gwent which has the dubious honour of being one of the sites of imprisonment for Rudolf *Hess after his capture during WW2. (Hess was Adolf Hitler's deputy who is best remembered for his long incarceration at Spandau Prison in Berlin from the end of the war to his death in 1987.).

ABERGELE RAIL DISASTER . . . a tragedy which occurred in August 1868 when a passenger train from Chester bound for Holyhead ploughed into a goods train carrying eight tons of paraffin. Thirty-three people died and the intense heat left only charred remains.

ABERGWESYN PASS . . . in Powys. Parts are still as isolated and lonely as in the days of George Borrow's '. . . wildest solitudes . . . '

ABERGYNOLWYN . . . in Gwynedd is the terminus of the Tal-y-llyn narrow gauge railway and, in 1923, saw the formation of the second branch of the *Urdd movement.

ABERHOSAN . . . a mere dot on the map which can lay claim to more bardic chairs (National and local eisteddfodau) than any other town in Wales – not through some bizarre twist of fate of poetic prowess or even the magical properties of the drinking water. Aberhosan is the place where most bardic chairs are crafted!

ABER IÂ . . . the original name of the mansion acquired by Clough Williams-Ellis in 1925 – later to become Portmeirion.

ABERMENAI FERRY . . . Before the advent of the bridges across the Menai Strait people used ferry boats to cross back and forth to Anglesey. In 1664 the Abermenai Ferry capsized and 79 out of the 80 people on board were killed. *Houdini

ABERTHAW . . . the town provided the special brand of brine-resistant lime used to build the Eddystone lighthouse in 1759.

ABERYSTWYTH 1 . . . a town in mid-Wales on Cardigan Bay. Wales' first university college was opened there in October 1872 – almost by accident. Over-ambitious railway builders hoped to sell package holidays to the Cambrian Coast and it was mooted that rail travellers would stay at resort hotels. Their £80,000 hotel (the name is academic) at Aberystwyth was not quite complete at the time of their bankruptcy and was bought for £10,000. Other colleges followed at Cardiff 1883, Bangor 1884 and Swansea 1920. At Aberystwyth University in 1872 there were a mere twenty six students. In 1998 there were approximately seven and a half thousand.

ABERYSTWYTH 2. This mid-Wales town saw the first use of explosives in Britain in c.1406 when the later Henry IV attacked Aberystwyth castle and used cannon against the supporters of Owain Glyndŵr.

ABERYSTWYTH and Brighton – old tourist guides referred to the town as 'The Brighton of Wales'.

ABERYSTWYTH'S CAMERA OBSCURA – A fully operational throwback to the Victorian era with a 14' (35.6 cm) diameter lens – the largest of its kind in the world. Tourists can find it at the top of Constitution Hill and see how it functions.

ABERYSTWYTH'S NATIONAL LIBRARY OF WALES – Entitled on request to a copy of every single publication printed in the UK – including this book!

ABERYSTWYTH WW1 FUND RAISING – the town's population raised more per capita for the war effort than anywhere else during the Great War of 1914-1918.

ABSE (Dannie) the poet who wrote *Exit* and *The Pathology of Colours* was born in Cardiff.

ABT (Dr) Roman . . . Deserves the credit for the rack and pinion system which enables the Snowdon Mountain Railway to ascend the highest mountain in Wales and England. Dr Abt's improvements on Riggenbach's rack and pinion railway up Mount Rigi in Switzerland (opened 1871) ensured the century and more of success that has been enjoyed by the Snowdon Mountain Railway since 1896.

ABUSE . . . In April 1998 Britain's longest enquiry to date into sexual and physical child abuse ended at Ewloe in northern Wales after 203 days of hearing one hundred and thirty-two witnesses, whose haunting evidence filled 30,000 pages.

ACADEMI GYMREIG, yr. An august institution established in 1959 as an association of Welsh writers (authors writing in the Welsh language). An English language section was added in 1968.

ACCENT . . . a 1990s survey voted the Welsh accent the most trustworthy.

ACES TURN UP TRUMPS . . . Maggie and Jessie Ace, daughters of the Mumbles lighthouse keeper, saved the crew of the wrecked 'Prinz Adalbert' on January 21, 1883.

ACTING DEBUT . . . *The Druid's Rest* was a comedy play written by Emlyn Williams of Fflint, in which Richard Burton made his London acting debut as a nineteen year old.

ACT OF UNION of England & Wales 1536 . . . Volumes, or quite possibly libraries, of learned books have been written on this topic. In a nutshell, Henry VIII wanted to ensure that Wales did not become a centre of resistance to his becoming head of the Church. The Act of Union, in which the Welsh had no say at all, purported to improve Wales' lot. For 'lot', read 'little'. These acts ended any remaining vestiges of independence enjoyed by Wales. Even the Welsh language was savaged, because English was henceforth to be the official tongue. Say no more – in all senses. Any Welsh laws or customs differing from those of England were declared illegal.

ADAM & EVE . . . no, we are not claiming Welsh nationality for the purported first humans. These are the names given to two boulders at the top of Tryfan mountain in the Glyderau range of Snowdonia.

ADEY-JONES (Sian) . . . North Wales-born beauty queen from Bodfari, Denbigh who won Miss United Kingdom in 1976 and came third in the Miss Universe contest. Now apparently living on the Mediterranean island of Ibiza.

ADMIRALTY . . . made an admirable move in 1885 when the entire British fleet (not just two thirds) was ordered to use Welsh coal.

ADMIRALITY SPY . . . John Vassall of the KGB involved in the infamous 1960s spy scandal was born in Monmouth. He died in 1996.

AERIAL FERRY . . . The Aeron Express Aerial Ferry across Aberaeron harbour is a carriage suspended on wire, and worked by a hand-operated pulley. It was originally built in 1885 and was the first passenger-carrying rope-way in the world.

AGINCOURT – on 12 October 1415 in a mere three bloody hours at the battle of Agincourt Henry V's army, with strong and capable sections of Welsh longbow men, slew six thousand French soldiers – fifteen hundred knights and four and a half thousand men-at-arms. Henry's casualties were minimal. The Welsh bowmen were able to fire six arrows per minute, keeping up the traditions of Crecy and Poitiers.

AGRICOLA . . . Famous Roman General who conquered northern Wales and even Anglesey – once he had negotiated the Menai Straits – and annihilated the druids. He was the father-in-law of the Roman historian Tacitus.

AGRICULTURE . . . In 1888 the University College of North Wales at Bangor opened a Department of Agriculture – the first such department at a British university. Its own 'College Farm' at Abergwyngregyn on the northern Wales coast was put up for sale in August 1999.

AIRCRAFT DISASTER . . . Wales' worst was at Llandow, Glamorgan in 1950 when there were seventy-four fatalities. The aircraft was an Avro Tudor V, carrying Welsh supporters home from an international rugby union match in Ireland.

AIRSHIP . . . the first airship to fly across the English channel was called *City of Cardiff* and was flown by Ernest Thompson Willows in 1910.

ALCOHOL . . . the county of Gwynedd has more booze outlets (pubs, clubs, off-licences, restaurants etc) per head of population that anywhere else in Wales and England. Home Office figures for 1999 said there were sixty-three licensed bars and restaurants per ten thousand people, compared to the meagre national average of twenty-three per ten thousand. Whose round is it? Hic! Iechyd da.

ALEXANDER (Ewart) . . . The Ystradgynlais writer has written over 120 tv dramas including episodes of *Juliet Bravo* and *Softly Softly* and the hospital drama *Maybury*.

11

ALIASES . . . Wales own 'Mr Nice', Howard Marks, the renowned former drug smuggler had no fewer that forty-three assumed names. Surely a record?

ALLAN . . . not a boy's name this side of Offa's Dyke; the word means 'way out' or 'exit'.

ALL BLACKS . . . The New Zealand Rugby Union Team of 1905 arrived in Wales on the back of a run of twenty-seven international matches unbeaten. The result of the Cardiff Arms Park match? Wales Three points, All Blacks nil.

ALLCHURCH . . . Ivor Allchurch the 'Golden Boy' of Welsh soccer in the 50s and early 60s. He made a then record sixty-eight appearances for Wales scoring twenty-three goals, along with making nearly seven hundred football league appearances for Newcastle United, Cardiff City and Swansea Town. Allchurch was awarded the MBE in 1966.

ALLEN (Keith) . . . (born 1953) in Llanelli. Actor who excelled in the TV series *Making Out* and, in 1999, *Jack of Hearts*. A fine character actor who first came to prominence in the *Comic Strip* series of the 1980s. Memorably made a brief cameo appearance in the film *Twin Town* which was directed by his brother Kevin. Also enjoyed chart success with the group 'Fat Les' who sang *Vindaloo* at the time of the 1998 soccer world cup.

ALLEN (Kevin) . . . writer and director of the 1990s cult movie *Twin Town*. Llanelli-born brother of actor Keith.

ALL WELSH RULE . . . in 1937 Welsh was declared the official language of the National Eisteddfod. English was still used on the stage, however, until a new constitution was formed in 1951 which insisted on the implementation of The All Welsh Rule.

ALUMINIUM FURNITURE . . . In the immediate post-war years New Period Furniture of Caernarfon made household furniture out of aluminum.

AMAZON . . . Margaret Evans or (Marged Uch Ifan) 1695-*c*.1801 of Penllyn, Cwm-y-Glo, Llanberis in Gwynedd. Of Amazonian reputation, she would probably have been more than a match for most TV 'Gladiators'. Her physical prowess and technical abilities are related by several contemporary visitors to Wales, including Revd W. Bingley and Thomas Pennant. Margaret was a boatbuilder, blacksmith, shoemaker, harp-maker and candle-maker. Her hobbies included rowing, playing the harp and fiddle and, at the age of seventy, she was still the best wrestler in the country, as well as being an excellent hunter, shooter and fisher. Thomas Pennant was informed by neighbours (who, doubtless wished to remain anonymous) that she had married a cissy in order to wear the trousers in her household.

AMEN CORNER . . . The famous 1960s pop group were led by Welshman Andy Fairweather-Low.

AMERICA . . . 16th Century Italian explorer Amerigo Vespucci or 15th century Sheriff of Bristol Richard A' Meryk, the anglicized form of 'ap Meurig' (son of Meurig). After whom was America actually named? The Sheriff, it is said, administered the landing of Sebastian Cabot in Nova Scotia of 1486 and was duly honoured with the explorer naming the land after Richard Ameryck.

AMERICAN INDIANS SPEAK WELSH . . . Iolo Morganwg suggested that Madog, who had sailed from Wales to America in the 12th century, would have established the Welsh language in America. In 1792 John Evans (1770-1799) of Waunfawr near Caernarfon went in search of Welsh-speaking Indians in the Mandan area. He found them but failed to detect any traces of the Welsh language – this quashes the notion that the Welsh start jabbering their own lingo when strangers appear! Evans went on to map the Missouri for nearly two thousand miles upstream of its confluence with the Mississippi.

AMERICAN WELSH . . . Civil War General Robert E. Lee was, as was frontiersman Daniel Boone. William George Fargo (of the Wells Fargo Express Company fame) was, along with silver screen legends Harold Lloyd and Bob Hope. All of these men were American Welsh as was Frank Lloyd Wright, the famous architect. Others with links include singer Andy Williams and statesmen Thomas Jefferson, as well as 'Tricky Dicky' Richard Milhous Nixon.

AMERICAN WAR OF INDEPENDENCE . . . (1773-1777) During the conflict the rebel John Paul Jones opened fire on Fishguard town after earlier seizing a ship belonging to local entrepreneur Samuel Fenton. He charged a five hundred guinea ransom which Fenton paid, but Jones still launched his attack causing some structural damage.

AMIS (Kingsley) . . . renowned author (a Booker Prize winner in the 1980s with *The Old Devils*) was once a lecturer at Swansea university.

AMLWCH PENNIES . . . For a period Mynydd Parys in Amlwch, Anglesey, was the copper capital of the world. The discovery of rich copper veins in 1768 marked the beginning of thirty frenetic years for the Parys Mines Company which employed fifteen hundred men, women and children. Shortage of low denomination coins meant that the company was authorised to mint pennies and halfpennies. The unbelievable number of copper pennies exceeded two hundred and fifty tons, while over fifty tons of halfpennies were minted between 1787-1793. Numismatists speak highly of the design of the Amlwch Pennies – a druid's head wreathed in oak leaves and acorns, while the reverse of the coin bore the words 'we promise to pay the bearer one penny' and showed the initials P.M.C. Valid until 1817, the edge of the coin bore the words 'on demand in London, Liverpool or Anglesey.'

AMPHITHEATRE . . . Wales' earliest all-seater stadium was built by the Romans at Isca (Caerleon-on-Usk). It had seating for about six thousand as well as boxes for the VIPs, and was built about 75 AD. It hosted Wales' earliest E.N.S.A.-type entertainment. Only in 1926 was it excavated.

AN AMERICAN WEREWOLF IN PARIS . . . the misty opening of this 1990s sequel was shot at Capel-y-Ffin near Hay-on-Wye.

ANCIENT CAPITAL . . . Aberffraw, a village on the isle of Anglesey was the seat of Llywelyn ap Iorwerth and acknowledged as the ancient capital of Wales. It held this position as Court of the Princes for half a millennium until the 13th century when Llywelyn the Last was defeated. It is said that the village inn 'The Crown' is built on the site of Llywelyn's court.

ANEIRIN . . . famous poet of the 6th Century whose work was written at the time of the wars against Northumbria under King Ida.

ANGLESEY . . . Ynys Môn the island county of North Wales is separated from the mainland by the Menai Strait and known historically as Môn, Mam Cymru (Mother of Wales) because, at one time, Anglesey produced enough grain to sustain the neighbouring mainland territories. The island has one hundred and twenty-five miles (two hundred kilometres) of coastline and, at one time, six of the then nineteen lifeboats in Britain were stationed around the island.

ANGLESEY ATTACK . . . Roman leader Paulus Suetonius launched an attack on the island in AD61 some seventeen years before Agricola's successful conquest of the Druids.

ANGLESEY LEG . . . This was invented and patented by James Potts of Chelsea. Picture the gory scene at the Battle of Waterloo in 1815. A cannon-ball de-legs Wellington's cavalry commander, Henry William Paget who, with typical stiff upper lip, says: 'By God sir, I've lost my leg!' The Duke of Wellington looks down and mumbles 'By God sir, so you have'. The upshot was that the shattered remains were amputated, without anaesthetic; Paget was entitled the First Marquess of Anglesey and needed a wooden leg. This was not a basic run of the mill version, but a super de-luxe purpose-built marque 1 (what else for a first Marquess?) which James Potts then used to make pots of money, especially for his descendants as the 'Anglesey Leg' was still in use in World War 1.

ANGLO-WELSH . . . usually refers to Welsh-born writers who work in the English language.

ANGOR yr . . . Liverpool's Welsh-language newspaper.

ANIMATION . . . Welsh TV station S4C has a prolific animation department.

ANNUAL LECTURE . . . The BBC Wales Annual Lectures have been broadcast since 1938. The most significant was that of Saunders Lewis in 1962 which led directly to the formation of the Cymdeithas Yr Iaith Cymraeg (Welsh Language Society).

ANTHRACITE . . . see coal

ANTHRAX ATTACK . . . During WW2 part of the Dinefwr Herd, a rare breed of Welsh cattle, was evacuated to the USA in case Hitler's Nazi Germany launched an anthtrax attack on the British mainland.

ANTI WELSH . . . See GILL A.A.

AP. . . . * AB

APOSTLE OF PEACE . . . this was the name given to Henry Richard (1812 – 1888) of Tregaron, Dyfed who founded the Peace Union which was a forerunner of the League of Nations, which itself foreran the UN.

'AR HYD Y NOS' . . . (All through the night). A popular Welsh tune since the late 18th century. The words were written by John Ceiriog Hughes.

AR WERTH . . . (For Sale) These are the words emblazoned on estate agents' sign boards throughout the country.

ARABIA . . . Lawrence of Arabia – no, he was Welsh.

ARAF . . . on a road sign means 'slow'.

ARCTIC CHAR . . . an amazing breed of fish, and a survivor from the Ice Age, which is found in Llyn Padarn near Llanberis in Gwynedd.

ARCHDRUID . . . The Welsh National Eisteddfod's first archdruid was David Griffiths (Clwydfardd), who held office for eighteen years from the Wrexham Eisteddfod of 1876.

AREAS OF OUTSTANDING NATURAL BEAUTY . . . Between 1956 and 1985 five areas in Wales were awarded AONB status. The first was the Gower Peninsula seventy-three miles of which were bestowed the title in 1956, closely followed by sixty square miles of the Llŷn Peninsula in 1957. Eventually, parts of Anglesey and the Wye Valley and the Clwydian Range also had beauty 'thrust upon them'.

ARENNIG FAWR . . . the 2,800 ft Snowdonian peak was struck by an American Flying Fortress plane in August 1943. The peak is also the subject of quite well-known paintings by J D Innes.

'ARE YOU READY?' . . . the first wireless message sent by Guglielmo Marconi was from Lavernock Point near Penarth to Flat Holm Island in the Severn Estuary.

ARITHMETIC . . . In 1540 Robert Recorde or Tenby (best known for inventing the equals sign =) published the first arithmetic book in English 'The Grounde of Artes'. By 1662 it had reached twenty-six editions. Sum achievement!

ARMS PARK . . . Cardiff Arms Park was the home of Welsh Rugby Union from its construction in 1874 until closure in 1997, to be replaced by the Millennium Stadium.

ARMY HISTORY . . . Lucy Ellis of Tywyn and Joanna Williams of Builth Wells became the first female members of the Welsh Guards Band in 1998 – making army history in the process. The band was formed some eighty odd years previously.

ARNOLD (Matthew) . . . the son of the former headmaster of Rugby school who was one of the foremost critics of his day. In 1864 he stayed in Llandudno and visited the National Eisteddfod. The conclusion of this 'great man' was simple. (a) 'The sooner the Welsh language disappears, the better; the better for England and the better for Wales itself'. And (b) the Welsh 'should not delay by a single hour' the spread of the English language.

ARTHEL . . . or Arddel. Late medieval border magnates sheltered criminals who acted as their bodyguards and so aggravated lawlessness. The practice was abolished by Henry VIII as part of the Act of Union.

ARTHUR . . . Legendary Brythonic/Welsh king whom the Normans usurped so as to prove their right to the crown of the British Isles. Arthur had been part of Welsh poetry and folklore for centuries, but, the first Norman chroniclers of the legends was Geoffrey of Monmouth according to whom the 6th Century 'king' was triumphant in wars with the Saxons and was able to pacify the Picts and Scots in the north before conquering Ireland and Iceland and ruling over 12 years of peace. Arthur then plans to conquer the rest of Europe and is adamant not to pay homage to the Romans. Whilst preparing to launch an assault on Rome he is betrayed by Methrod back in Britain and is forced to return. Arthur is then wounded in battle on the banks of the Cornish river Camel and is ferried away to the isle of Avalon where his wounds can heal. Other versions of the tale are tenfold. King Arthur has been the subject of over six hundred English language books since Geoffrey of Monmouth's version.

ARTHUR TUDOR (1486-1502) . . . Henry Vll, keen to capitalise on his Welsh origins, named his son Arthur after the ancient Brythonic king whose 'return' had been long-promised by the bards. However, the sickly Tudor died in his youth leaving his younger brother (later Henry Vlll) to inherit the throne as well as his widow, Catherine of Aragon.

ARTISTS' VALLEY . . . the name given to Cwm Einion in Ceredigion – reasons are obvious.

ARVONIA . . . a settlement of Welsh immigrants in Kansas, USA in the 1870s.

ASHLEY (Laura) (1925-1985) . . . Merthyr-born fashion designer of renown. Born Laura Mountney, she married Bernard Ashley in 1949 and set up a business designing clothes. Her work was characterized by use of soft and natural fabrics, often in a romantic style.

ASKEY . . . diminutive entertainer Arthur Askey, who died in 1982 served in the Welch Regiment after WW1. 'Another legendary Arthur', which he was.

ATHEQUA . . . Catherine of Aragon's Spanish chaplain was the Bishop of Llandaf. He had a lot in common with his flock as neither they nor he could speak English.

ATLANTIC COLLEGE . . . at St Donat's Castle. Established in 1962 by German educationalist Kurt Hahn who earlier founded Gordonstoun school. Atlantic College was the first of six United World Colleges aiming to foster international understanding and serve the community. The three hundred and fifty or so pupils hail from around sixty different countries.

ATPAR . . . Carmarthenshire town which can proudly boast a first and last . . . Firstly, in 1718 Isaac Carter established the first permanent printing press in Wales on which he printed a Welsh ballad about tobacco in 1719. Lastly, . . . in 1872 Jack Foster spent three hours in the stocks at Atpar the last use of the stocks as a punishment in Britain. He was found guilty of drunkenness.

ATTRACTIONS . . . To qualify for a directional road sign tourist attractions need to draw in more than five thousand visitors per annum and, if they are a castle, they need a custodian on duty.

AUGUST . . . a mid-1990s film by Sir Anthony Hopkins set and filmed in the heart of the Llŷn Peninsula.

AUGUSTUS William (also known as Will Awst). An 18th Century weather prophet from Llandovery (Llanymddyfri) in Carmarthenshire. He wrote a bilingual collection of weather lore called *The Husbandman's Perpetual Prognostication* and, folklore dictates, he was able to predict the onset of all manner of weather conditions within an hour.

AUKS . . . The best known colony of auks in the UK reside at Stacks Rocks off the coast of Pembrokeshire (*Penfro*).

AUSTRALIAN COAL . . . Lewis Thomas (1832-1913) . . . was a pioneer of

Australian coal-mining. Born in Ceredigion he emigrated at the age of 27 and opened up the Aberdare colliery in the Bundumba coalfield where he had cut the first ton of coal.

AUSTRALIAN PM . . . William Morris Hughes. 'Billy' (1862-1952) London born to Welsh parents. Australian statesman who was Prime Minister between 1915 and 1923. Aged 7, on the death of his mother, he moved to Llandudno and was brought up by an aunt. He later settled in New South Wales and became a qualified barrister and a Labour MP in 1894. By 1908-13 he was Australia's Attorney general before being elevated to the position of PM. He remained an MP until his death – 58 unbroken years in parliament. In 1915 he visited Llandudno once again and was given the freedom of the city of Cardiff. He also shared a platform with Lloyd George, when they were both in favour of the introduction of conscription.

AWARD-WINNING BEACHES . . . Anglesey boasts the greatest concentration of Seaside Award beaches in Wales.

AWDL . . . a long poem written in the traditional metres. At the National Eisteddfod the prize for the best awdl is the Bardic Chair.

AXE FACTORY . . . About 2000 years BC, Neolithic man mass-produced stone axes and picks on Penmaenmawr's rocky slopes. The geologist described his discovery in 1919 as a 'prehistoric Sheffield'. Hundreds of tough stone tools which were crafted in Penmaenmawr have also been found in England, Scotland and Ireland.

BABIES . . . In Wales, babes in arms speak Welsh so it must be an easy language to learn !

BACH . . . The Welsh word for small and often used with affection especially in the nicknames of those short of stature. John Bach, Dai Bach, Gwyn Bach, Gareth Bach, Mike Bach . . . not an American family pop group, all tiddlers from Wales. John Bach is to the Welsh pub what the major is to the English pub 'Is the major in?' 'Not due till 9ish'.

BACHEGRAIG . . . a Denbighshire house built in 1567 by Sir Richard Clough is said to be the earliest use of Welsh brick in home-building.

BACON (Anthony) (1718-1786). The English iron-master who developed Merthyr Tydfil from a mere hamlet to Wales' most densely populated town –

greatly aided by the War of American Independence (1775-1883) as Merthyr made cannon ball and iron for guns.

BACON HOLE CAVE . . . On the Gower peninsula which contained the bones of prehistoric animals including elephant, bison, rhinocerous and hyena. Similar finds were made at other caves in the area including Michin Hole Cave.

BAISTER . . . Brian Baister the Chairman of the English Rugby Union and ex Deputy Chief Constable of Cheshire was born in Llandudno.

BAKER (Elizabeth) . . . An 18th Century diarist born in the Midlands. She moved to the Dolgellau area (living for some time at Hengwrt) as she had acquired the right to prospect for metals in the area. The plan failed due to lack of support from her partners. She later died destitute and was buried in Dolgellau cemetery in 1789.

BAKER (Stanley) . . . Screen actor who appeared in such classic movies as *Zulu The Cruel Sea* and *The Guns of Navarone*, was born in the Rhondda. He died of lung cancer in 1976.

BALA . . . Town in Snowdonia and also a lake (Llyn Tegid) which is the largest natural lake in Wales and home to a unique species of fish called *gwyniad*.

BALA LAKE RAILWAY . . . In 1972 the Bala Lake Railway became the first company to be registered in the Welsh language as Rheilffordd Llyn Tegid Cyf.

BALDWIN Archbishop (of Canterbury) who toured Wales in 1187 seeking support for the third Crusade. He was the first archbishop to visit Wales.

BALL . . . Singer Michael Ball is not strictly Welsh (being born in Droitwich does not qualify). He does, however, have family links with Mountain Ash. The star caused disenchantment in the Valleys in 1997 when he appeared at Wembley to sing the English national Anthem before a soccer World Cup clash between England and Italy – only two years earlier he had recorded *Bread of Heaven* the official Wales song for the 1995 Rugby World Cup!

BANANAS (Dai) . . . Nickname given to Sir David Maxwell Fyfe, Minister for Welsh Affairs 1951-54.

BANDO . . . a particularly rough game enjoyed in Glamorgan before it was overtaken by Rugby. Goals were often a mile or more apart and teams consisted of between twenty and thirty players, using hurley-style sticks.

BANGOR . . . university city of North Wales. The town was featured in the 70s novelty hit record *Day Trip To Bangor* by Fiddler's Dram who warbled about the fun time they'd had on a day out. Unfortunately, the real place they had visited was about 30 miles (48 km) further up the North Wales coastline but 'Day Trip to Rhyl' wouldn't scan or fit the lilting melody.

BANGOR . . . Once proud to have been called 'The Athens of Wales' on a welcome sign until mischievous students removed it. It was never re-erected.

BANGOR CATHEDRAL . . . the oldest in Britain (predating Canterbury by about 81 years) was established *circa* 546 by St Deiniol.

BANGOR FLOWER GARDEN . . . The Gwynedd city has a unique Biblical garden in which the flowers grow in the same order as they are mentioned in the Bible.

BANGOR UNIVERSITY . . . A team from the University College of North Wales reached the semi-finals of the 1999 series of 'University Challenge'.

BANGOR-ON-DEE (Bangor-Is-coed) . . . About five miles from Wrexham, the racecourse there holds monthly National Hunt race meetings and is the oldest racecourse in Wales which opened in 1860.

BANGOR RUGBY CLUB . . . The Gwynedd club were the only northern Wales representatives at Neath in 1881 when the Welsh Rugby Union was founded.

BANGORIAN CONTROVERSY . . . This was a dispute over the theory of the Divine Right of Kings in which Bishop Hoadly of Bangor was embroiled. Of Bangor? No, he couldn't be. In his five years as Bishop he never once set foot in Bangor.

BANK . . . ABERYSTWYTH'S BANC Y LLONG . . . (The Ship Bank), was the first bank to be established in Wales (1762).

BANK OF ENGLAND . . . a branch opened in Swansea in 1826.

BANKS (Jeff) . . . The presenter of TV's 'The Clothes Show' was born in Ebbw Vale where his father was a steel worker. The family left Wales when the designer was nine. He was once married to singer Sandie Shaw. (No relation!)

BARA BRITH . . . speckled bread, literally.

BARCLODIAD Y GAWRES and Bryn-celli-ddu in Anglesey are Neolithic burial tombs. These circular cairns were possibly collective graves and built between 4000 and 2000 BC.

BARD (The) . . . A poem written by Thomas Gray in 1757 which spread the idea that Edward 1 in his conquest of Wales had 'killed' the Welsh muse. He had sounded the death knell of the Welsh bards and Gray suggests that, without the benevolence of the Welsh princes and leading families, Welsh culture would die.

BARDSEY ISLAND . . . island off the Llŷn Peninsula (*Enlli).

BARDSEY SOUND . . . home of the seventh fastest tidal race in the world and consequently treated with caution by the sailing fraternity. King Arthur's ship Caswennan is said to have sunk in the sound – the first of many.

BARMOUTH (Y Bermo) . . . pretty Gwynedd coastal resort where an enterprising hotelier once tried to foster rumours of a 'Beast of Barmouth' along the lines of the Loch Ness Monster. Unfortunately, the story never took off in the way that Nessie has contributed millions of pounds to Scottish tourism.

BARMOUTH'S St JOHN'S CHURCH . . . Mrs Dyson Perrins of the sauce family sourced the finance for the building.

BARRY also known as Barry Island. The docks were built in 1889 by David Davies of Llandinam, owner of the 'Ocean' group of coalmines in the Rhondda Valley. 'Davies The Ocean', who also built bridges and railways, had to avoid the paralyzing delays and high charges of Cardiff docks. By 1911 Barry exported eleven million tons of coal, a record for any Welsh port. A statue commemorating David Davies stands outside the docks – it was sculpted by Sir Alfred Gilbert who also created the statue of Eros in Piccadilly Circus.

BARRYMORE (Drew) . . . the Hollywood star married Newport born club owner Jeremy Thomas in 1994 after a five week liaison. The marriage lasted marginally longer. Drew starred in the film E.T. as a child, but this was a case of 'Jeremy, phone home'

BASKING SHARK . . . the harmless creatures that can be seen at times off the Welsh coastline are protected under the Wildlife and Countryside Act.

BASSEY (Shirley) Big-voiced international singing star who hails from the Tiger Bay area of Cardiff. Her charisma and stage presence is always coupled with awesome costumery. Hits include *Hey Big Spender, Something* and several themes from James Bond movies.

BATS . . . of the fourteen species of bat that occur in Britain, eleven can be found in Wales.

BATTLE OF CHIRK BRIDGE . . . In December 1830 Rhosllanerchrugog coalminers were involved in a demonstration against iniquitous truck shops. (Would you like your wages paid partly in vouchers which had to be spent in the boss' shop, especially if the boss had a very narrow range of goods and was partial to West End of London prices?) In the skirmish the yeomanry fired on the crowd and later two of the leaders of the demonstration were gaoled. Within six months South Wales saw the Merthyr Riots.

BAULCH . . . Jamie. The Risca-born sprinter who is an Olympic silver medal winner.

BEATLES THE, . . . Ringo Starr once worked on the pleasure steamers plying from Liverpool to Llandudno and at Butlin's Holiday Camp in Pwllheli before joining the Fab Four. In August 1967 The Beatles were with the Maharishi Mahesh Yogi at a conference in Bangor when they learned of the death of their manager, Brian Epstein.

BEASTS OF . . . Bala, Bodmin, Bont, Llanaelhaearn, Mallwyd and Tregaron and, no doubt elsewhere. Elusive large cat-like creatures that have been spotted in these areas at various times could be pumas.

BEAUMARIS . . . Anglesey town whose name is taken from the French for 'beautiful marsh'.

BEAUMARIS CASTLE . . . Edward l in 1295 once again instructed the master builder James of St George to build another magnificent fortress to overawe the Welsh. Beaumaris was James' eighth castle-building project. As usual Edward 1 demanded sea-access for obvious reasons. One consolation was that, unlike Rhuddlan Castle, there was no need to import thousands of 'ditchers' to divert the river. Although never completed, Beaumaris Castle is included on the World Heritage List as a site of outstanding universal value. It cost £14,344-8-10. Within a year of commencement a vast labour force was engaged including four hundred masons, two hundred labourers, two hundred quarrymen and countless smiths and carpenters. The king forced the native population of nearby Llanfaes to move to a new borough (at Newborough) about ten miles away as he needed their homes for the influx of builders.

BEAUMARIS JAIL . . . was designed by Hansom (of Hansom Cab fame) and is one of very few in Britain to be open to the public. Built in 1829 it has a unique treadwheel, thirty-two cells, gallows bell and, of course, condemned cell. The last person to be hanged at Beaumaris jail was Dic Rolant in 1862. Rolant was executed for the murder of his father-in-law. He protested his innocence to the last and put a curse on the church clock – for years it failed to keep the correct time. Rolant was the last – there was only one other hanging carried out. That was in 1830 when a certain William Griffith was executed for attempting to murder his two wives!

BEAUMARIS PIER . . . the first in Wales was built in 1843.

BEAUMARIS WATER PORT . . . the town claims to have a larger deep-water port than the Pool of London.

BEAUMARIS/BIWMARES . . . the Welsh version of the name was adopted in the late 50s on the suggestion of the Board of Celtic Studies.

BEAUMARIS HINGED DOOR . . . According to the Guinness Book of Records, the large single-hinged door stands at 30 feet high by 12 feet wide (9 metres by 3 metres) and is at the 17th century Ye Olde Bull's Head in Beaumaris.

BEDDARTHUR (Arthur's Grave) . . . the burial site of the ancient Celtic king is above Crymych in the Preseli mountains in Dyfed – at least, one of them is there. N.B. Don't believe any wild unsubstantiated corny Cornish claims about the final resting place of Arthur.

BEDDGELERT . . . a town in the Snowdonia National Park famous for the legend of *Gelert.

BEDDGELERT IN BLOOM . . . the village consistently tops the poll in the Wales in Bloom competition.

BEECHING AXE . . . the now infamous 1960s report on the railway lines of the country. As a result of Dr Richard Beeching's report some three hundred and thirty-eight stations in Wales were closed, along with several minor lines.

BEERTENT . . . 'a beertent black with parchs' is one of Dylan Thomas's better-known expressions. Parch is the abbreviated form of parchedig meaning reverend as in minister of religion, so this a good example of Thomas' 'black humour'.

BELGIAN WALK . . . The name given to the promenade in Menai Bridge, Anglesey which was constructed by Belgian refugees during WW1.

BELL (Richard) (1859-1930) . . . Trade Unionist and M.P. He was general secretary of a Railway Union when the Taff Vale Dispute of 1900 led to the unions being successfully sued by the company, which resulted in a change to Trade Union Law. Secondly, under the secretaryship of Bell, trade unions were allowed by law to levy a political toll on their members. This came about after the famous Osbourne case. Richard Bell was born in Brecknock (*Brycheiniog*) and was a fluent Welsh speaker.

BELLS . . . St Woolos Cathedral in Newport has Wales' largest peal of bells.

BELLS OF ABERDYFI . . . a song from the late 18th Century opera *Liberty Hall*.

BENNETT (Elinor) . . . world-famous Welsh harpist and wife of Plaid Cymru politician Dafydd Wigley. In 1999 she provided the backing harp for a track on the Catatonia album *Equally Cursed & Blessed*.

BENNETT (Gordon) . . . the tough boss of the New York Herald instructed one of his reporters to find the missing British explorer, Dr Livingstone. Henry Morton Stanley* did so.

BENNETT (Phil) . . . A Welsh Rugby Union all-time legend who won twenty-nine caps for his country and played in eight British Lions test matches. He captained Wales in 1977-78 and the British Lions in 1977.

BERSHAM . . . near Wrexham is where John Wilkinson's foundry made perfectly straight barrels for cannon. In the early 19th century Bersham boomed due to the warring of the time.

BERWICK ACT . . . the act of 1747 stated quite simply that the word 'England' in any legislation also meant Wales. (Not unlike some entries in the *Encyclopaedia Britannica*, which said 'For Wales, see England'.

BERWYN (Richard Jones) (1863-1917) . . . born at Glyndyfrdwy. He was one of the leaders of the first group of Welsh emigrants to settle in Patagonia, Argentina where he became the first postmaster in the colony and also private secretary to the first governor. He was also co-author (with Thomas Pugh) of the first Welsh book to be printed in South America.

BESTALL (Alfred) . . . NOT in fact the creator of Rupert The Bear (that was Marie Turtel) but he did draw the Rupert cartoon strip that appeared in the Daily Express for over thirty years. Bestall lived near Beddgelert until his death at the age of ninety-three in 1986. Many of the adventures Rupert experienced were set in the hills surrounding Bestall's home.

BEST-KNOWN OPENING LINE . . . Felicia Dorothea Hemens (1793-1835) is the authoress of one of the best known opening verses of a poem (though few know the actual title and author) 'The boy stood on the burning deck . . . ' is the opening line of *Casabianca*. Mrs Hemens lived near St Asaph. The second line, for your information is 'Whence all but he had fled?'

BETHESDA . . . in the beautiful Dyffryn Ogwen (Valley) in Snowdonia. The village was originally called Cilfodan but changed its name in 1819 when Bethesda Chapel was built.

BETHESDA – PORT-PENRHYN RAILWAY . . . Opened in 1801, it was the first narrow gauge horse-drawn railway in Wales and was used for transporting slate from Penrhyn Quarry, Bethesda to Porth Penrhyn.

BETHLEHEM . . . the Carmarthenshire village post office receives in excess of five thousand visitors in the build up to Christmas each year as the visitors wish to send mail carrying the name of Jesus' birthplace.

BETWS Y COED – ARTISTS' COLONY . . . go there and see why!

BEVAN (Aneurin) (1867-1960) Welsh labour M.P. born in Tredegar who instituted the National Health Service after World War 2. He resigned his post when the government introduced charges for NHS services in 1951. Bevan became deputy leader of the party in 1959.

BEVAN (Madam Bridget) (1698-1779) A main patron of the highly successful circulating schools of Griffith Jones, she carried on the crucial work as their organizer, after Jones' death in 1761.

BEYNON (William) (c.1884-1932). British bantam-weight boxing champion born at Port Talbot. Tragically killed in a coalmining accident.

BIBLE . . . first translated into Welsh by Bishop William Morgan in 1588, but the first Welsh Bible actually printed in Wales was at Carmarthen in 1770.

BIBLICAL NAMES . . . Nazareth, Bethlehem, Carmel, Cesarea, Golan . . . all names of places featured in the Bible, and all of which can also be found in Wales.

BIG BEN . . . the bell in the famous clock was named after Sir Benjamin Hall (Lord Llanover of Abergavenny) (1802-67). Hall was MP for Monmouth Boroughs and was the government's first Commissioner of Works in 1858. The 13.7 tonnes bell in the clock tower of the House of Commons bears his name. Big Ben (the man) was 6' 4".

BIG LOVE SPOON . . . the largest in Wales stands at 4 feet (1.2 metres) tall and is the work of former miners. It was hewn from a former pit prop and can be seen at the Greenfield Valley heritage Park, near Holywell in Flintshire.

BIGGS (Norman) (1870-1908). Cardiff-born rugby wing three-quarter whose most memorable match for Wales was at Murrayfield against Scotland in a match that Wales won (thanks to Biggs's performance), to win the 'Triple-Crown' for the first time in 1893.

BILLION DOLLAR MAN . . . Robert Edwards left Llanymynech around 1800 and acquired swampy land in America, which he leased to tenants. By today the Edwards Heirs Association is involved in a landownership dispute because the former swamp includes Wall Street and Broadway, worth an estimated $680 billion. Naturally, the number of heirs is growing.

BILLY THE KID was Welsh. He is the regimental goat of the Royal Welsh Fusiliers. Based at their Caernarfon barracks he weighs in at about 16 stones (102 kilograms) and leads ceremonial parades.

BIOTECHNOLOGY ENTREPRENEUR . . . Dr Chris Evans, born in Port Talbot in 1958, started the company Enzymatix in 1987 after completing a fellowship in research into microbiology. In 1998 he was worth an estimated £75 million and was amongst the top ten richest people in Wales.

BIRT (John) . . . the one time BBC director general once bought a cottage at Crickadarn near Builth Wells.

BIRTH OF A QUEEN . . . Sir David Davies, Ceredigion born in 1792, became a doctor rising to the post of first Professor of Medicine at University College, London. He treated King William IV during his last illness, as well as attending at the birth of the later Queen Victoria – though not at the same time.

BLACK BART THE PIRATE . . . better known as Barti Ddu (Bartholomew Roberts of Little Newcastle, Pembrokeshire (Penfro). (1680-1722). Only in his later years did he indulge in piracy. In fact he was just a bold tar until 1719. If his 'haul' of four hundred ships in two years as legend dictates is to be believed, then he must have had a turbo-powered pirate ship, together with a crew of ex-SAS men. Interestingly, he became a buccaneer accidentally! He was serving as second mate on the ship *Princess* which was attacked and overwhelmed by pirate Howel Davis and crew, and was pressed into service. Six weeks later Davis was killed and the crew elected Roberts as their new captain because they had been so impressed by his cunning, bravery and skill. Roberts soon gained a fearful reputation and struck terror all over the seven seas. On one occasion his ship sailed into a Newfoundland harbour and the crews of no fewer than twenty-two ships fled. One of his most famous captures was a frigate of the Royal African Company which he renamed *Royal Fortune*. When he was killed in February 1772, his body was buried at sea in full pirate 'honours'.

BLACK BOOK OF CARMARTHEN . . . (Llyfr Du Caerfyrddin) – oldest surviving Welsh language manuscript, written about 1250. It consists of one hundred and eight pages of poetry on themes including religion and legend (especially Arthurian).

BLACK CHAIR, THE. Held at Birkenhead in 1917 on one of the few occasions that the National Eisteddfod was held outside Wales. So named because the winner of the Chair was Ellis Humphrey *Evans, 'Hedd Wyn', who had just been killed in WW1 in France. *DEAD POET

BLACK HUNDRED SOCIETY . . . they meet and feast at Llantrisant every

May to commemorate the glorious part played by Welsh archers under the Black Prince at Crecy in 1346.

BLAENAU FFESTINIOG . . . the railway tunnel here stretching almost two and a quarter miles was opened in 1879 and is the longest in Wales.

BLAIR . . . Tony Blair's step-mother Olwen once lived at Radyr near Cardiff.

BLAS AR GYMRU (Taste of Wales) . . . eateries boasting a distinctive culinary identity involving recipes (old or new) based on Welsh local produce e.g. beef, lamb, seafood, cheeses etc. Establishments display an attractive plaque (including the ubiquitous red dragon) and make as much as possible of the old Welsh Croeso.

BLEEDING YEW TREE . . . the tree in Nevern (Nyfer) churchyard in Pembrokeshire has oozed red resin since medieval times. A monk accused of a heinous crime was sentenced to death by hanging. He apparently protested his innocence to the end and swore that the tree would 'bleed' for ever more in proof of this.

BLIND HARPIST . . . John Parry (c.1710-82) was born on the Llŷn Peninsula at Nefyn and was a most gifted harpist of his time despite his disability, and performed at events in London, Dublin and Oxford.

BLITHE SPIRIT . . .was written by Noel Coward whilst staying at Portmeirion.

BLODWEN . . . The first Welsh language opera was first performed at Aberdare in 1886. It was the work of Dr Joseph Parry who also composed the hymn tune 'Aberystwyth'.

BLONDIN . . . the rope used by the tightrope walker to famously cross Niagara Falls was made by James Frost, who had a home in Old Colwyn.

BLOODY SUNDAY . . . 'The Bloody Sunday of Mwnt' in 1155 saw Flemish invaders landing on the Pembrokeshire coast, and were met with ferocious Welsh resistance. This victory over the French was celebrated annually on the first Sunday in January for many years.

BLUE BOOKS . . . ' The Welsh language is a vast drawback and a manifold barrier to the moral progress and prosperity of the people. It is not easy to overestimate its evil effects.' . . . So said the 1847 reports on education in Wales, which became known as 'the treason of the blue books'.

BLUE FLAG BEACHES . . . Wales has got 'em!

BLUESTONES . . . of the inner circle of Stonehenge on Salisbury Plain are the same as from the Preseli area of Pembrokeshire. Of that there is no doubt. The puzzling question is that of haulage. Were the 'beaker folk' of that era long distance hauliers? The distance involved was about 180 miles (288 km) over land and sea. Did they use rollers, sledges and rafts? Did they use slave labour? How many men were involved? Experiments conducted in the early 1950s showed that such a monumental task was possible but perhaps the Institute of Geographical Science suggestion is the simplest. The bluestones were carried by glacier ice.

BODELWYDDAN MARBLE CHURCH . . . with a 202 foot (60.6 metres) spire it was built in 1856. An ornate building which is a landmark on the A55 coast road into North Wales.

BODNANT GARDEN . . . at Eglwysbach, Conwy is one of the finest gardens in Britain and famed for its Laburnum Arch. It's eighty acres overlook Snowdonia and the majestic Afon Conwy.

BOG SNORKLING . . . a competition devised by the enterprising traders of Llanwrtyd Wells. World championships have been held there since 1986.

BONESETTERS . . . The Thomas family of Anglesey provided six generations of bonesetters between c.1700 and 1920. In the 18th century the family of healers showed that amputation was not a cure. They set bones and cripples walked again. Hugh Owen Thomas (1834-91) who established a surgery in Liverpool is regarded as the father of modern orthopaedic surgery. His pioneering work is described in his 1875 book *Diseases of the Hip, Knee and Ankle* and thousands of 'Thomas splints' were used in WW1.

BOOTH (Emma) . . . as a 15 year old schoolgirl, Bridgend-born singer Emma Booth was Britain's unsuccessful entry in the annual Eurovision Song Contest (1990).

BOOTH (Richard) . . . the man behind the Hay-on-Wye Second Hand books bonanza.

BOOTS (John George) 1874-1928) Rugby forward born in Monmouthshire. He is remembered as the 'Peter Pan Of Rugby' because he played at the top level for thirty seasons.

BORDER . . . what border? At least there are no Customs, passport control or currency changes (yet!).

BORDER COLLIES . . . The most intelligent members of the canine world are common sights in farms across the Principality.

BORE DA . . . (Good morning) The phrase that should be on the tip of your tongue as soon as you see the 'Croeso' or 'Welcome to Wales' sign.

BORROW (George) (1803-1881) . . . An agent for the British and Foreign Bible Society who travelled widely in Wales, and his book *Wild Wales* (1854) is an account of the people, language and scenery. He was a competent linguist who was reasonably fluent in Welsh, which he possibly found easier-going than his effort at translating the New Testament into Manchu !

BOWDLER (Thomas) (1754-1825). Born near Bath. A man of letters who is best remembered for his editing of the 'Family Shakespeare' in 1818, in which all passages which he considered unfit for family reading were omitted. The term 'to bowdlerize' is synonymous with puritanical censorship of this nature. Died and was buried at Oystermouth, The Mumbles near Swansea.

BOYCE (Max) Much-loved Welsh entertainer (born 1945) who sprang from obscurity after winning Opportunity Knocks in the 70s. His song and comedy act was intertwined with the unprecedented success at the time of the Wales Rugby Union side but as their success dwindled so, it appeared, did the career of Max Boyce . . . at the time of writing on the eve of the 1999 World Cup, the Wales national team have just completed the eighth match undefeated in a row. Watch out for the Max Boyce world comeback tour any day!

BOY SCOUT TROOPS . . . The first foundations in Wales were in Carmarthen and Cardiff in 1908. They were definitely not in Caerfyrddin and Caerdydd.

BOXING . . . John Graham Chambers of Llanelli in 1867 revised the Queensberry Rules which govern the sport.

BOXING 2 . . . the first women's official boxing bout was held at Whitland, west Wales in October 1997. Marie Leefe beat Marie Davies after three one minute rounds in front of a packed house. Both girls were 16 year old college students from St Clears (Sanclêr), Carmarthenshire. Was boxing the last male sporting preserve?

BRADSHAW (John) (1602-1659) of Presteigne was one of the first regicides to sign the death warrant of Charles l.

BRAINTREE . . . the Essex market town. In 1999, travel writer Bill Murphy said that Braintree residents were 'the ugliest collection of people in the UK outside of Wales'.

BRANDING . . . What is the perception of Wales in the new Millennium? Are we still sooty-faced hymn-singing miners?

BRANDY COVE . . . in West Glamorgan was a smugglers' haunt.

BRASS BAND 1 . . . The Royal Buckley Town Band is the oldest brass band playing in the UK. It was established in 1822 and is one of only two 'Royal' brass bands. The 'Royal' accolade was conferred in 1889 thanks to Gladstone. The PM got the band a gig playing before the then Prince of Wales (later Edward VII).

BRASS BAND 2 . . . the first working man's brass band in Britain was formed at Brown's Ironworks in Blaenau Gwent in 1832.

BRAZIL . . . their national football team defeated Wales in the quarter finals of the 1958 World Cup. The only goal of the game was scored by a 17 year old player of some promise . . . his name? Pele ! Wales have not qualified for the final stages of any major tournament since 1958.

BRAZILIAN SETTLEMENT . . . at Rio Grande do Sol in 1850 Evan Evans of Nant-y-glo established a Welsh settlement. Called Nova Cambria, it bit the dust a year later – at least the dust settled!

BREAKWATER . . . the breakwater at Holyhead on Anglesey took twenty-eight years to build (started 1845), is the largest in Britain, involved excavating seven million tonnes of stone from the adjacent mountain and eventually created a six hundred and sixty-seven acre harbour.

BRECHFA FOREST . . . in Dyfed is Wales' largest conifer plantation.

BRECON BEACONS – One of the National Parks of Wales which was established in 1957. It covers an area of over 550 square miles and encompasses the peaks of Corn Du, Cribyn, and Pen y Fan, and these three are the 'beacons' of the name. Writer Daniel Defoe travelled the Beacons in 1724 and found them most unappealing. He wrote: '. . . horrid and frightful, even worse than those mountains abroad'.

BRECONSHIRE AGRICULTURE SOCIETY . . . The Breconshire Ag. Soc. Was founded in 1755 by Howell Harris and others and was one of the earliest such organisations in Britain. The idea was to improve farming in general in this period of the so-called 'Agrarian Revolution'.

BRECON JAZZ FESTIVAL . . . Britain's most popular annual jazz event.

BREWERY . . . the smallest in Wales is at Tynllidiart Arms, Capel Bangor, Aberystwyth. Licensee Tim Hughes brews only nine gallons a week of 'Rheidol Reserve' – its recipe remains a secret.

BRIANNE . . . (Llyn) the Dyfed dam and reservoir which serves Swansea (Abertawe) city is 300 feet (92 metres) high, covers 520 acres with 13,400 million gallon (61,000 million litres)reservoir. It is the highest man-made lake in Britain and the largest rock-filled dam in Europe. The growth of Swansea meant increased demand for fresh water. Nearby Cwm Senni was to have been the home of a man-made reservoir but the vocal locals swayed the authorities to abandon the scheme (which would have meant evacuating the Cwm Senni community) and Llyn Brianne was built instead.

BRICKS . . . a nice little earner for a number of brickworks was the Severn Railway Tunnel. 76,400,000,000 bricks were used in the construction of the 4.5 mile (7.2 km) long tunnel which took twelve years to build until it was finally opened in September 1885.

BRIDGEND . . . the munitions factory in the Glamorgan town employed thirty-seven thousand people during WW2 – the largest of its type in Britain.

BRITANNIA TUBULAR BRIDGE . . . across the Menai Strait was built by Robert Stephenson in 1850 to link the London to Holyhead railway with Anglesey. It was the world's first tubular bridge and cost £674,000 which was then the most expensive bridge in the world.

BRITISH BROADCASTING CORPORATION . . . (BBC) During WW2 the

Light Entertainment broadcasts were made from Penrhyn Hall in Bangor, Gwynedd (now a modern shopping mall). Perhaps the best known programme was Tommy Handley's I.T.M.A.

BRITISH AND FOREIGN BIBLE SOCIETY . . . co-founded by Revd Thomas Charles of Bala in 1814. By today it issues Bibles in two hundred and eighty-three different languages.

BROADCAST . . . the first royal broadcast from Wales was the 1927 opening of the National Museum of Wales by George V.

BRONTË (Charlotte) . . . the 19th century novelist spent her honeymoon at Conwy.

BROTHERLY LOVE . . . Owain Goch was imprisoned for 20 years (1255-1275) by his younger brother, Llywelyn The Last.

BROOME (David) . . . Cardiff-born showjumper who won many equestrian titles including the World Championship in 1970 on his famous horse 'Beethoven.' In the same year he won the Welsh Sports Personality of the Year award. His sister, Liz Edgar, is also a highly-regarded showjumper.

BRUNEL (Isambard Kingdom) (1806-1859) . . . one of the most gifted engineers to work in Wales – skilled in the building of railways, railway tunnels, railway viaducts, Llansamlet's 'flying bridge', bridges, docks (at Milford Haven), harbours and steam ships – mainly in south Wales.

BRYMBO . . . Wales' oldest man was discovered in Brymbo near Wrexham in 1958. Near him was a flint knife and a waisted beaker. Born in the Bronze age about 4000 years ago (he was, naturally, dead!), he became known as *Beaker Man*. He had been buried in a chamber between stone slabs.

BRYN . . . means 'hill' and is a common prefix in Welsh placenames.

BRYN-CELLI-DDU . . . A Neolithic (4000-2500 BC) circular burial chamber on Anglesey. This stone Age cairn is one of two similar collective graves on the island. Barclodiad y Gawres is the other.

BRYN MAWR . . . town in Gwent at 1300 feet (480 metres) above sea-level is Wales' highest town and consequently has the highest bank in Wales, the highest public lavatories in Wales, the highest golf tee in Wales etc, etc.

BUILTH WELLS . . . the Spa town which in the 19th Century offered 'waters to cure all ills', especially bladder and kidney ailments. The X factor was the high sulphur content. The town is the permanent home of the Royal Welsh Show.

BULKELEY Richard, Sir (1533-1621) . . . One of the foremost of Anglesey's gentry families, the Bulkeley's lived in Beaumaris. Sir Richard built the well-known Penmon Dovecot, spacious enough for over one thousand nests. Fresh meat in winter from dove and pigeon possibly contributed to his longevity. He reached a nice ripe eighty-eight years.

BUFFALO BILL (William Cody) the famous wild-west showman visited North Wales in 1903.

BULL DOG . . . The biggest bulldog in the world was once owned (albeit briefly) by a Welshman . . . This is no bull, but the hound was *en route* through war torn Europe to his intended home at Rhiwlas near Bala, Gwynedd. The Balkan-born bulldog was waylaid in Paris during the Prussian siege of 1870. As every schoolboy knows, a starving Parisian cannot resist a portion of hot dog . . . and the rest is history. The owner of the luckless hound was a legend in his own lifetime. R J Lloyd-Price, squire of Rhiwlas was a whisky distiller and pioneer of sheepdog trials. Whether the bulldog was scheduled to round up flocks is unclear because, sadly, he ended up as dead meat.

BULL SLAUGHTER BAY . . . a real Welsh placename on the Gower.

BURIAL CHAMBER . . the Tinkinswood Chamber near Barry in South Glamorgan dates back to around 4000 BC and has the biggest capstone of any British burial chamber, weighing in at 40.6 tonnes.

BURBERRY . . . the famous Burberry raincoats are made in Treorchy.

BURNS NIGHT . . . and other Scottish celebrations are missing in Wales, which is a pity as Welsh bards far outnumber their Scottish counterparts.

BURROWS (Stuart) . . . the acclaimed tenor who hails from Cilfynydd.

BURTON (Sir Richard) . . . South Wales-born actor (1925-1984). Born Richard Jenkins as the tenth child of a coalminer. Encouraged by his English teacher Philip Burton, the young Jenkins excelled at English and acting and won a place at Oxford. He changed his name to Burton in honour of his mentor and served with the RAF before making his screen debut in 1948. Memorable screen roles included Mark Anthony in *Cleopatra*, and a drunken writer in *Who's Afraid of Virginia Woolf*. His on-off relationship with actress Elizabeth Taylor was one of Hollywood's most tempestuous and the couple married twice. Burton died in Switzerland.

BUSIEST PHONE BOX IN WALES . . . is in Ebbw Vale with more than forty-five thousand calls every year.

BUTE TOWN . . . in Cardiff is the site of one of the oldest cosmopolitan societies in Britain.

BUTLIN'S . . . A former holiday camp outside Pwllheli, Gwynedd which was one of several set up by South African entrepreneur Billy (later Sir Billy) Butlin before and after WW2. During the war Butlin's Pwllheli was a Royal Navy training centre known as HMS Glendower and was attended by the now Duke of Edinburgh. Billy Butlin met his future wife at Butlin's Pwllheli. Butlin's metamorphasized into StarcoastWorld in the 1990s and then became a Haven All Action Centre in 1999. A similar holiday camp at Barry Island in South Wales was closed in the 1980s.

BUTTLE Liz of Lampeter, Ceredigion became the oldest new mother in Britain at the age of sixty after fertility treatment in the late 1990s.

BUTTON (Sir Thomas) . . . Welsh explorer who died in 1634. He was one of several of his ilk who explored Hudson Bay in an attempt to find a North West Passage to Asia. He was knighted in 1613 by James 1.

BWLCH Y SAETHAU . . . near the top of Snowdon where Arthur supposedly slew Rhita Gawr.

BYRON (Lord) the poet who was 'mad, bad and dangerous to know' visited Capel Curig, Gwynedd.

C.K. TOOLS . . . the world-renowned tool making firm have their head office and main packing and distribution centre in Pwllheli, Gwynedd.

CABINET . . . In 1905, Lloyd George became the first Welshman to join the cabinet since 1855. MP for the Radnor Boroughs George Cornewall Lewis was the previous token Welshman. *POOR LAW LEWIS

CABLE BAY . . . (Porth Trecastell) on Anglesey is so named because one of the

36

undersea cables to Ireland enters the sea here.

CABLE TRAMWAY . . . The Llandudno Cable Tramway, built in 1902, is not quite unique. There are two others in the world, in San Francisco and in Lisbon.

CADAIR IDRIS . . . Southern Snowdonia mountain near Dolgellau in Gwynedd, which rises to a peak of 2927 feet. Legend dictates that the name came about because the mountain was the chair of the giant Idris.

CADFAN'S STONE . . . a seven foot pillar at Tywyn, Gwynedd with traces of the earliest form of written Welsh dating from the 7th Century. A rough translation of the inscription is 'The body of Cingen lies beneath'.

CADW . . . (Welsh Historic Monuments) is not unlike the body 'English Heritage'. The meaning of 'Cadw' is to preserve, to keep. Cadw is responsible for thousands of castles, mansions, churches, bridges, lighthouses and so on in Wales.

CADI-FFAN . . . an effeminate male.

CADWALADR . . . Prince who died in 664. Known not for his reign as a ruler of Gwynedd but rather for his presence in the prophecies of Merlin as related by Geoffrey of Monmouth. Cadwaladr was another one who would return to lead the Britons to victory over the Saxons. Later, Henry VII claimed descent from Cadwaladr 'in the 22nd degree.'

CADWALADR (Dilys) . . . (1902-1979) of Y Ffôr, near Pwllheli. In 1953 she became the first woman to win the Crown at the National Eisteddfod.

CAERLEON . . . In 1926 archaeologists removed 20,000 tons of soil from a hollow here. Financed by the American Knights of the Round Table, they were seeking King Arthur's fabled round table. Instead they found the only fully excavated Roman amphitheatre in Britain.

CAERNARFON. Main town of North West Wales and home to one of the impressive medieval Norman castles that ring the county of Gwynedd. Natives of Caernarfon are known as Cofis (Covveys). The town was the birthplace of Edward II and until the 1536 Act of Union it was the centre of Welsh government.

CAERNARFON CASTLE . . . as it was not near any flight path, during WW2 the castle was used to house priceless armour from the Tower of London. (c.f. Manod Quarry, the BBC in Bangor . . . etc, etc.).

CAERNARFON GRENADIERS . . . a Dad's army-type militia of around four hundred of Lord Newborough's estate workers who were banded together and armed by his Lordship to guard the entrance to the Menai Straits during the Napoleonic Wars.

CAERFFILI . . . Caerffili castle was the location of the movie *Restoration* starring Meg Ryan and Robert Downey Jnr. This was not the building's first sortie into film as it also featured in the Peter O'Toole movie *Rebecca's Daughter*. It is the largest castle in Wales, the second largest in Europe.

CAERFFILI 2 . . . Twinned with Italian city of Pisa? No, but it does have a leaning tower at the castle, that was caused by damage sustained during the English Civil War.

CAERPHILLY CHEESE . . . at one time this was the only cheese Wales commercially produced.

CAERWENT . . . was Venta Silurum, a Roman city, the third largest in south western Britain (after Cirencester and Bath). *CERINIUM

CAERWYS . . . in Flintshire is Wales' smallest town. In 1568 Elizabeth I granted the town permission to hold an annual eisteddfod.

CALDY ISLAND . . . Trappist monks have inhabited the island off Tenby since 1929. Sales of their perfume made from lavender and broom help finance their existence.

CALDY MONKS . . . in Wales, Welshmen who arrive in the alehouse and order a fruit juice and decline a cigarette because they are 'now into clean living' are asked 'Why don't you go the whole hog and go join your mates on Caldy?'

CALENNIG . . . a traditional New Year's gift.

CALLAGHAN (James) . . . (born 1913) created Baron Callaghan of Cardiff in 1987, he had served the city as an MP for many years. One time leader of the Labour party (succeeding Harold Wilson). As Prime Minister he was ousted in the 1979 General Election after the so-called *Winter of Discontent*.

CAMBRIA DAILY LEADER . . . established in 1861 in Swansea, it was the first daily newspaper in Wales.

CAMBRIAN, Precambrian, Ordovician and Silurian are geological periods with names that have a Welsh connection, because Wales was so rich in study material.

CAMBRIAN (the) was the first weekly newspaper to be founded in Wales. Established in Swansea in 1804.

CAMBRIAN COAST RAILWAY . . . so few trains, apparently so many accidents. The railway has a shocking record.

CAMBRIAN SHAKESPEARE . . . Thomas Edwards (1738-1810) . . . (AKA 'Twm o'r Nant') of Llannefydd, Denbighshire. (*Sir Ddinbych*). He has been called 'the Cambrian Shakespeare.' He was chiefly a writer of interludes (or 'anterliwtiau') which were short plays for actors and a narrator – not unlike medieval morality plays with the characters personifying morality, greed, miserliness and so on. Twm o'r Nant was one of the few Welsh dramatists between the middle ages and the 20th Century.

CAMBRIOL . . . a Welsh colony founded in 1616 in Newfoundland by Sir William Vaughan of Llangyndeyrn, Carms. The colony fizzled out in 1637.

CANOLFAN IAITH GENEDLAETHOL . . . see Nant Gwrtheyrn

CANT . . . Welsh for one hundred.

CANTILEVER . . . A huge rock, twenty-five feet (8.5m) long found on Glyder Fach (3261 feet/979m) in Snowdonia. A much photographed phenomenon. Thomas Pennant referred to the Cantilever in 1778 in his *Tours in Wales*.

CANTREF . . . a regional division of land referring to a hundred hamlets.

CANTRE'R GWAELOD . . . a drowned *cantref* in Cardigan Bay. Legend has it that a drunken nightwatchman, whose task it was to close the city gates on the incoming tide, fell asleep on duty . . . cue a watery grave.

CANTERBURY TALES 1 . . . The earliest surving manuscript of Chaucer's work is known as *The Hengwrt Chaucer* because it was just one of the collection of more than five hundred manuscripts known as the 'Peniarth Manuscripts' collected by Robert Vaughan of Hengwrt near Dolgellau, Meirionydd. Vaughan, an avid collector of manuscripts, amassed writings in Welsh, English, Latin, French and Cornish.

CANTERBURY TALES 2 . . . an animated version of Chaucer's medieval saga was produced by the Welsh TV company S4C in 1999. It was shortlisted for Oscars.

CAPEL-Y-FFIN . . . near Hay-on-Wye. 'On the Black Hill' the film of Bruce Chatwin's novel was shot here. (cf. An American Werewolf in Paris').

CAPITAL OF WALES . . . The capital of Wales was 'W' until, in the mid 1950s it was decided that the Principality was in need of a capital city. There were four contenders. Aberystwyth, Caernarfon, Cardiff and Swansea. Cardiff won the day.

CAPRICE . . . the supermodel once ate egg on toast at Caernarfon's Palace café whilst filming *Caprice's Travels* for cable TV.

CAPTAIN COOK . . . Dafydd Samwell (Dafydd Ddu Feddyg) (1751-1798) of Nantglyn, Denbs. Was an author and doctor who was expedition surgeon on Captain Cook's ship *The Discovery*. He witnessed the death of Cook at the hands of the Hawaiians in 1779. Samwell wrote *A narrative of the Death of Captain James Cook* in 1786.

CARADOG . . . the brave British tribal leader who fought the Romans *circa* 43-47AD, who retreated into Wales. Known also as Caractacus, he was defeated at Caer Caradog near Cerrigydrudion and taken to Rome where, amazingly, Claudius spared his life.

CARDI . . . natives of Ceredigion continue to enjoy a reputation for being miserly. Such is their alleged tight-fistedness that Shylock and his ilk journey to that part of Wales on refresher courses (provided that the courses are grant-aided of course).

CARDIFF (Caerdydd). Principal city of Wales. Standing on the rivers Taf, Ely (Elai) and Rhymni. Dates back to Roman times. Cardiff gained city status in 1905, became capital in 1955 (it was then Europe's youngest capital city), and is the home of the Welsh Assembly. Also home to the Welsh National Opera,

The Welsh National Folk Museum at St Fagans, Llandaf Cathedral, loads of Welsh language tv stars, Cardiff RFC and Cardiff *City F.C. who currently languish in the Nationwide League division two. Cardiff's Norman castle was once the home of the marquesses of Bute.

CARDIFF CITY F.C. It was 1927. Cardiff City had reached the FA Cup Final for the second time in three years. This time, they beat Arsenal 1-0 and the trophy left English soil for the first and, to-date, only time. Controversy reigned however in that it appeared as though the Arsenal goalkeeper, Dan Lewis, had failed to stop an innocuous shot from Cardiff's Hugh Ferguson. Lewis later blamed his gloves, which he was wearing for the first time, but snide comments abounded because Dan Lewis was a Welshman!

CARDIFF CITY 2 . . . In 1924 at a Wales v Scotland international soccer match, both captains were Cardiff City players – Fred Keenor (Wales) and Jimmy Blair (Scotland).

CARDIFF DEVILS . . . one of the leading Ice Hockey teams in the UK.

CARDIFF DOCK . . . Built in 1839 by the second Marquess of Bute. It cost £350,000 which is, possibly, the most expensive business venture by one man at his own expense in Wales.

CARDIFF MEN . . . FHM magazine, one of the best-selling men's magazines in the UK, said that 'fat necked, stunted blokes outnumber presentable women by about 44 to one' in 1998.

CARDIFF WOMEN . . . in the same issue, the magazine referred to the womenfolk of Cardiff as if they had 'been at their faces with wire wool'.

CARDIGAN BAY – the vast sweep of coastline of Wales which is the largest natural bay in the United Kingdom. Technically Cardigan Bay stretches from Aberdaron on the Llŷn Peninsula down to St David's.

CARLO . . . Singer Dafydd Iwan in 1969 (Investiture year) sarcastically and melodiously sang of Prince Charles (Carlo) playing polo with his pater.

CARMARTHEN (Caerfyrddin) . . . the west-Wales town is the site of Wales' only Crimean War Memorial. It also has a Boer War Memorial.

CARMARTHEN . . . In 1546 Henry VIII granted the town the unique honour

41

of a sword to be carried in front of the town mayor on ceremonial occasions. He also granted special licensing laws allowing longer opening hours.

CARNARVON . . . probably the most westerly part of Western Australia. The port was established in 1883 and has a population of 9,000. How it got the name is a mystery.

CARNO . . . home of Laura Ashley's first effort.

CARRY ON CRUISING . . . *Orunda* was the vessel on which five hundred Urdd members cruised to Scandinavia in 1933 on the movement's first cruise.

CARRY ON UP THE KHYBER . . . one of thirty Carry on films, it was filmed partly on location in Snowdonia in 1968. India, Afghanistan and Wales all enjoy scenically filmable passes.

CARTOGRAPHY . . . John Evans (1723-1795). Cartographer born near Llanymynech. His large scale maps of Pistyll Rhaeadr and two of North Wales are his best known works. In particular, his 1795 map of North Wales on a scale of one inch to the mile was the biggest and best map of the area until the inception of the Ordnance Survey.

CASH FOR QUESTIONS . . . Neil Hamilton the ex-Tory minister in the 'Cash for Questions' scandal of the late 1990s was born at Fleur-de-lis near Blackwood. His father was an Aman Valley pit engineer and his grand-dad was a Gwent colliery worker.

CASTELL COCH . . . near Tongwynlais, Glamorgan (*Morgannwg*). The fabulously wealthy Third Marquess of Bute rebuilt Castell Coch in true medieval style between 1875 and 1900. Not many medieval castles have fully furnished rooms, a working portcullis and drawbridge and water proof roofs. The name is derived from the colour of the stone of the original castle of 1270-1300. It has been used in the making of many films involving medieval castles, including *Ivanhoe*.

CASTLES – North Wales' famous castles include *The Ship and Castle* in Porthmadog High Street, *The Castle Hotel* in Cricieth and Pwllheli's *Y Castell*. All are open all day. On a serious note, Wales has six hundred castles in eight thousand square miles and is therefore the most densely fortified country in Europe.

CASTLES OF GWYNEDD . . . the writer Thomas Pennant referred to these as 'the magnificent badge of our subjection'.

CASTLE MARTIN . . . the Royal Armoured Corps used Castlemartin as a firing range. Flag poles, control towers and lights were sufficient warning to keep clear.

CATALINA FLYING BOATS . . . these were built in Beaumaris, Ynys Môn during World War ll.

CATATONIA . . . critically acclaimed as one of the best pop groups of the 1990s – everyone knows that they are Welsh and definitely proud of it. One of their concert anthems includes the refrain 'Every day when I wake up I thank the Lord I'm Welsh'. Quite.

CAT BURGLAR . . . Ray Jones (Ray The Cat) born 1916. Self-confessed Welsh cat burglar who, in May 1960, stole jewels worth £185,000 off Sophia Loren, who was (type cast of course) filming 'The Millionairess' with Peter Sellers. 'The Cat' sat on the matter of his confession until 1993.

CATI (Twm Siôn) . . . was a latter-day Welsh Robin Hood who hailed from Tregaron, Carms in Elizabethan times. In 1828 Thomas Llewelyn Pritchard cashed in on his heroic deeds by publishing a best-seller *The Adventures and Vagaries of Twm Shon Catti* often said to be the first Welsh novel in the English language.

CATTLE ACT . . . Welsh cattle farming was greatly helped in 1666 by the passing of the Irish Cattle Act, which stated that no Irish cattle could be imported to England and Wales.

CAVE SYSTEM . . . Mynydd Llangatwg has more than sixty miles of caves and passages, including Ogof Agen Allwedd, Ogof Darren Ciliau and Eglwys Faer.

CAWL . . . the Welsh dish of soup or broth or gruel.

CEDAR TREE . . . one planted in the grounds of Gwydir Castle to honour the 1627 wedding of Charles I to Henrietta Maria still flourishes.

CEFN . . . Caernarfon-based Welsh civil rights group.

CELTIC GRAND TOUR . . . for toffs and culture buffs during the French Revolution and Napoleonic Wars. Welsh waterfalls, mountains, flora and fauna were 'discovered' as they could be enjoyed in politically stable conditions.

CELTIC LANGUAGES . . . there are six. Welsh, Irish, Scottish Gaelic, Breton, Cornish and Manx.

CELYN (Llyn) . . . the lake feeds north-eastern Wales and Cheshire with water.

CENSUS . . . the national survey of 1891 was the first to record statistics regarding the Welsh language – incidentally, it was the only one in which Welsh speakers were the majority. (*ARNOLD [Matthew])

CENTRE FOR ALTERNATIVE TECHNOLOGY . . . (C.A.T.) at Corris near Machynlleth is one of Europe's leading Eco centres. Established in a disused slate quarry in 1975.

CERDD DANT . . . the art of singing a counter melody to the accompaniment of a harp.

CEREDIGION MUSEUM . . . in Aberystwyth, formerly the Coliseum Music Hall on whose stage Gracie Fields and Max Miller appeared.

CERNIOGE . . . An 18th Century milestone in the vale of Maentwrog, Gwynedd advises travellers that London is 200 miles, Barmouth 20, Caernarfon 23 etc. It also states that Cernioge is 20 miles. It was not a town but an isolated inn where travellers could seek accommodation. It is now a farmhouse near Cerrigydrudion.

CESAREA . . . former name of a Gwynedd hillside hamlet overlooking the Menai Strait, latterly re-dubbed Upper Llandwrog (how's that for delusions of grandeur?) It is now known as Y Fron.

CHAIR . . . Traditionally at the National Eisteddfod a chair is awarded for the best awdl (a poem in strict metre). The chairing of the winning poet is a ceremony rich in pageantry. Only five women have won a chair to date.

CHAMBERLAIN (Brenda) . . . born 1912, authoress told of her life on Ynys Enlli in the autobiographical book *Tide Race* (1962).

CHAPELS . . . of the five thousand built in Wales during the 19th century, at least one disappears every week.

CHAPLIN (Charlie) . . . the masterful silent screen performer, writing in his autobiography, told of an encounter with 'a human frog' whilst staying at an Ebbw Vale guesthouse.

CHARLES (John) . . . The 'Gentle Giant' of Welsh soccer. Equally adept at centre forward or centre half. Played for Leeds United in the early 50s and became one of the first players to subsequently sign for an Italian club (Juventus) in 1957, for a then record fee.

CHARTISTS . . . a political reform movement of the early 19th Century who campaigned, sometimes violently, for male suffrage for all at the age of 21, amongst several other points. Llanidloes in Powys was the scene of Chartist riots in April 1839. The rioters held the town for a week and wrecked the Trewythen arms where the London police were billeted. It was up to the Brecon Infantry and Montgomeryshire Yeomanry to restore order. One leader was transported for fifteen years whilst two others received seven years in the colonies.

CHATWIN (Bruce) *On the Black Hill* his 1982 novel won the Whitbread Literary Award.

CHEETHAM (Arthur) . . . pioneer of film in Wales. He filmed people, events and charged the public to see themselves. The owner of five cinemas in North & Mid Wales, he filmed Buffalo Bill Cody in his ten gallon hat in Rhyl, the Holyhead mail boat, a royal visit in 1899 and so on. He opened North Wales' first permanent cinema in Rhyl in 1906.

CHEPSTOW . . . town above the River Wye. It was the site of the first stone castle in Wales, built by William Fitzosborn in 1067.

CHEPSTOW RACECOURSE . . . the largest in Wales and the newest in Britain (opened 1926). The home of the Welsh Grand National.

CHESS . . . The *Evans Gambit* in chess is named after a Welshman.

CHESTER . . . English city unhealthily close to the Welsh border. It is proud to enjoy the protection of an unrepealed by-law (passed in 1408) which states that any Welshman found within the city walls after dark is liable to decapitation.

CHINESE TIMMY . . . Timothy Richards (died 1915) of Ffaldybrenin outside Lampeter also had a Chinese name, Li Ti Mo Tai. He was a Baptist missionary and scholar who left for China in 1869 and so impressed the authorities that he was made a mandarin of the highest rank, and a member of the Order of the Double Dragon.

CHIRK CASTLE . . . in Flintshire has enjoyed continuous occupation for over seven hundred years.

CHOIRS . . . Wales has at least three hundred male voice choirs.

CHOLERA . . . Cefn Golau, Tredegar is an abandoned cemetery whose grave stones indicate that it once 'specialised' in cholera victims.

CHRISTIE (Julie) . . . the famous actress (*Dr Zhivago*, *Don't Look Now* and more . . .) owns a farm in mid-Wales at Llandysul.

CHURCH (Charlotte) . . . born Llandaff, Cardiff. A heavenly child soprano whose breakthrough came in 1998, when she was a mere 11 years old. Signed up by Sony – she apparently earned £6,000,000 during 1999 – hence the expression 'a nice little earner'!

CHURCH IN WALES . . . According to 1996 figures there are 1,129 parishes in the country, with 1,522 church buildings. There were nearly seven hundred ordained clergy attending to nearly sixty-four thousand regular worshippers.

CHWARAE TEG . . . Welsh language version of 'fair play', as in 'Fair play, referee'.

CHWAREL FFOS LAS . . . an open cast site near Cydweli, which is the largest man-made hole in Wales.

CHWARELWR, Y . . . The first Welsh language 'talkie', filmed in Llechwedd Quarry, Blaenau Ffestiniog in 1935.

CHWISGI . . . a modern Welsh whisky.

CIGARETTES . . . Dylan Thomas smoked a 'conscious woodbine'.

CILFYNYDD, Pontypridd . . . a mere village which has produced two major international male opera stars in Sir Geraint Evans and Stuart Burrows.

CILMERI . . . village near Builth Wells in Powys. On December 12, 1282 it saw the death of Llywelyn ap Gruffudd, the last Prince of Wales. At the Treaty of Montgomery in 1267 Henry III had officially recognised Llywelyn as the Prince of Wales. The memorial to Llywelyn at Cilmeri is a national rallying place.

CINCINATTI . . . Ezekiel Hughes (1766-1849) was an early Welsh settler of the far west of the USA. When he arrived in Cincinnati in 1796 he noted it to be 'about the size of Machynlleth'. By 1996 Cincinnati had a population of almost 400,000 compared to Machynlleth with just over 2000 – typical American hyperbole.

CIRCLE OF THE WHITE ROSE 1710 . . . a Jacobite society based in Denbighshire who sympathized with the exiled Stuarts.

CIRCULAR CHURCHYARD . . . Pennant Church, two miles from Llangynog, has one.

CIRCULATING SCHOOLS . . . very successful 18th century schools which taught reading. The magic ingredient was simple. Griffith Jones (1683-1761), born Penboyr, Carms, had one aim – Bible reading in the Welsh language. Over 300,000 obtained the rudiments of reading by attending classes that were taught by travelling teachers who would stay in an area for up to three months. Many of the gentry became supporters as they read *Welch Piety* the annual report on the schools. Even Catherine The Great of Russia asked for a report on their success. The result was a highly literate population, but one that was deemed illiterate in the mid 19th century because it was not literate in English.

CISTERCIANS . . . an order of monks known as 'White Monks' because their habits were of undyed wool.

CLEAN AIR . . . In the UK only Northern Scotland has less air-pollution than Wales.

CLEAN BEACHES . . . Wales has 'em!

CLECIADUR (Y) . . . a 1996 guide to the strict metres of poetry by Medwyn Jones.

CLIFF RAILWAY . . . at Aberystwyth. The largest electric powered cliff railway in Britain. It has a 2 in 1 gradient and the top speed is 4 mph (6.5 kph).

CLIMBING . . . The British Alpine Society was founded in 1857. John Clough Williams-Ellis of Llanfrothen, Gwynedd, a well-known climber, was a co-founder.

CLINTON (Hilary) . . . President Bill's First Lady is a fourth generation Welsh American.

CLOAK OF BEARDS . . . the Celtic giant, Rhita used the beards of defeated enemies to weave a cloak for himself. He once challenged King Arthur to a duel with the victor claiming either the cloak (if Arthur won) or the king's beard (should Rhita have been victorious). They fought . . . Arthur won.

CLOGWYN DU'R ARDDU . . . In 1798 this Snowdonian peak saw the first recorded rock climb.

CLONED SHEEP . . . 1996 saw the creation of Dolly the first cloned sheep. She was later mated with David, a Welsh mountain ram who was chosen because of his relatively small size and post-coital manners. The result was Bonnie – the rest is history.

CLYDOG . . . Saint and martyr who lived around 500 AD. Best remembered for the story of his death. He was slain by a jealous follower on the banks of the Afon Mynwy (Monnow river). All attempts to remove his body failed so he was buried where he fell.

CLYWEDOG (Llyn) . . . in Powys is a man-made reservoir which serves the Midlands of England. It was constructed in 1967, is 6 miles (10 kilometres) long and has Britain's tallest concrete dam at 237 feet (71 metres).

CNEWR ESTATE . . . above the Tawe valley in the Brecon Beacons is Wales' largest working sheep farm.

CNICHT . . . this 2,265 foot (680 metres) Snowdonian peak has been termed 'the Matterhorn of Wales' – because of the similarity in shape from the Western aspect.

COAL . . . at its peak in 1913, the coal industry in South Wales saw 233,000 miners producing six million tons of coal at six hundred and twenty coal pits. With over eight hundred fatalities as a result of accidents.

COBB (Joseph Richard) (1821-1897). English born lawyer and antiquary whose connection with Wales was the construction of the Brecon and Merthyr Railway.

COBBLERS . . . Llanerchymedd on Anglesey was known as 'Little Northampton' in the early part of the 20th century because the small town had over two hundred bootmakers. Bless my sole!

COCKLE BARD . . . John Evans (1827-1895) was known as *Y Bardd Cocos* (The Cockle Bard). An Anglesey born and bred eccentric whose outrageous costumery brought him fame, he lived at Menai Bridge (*Porthaethwy*) and sold shellfish (hence the nickname). Once famously proposed to Queen Victoria.

COED Y BRENIN . . . area of forestry in Meirionnydd which was planted in honour of George V.

COETEN ARTHUR . . . at St David's Head, Penfro is yet another of King Arthur's burial places.

COFFIN (Walter) (1784-1867) . . . Bridgend born colliery pioneer who was one of the first to set up pits in the Rhondda in 1815.

COLUMBUS . . . Christopher Columbus was allegedly beaten to the North American continent by Madog ab Owain Gwynedd who sailed from Abercerrig (near Rhos-on-Sea) in the 12th century and landed at what is now called Mobile Bay in 1169 or 1170. Unfortunately, the Vikings still got there first according to archaeological evidence. Of course, the Native Americans had been there for a long time already, but they were of no importance to imperialist statisticians.

COLWYN . . . the ancient Welsh word for spaniel. Hywel Dda's laws valued this hunting dog at £1-0-0, the same value as a perfect stallion, whilst a bondsman's house dog was worth one penny.

COLWYN BAY . . . Town in Conwy Borough, North Wales which has probably the longest promenade (over three miles) in Wales.

COLWYN BAY PIER . . . built in 1899 with a 2,500 seater pavilion, which burned down within a year.

COMMANDO RAID . . . the famous WW2 commando raid on St Nazaire, Britanny was rehearsed at Cardiff docks in 1942.

COMMITTEE . . . Thomas Edwards (1779-1858) was a lexicographer who produced an English-Welsh dictionary which contained many new words invented by Edwards himself to coincide with existing English words. Even today committees are employed in this same process – incidentally, the word for committee in Welsh (pwyllgor) was one invented by Edwards !

COMMONWEALTH GAMES DOUBLE . . . in Edinburgh in 1986, Welsh middle distance runner Kirsty Wade won the 800 and 1500 metres gold medals.

COMMUNITY NEWSPAPER . . . the first Welsh language community newspaper was *Y Dinesydd*, launched in Cardiff in 1973.

COMPULSORY PURCHASE . . . 'Get off moi land' roared Edward I to the monks of Conwy and the villagers of Llanfaes on Anglesey as he required their homes for the influx of builders working on the castles of Conwy and Beaumaris.

COMUS . . . a masque written by John Milton refers to Wales as 'an old and haughty nation proud in arms'.

COMPREHENSIVE SCHOOL . . . the first comprehensive school in Britain was opened in 1949 at Amlwch on Anglesey (*Ynys Môn*).

CONCRETE . . . the 50,000 tonne pressure vessels at Anglesey's Wylfa Nuclear Power Station are the biggest pre-stressed concrete structures in the UK.

CONCRETE BUILDING . . . Gregynog Hall, built in 1860 near Newtown, Trefaldwyn (Montomeryshire) by David *Davies of Llandinam, was one of the first concrete buildings in Britain.

CONEY BEACH . . . at Porthcawl. In 1921 an amusement park was built on the site of a former industrial tip.

CONWY CASTLE . . . another masterpiece in castle-building by James St James of Savoy, 'Master of the King's Works in Wales'. The orders of Edward I were clear. He wanted sea-access, impregnability and a walled town. Work began in 1283 and the castle and walls were completed four years later at the cost of £13,690. The town walls, some three quarters of a mile (1.2 km) long, together with twenty-one towers and four gates remain almost intact. By 1628 the castle had fallen into such disrepair that it was sold to Viscount Conway for a mere £100,000. Conwy Castle and walls are on the World Heritage List of sites of outstanding universal value. This is indeed an accolade because only four such World Heritage Sites exist in Wales.

CONWY HMS . . . a naval training vessel moored in the Menai Strait. A relic of the Napoleonic wars, its famous 'old boys' included ex-poet Laureate John Masefield and Captain Matthew Webb (the first swimmer of the English Channel).

COOK (Arthur James) (1884-1931). English born South Wales miners' leader. During the 1926 General Strike he coined the slogan 'Not a penny off the pay, not a second on the day', which became the cry of miners nationwide.

COOPER (Tommy) . . . the late entertainer was born in Caerffili's Llwyn-onn Street before moving on.

CO-OPERATIVE . . . the first Co-op shop in Wales opened in 1860 at Cwm Bach near Aberdare. It was a boon for the working class who now had the choice of not using the company shop of their employer.

COPE (Julian) . . . the leader of 1980s post-punk band 'The Teardrop Explodes' was born in the Rhymni valley in 1958.

COPPER . . . see AMLWCH PENNIES

COPPER BOTTOMED . . . Thomas Williams, the 'Copper King', owned the world's largest copper mine at Mynydd Paris on Anglesey. In Holywell he had a copper rolling mill to make sheathing for wooden hulls of ships to protect the wood from parasites in tropical waters. This was all well and good until the iron bolts corroded, which led the Copper King to produce copper bolts as strong as iron.

CORACLES (Cwrwgl) . . . Since pre-Roman times small, almost square, boats have been used for netting salmon in Wales. Very light and manoeuvrable and made of a wicker-work frame, coracle fishing is now restricted to just three rivers, the three T's Taf, Teifi and Tywi.

CORDELL (Alexander) (1914-1997) Formerly Major George Alexander Graber. He moved to Wales in 1950 and began writing novels. His best known are a trilogy about life in 19th century industrial Wales (Trade Unions, workers' rights, class clashes etc). *Rape of the Fair Country* (1959) *Hosts of Rebecca* (1960) and *Song of The Earth* (1969). He wrote about twenty novels which have been translated into around seventeen languages.

CORGI . . . breed of dog favoured by Her Majesty Queen Elizabeth ll. In 1996 there were ten royal corgis but none bore Welsh names unless Kelpie, Flor and Phoenix can be pronounced as Mot, Nel and Smwt. The present queen had her first corgi, Susan, when she was 18 years old.(QE2 that is, not the corgi). The Duke of York (later George Vl) bought the first royal corgi in 1933 and the following year the breed gained recognition from the Kennel Club. The corgi is the only British spitz breed of dog and comes in two varieties, 'Cardigan' and 'Pembroke'. They are particularly adept at herding cattle.

CORN IS GREEN (The) . . . the 1945 film version of the book by Emlyn Williams was filmed partly on location at Ysbyty Ifan in Conwy and featured movie-legend Bette Davis as Miss Lily Moffat.

CORY FAMILY . . . as a colliery-owning family who exported huge quantities of coal in their own ships from Barry and Cardiff, John Cory (1828-1910) and Richard Cory (1830-1914), after about 1860, realised that steam-ships needed ports-of-call with coal. With eighty depots, they soon became the world's biggest suppliers of coal to shipping, which used their bunkering service on worldwide shipping routes. The first was at Suez and opened in 1869.

COUNTERFEITING . . . Just before the Dissolution of the Monasteries by Henry VIII in 1536, one of the monks of Strata Florida was found guilty of counterfeiting in his monastic cell which promptly led to a prison cell at Carmarthen gaol.

COUNTIES MAP . . . in 1579 Christopher Saxon published the first map of Welsh counties.

COUNTING CHICKENS . . . talk about putting the cart before the horse... Assuming that the new London – Ireland route would pass through his new town of Tremadog in Gwynedd, William Madocks named the main thoroughfares Dublin Street and London Road, and the local pub *The Union*.

COVENTRY . . . more unfriendly than Wales. Well, so said some listeners who called up Radio Five Live's phone-in programme in 1998.

COVENTRY CATHEDRAL . . . was designed by Sir Basil Spence whose main claim to fame in Wales is his plan for Trawsfynydd's former nuclear power station in Gwynedd.

COWBOYS . . . they were not. Drovers were trustworthy souls who had a government licence so as to distinguish them from bands of vagrants.

COWLYD (Llyn) . . . the deepest Welsh lake at 222 feet (66.6 metres).

CRACHACH . . . the Welsh word for 'toff', or indeed anyone to whom you feel inferior because they have a bigger, more expensive car, a ride-on-mower – with headlights, posher houses, hyphenated surnames, kids at private schools, kids without headlice, bigger-better heated swimming pools with designer water filter systems, CD players, more slaves than you, a member of an older Masonic lodge than you, attend a bigger chapel than you, have an inside w.c. whilst your privvy's positioned in the yard, they have inside plumbing, they order Iceland Home Delivery, they use taxis, they wear a tie, they actually marry before pregnancy – now that is middle class, they own a poodle – you own a mongrel etc, etc, etc.

CRADDOCK (Sir Matthew) (died 1531). A Royal courtier whose main claim to fame is that he married the widow of the Pretender, Perkin Warbeck. Craddock was born in South Wales where he wielded considerable power.

CRAFNANT (Llyn) . . . this lake gets its name from the garlic (craf in Welsh) which grows in the Crafnant valley above the beautiful Afon Conwy.

CRAIG Y NOS 1 . . . in 1878 this Glyntawe mansion became the retreat of the renowned soprano Adelina Patti, the 'Queen of Song'. Of Italian parents, the diva was born in Madrid and brought up in New York. Verdi regarded her as the best of the day. The highest paid female opera star ever, Adelina (1843-1919) chose Wales for relaxation between world tours.

CRAIG Y NOS 2 . . . in the 1971 film *Young Winston* the train-ambush scene was shot on location on the railway line near here.

CRASH COURSE IN WELSH . . . one of the shortest was that of Prince Charles at Aberystwyth university before his 1969 Investiture.

CRAWSHAY . . . (Family of Cyfarthfa, Merthyr Tudful). Known as 'The Iron Kings'. The dynasty started with Richard (born 1739) and ended with Robert who died one hundred and forty years later although the family were still involved with the manufacture of iron until the firm (then called Messrs. Crawshay Bros.) were taken over in 1902.

CRECY . . . The Battle of, in France in 1346 in which Welsh long bowmen caused havoc among the French with their deadly accuracy and rapidity of fire. The Welsh wore green and white hats and coats, and it is argued that this was the first occasion on which military uniform was worn. At Crecy on August 26 1346 the number of Welsh exceeded five thousand men. One of their leaders was Hywel ap Gruffudd, known as Hywel y Fwyall (Hywel the Axe) – a Welsh gladiator whose ability with a battleaxe was unsurpassed).

CREDO CYMRU . . . a group of around one thousand clergy and laity who were opposed to women priests.

CREMATION . . . Dr William Price of Llantrisant was a preacher, doctor, druid, and a pioneer of cremation which he helped legalise in 1884. After police prevented his attempt to cremate his infant son, he won the ensuing legal battle. This eccentric fathered a child at the age of 90; the mother was Gwenllian his housekeeper. His own cremation was attended by thousands, who drank the pubs dry, naturally.

CRIB GOCH . . . an awesome ridge walk to Snowdon which is certainly not for the faint-hearted.

CRICIETH . . . a picturesque seaside town in Gwynedd known as 'The Pearl of the Cambrian Coast', which was lost when Regional Railways omitted it from a 1999 time table map.

CRICKET . . . Not until 1921 did Glamorgan join the County Cricket Championship.

CRIMEA NURSES . . . Elizabeth (Betsi) Cadwaladr (1789-1860) of Llanycil, Bala, Meirionnydd volunteered to serve in the Crimea with Florence Nightingale, at the age of 65. A society for Welsh-speaking nurses was founded in her name in 1970.

CRITICS . . . Recent so-called celebrity critics of Wales and the Welsh include Simon Heffer (who?) A.N. Wilson (A.N. Other who?), Jeremy Clarkson (boy racer) and Ian Wooldridge(who, again?).

CROESO . . . 'Welcome'. Apparently, at O'Hare Airport in Chicago the Welsh word is the last of many different languages used on a board in the arrivals lounge.

CROFT (Robert) . . . Glamorgan and England spin bowler of renown. He grew up in the village of Hendy in Glamorgan.

CROMLECH . . . a Neolithic burial chamber, otherwise known as a dolmen. These barrows or tombs were topped with a big capstone supported by upright stone pillars, with dry stone walls filling the spaces between the pillars.

CROSSBAR . . . In the autumn of 1993 Wales were only the width of a crossbar away from qualifying for the finals of the Soccer world cup in the USA. Wales, who had not qualified for any finals since 1958, were entertaining Rumania at the old National Stadium in Cardiff. With the game finely poised at 1-1 Wales were awarded a penalty. In a team that featured Ian Rush, Mark Hughes, Dean Saunders and Ryan Giggs (all world class attacking players), up stepped the Swindon Town left back, Paul Bodin, whose shot struck the bar. Clearly elated by their let-off the Rumanians went on to win the game and so qualified for USA '94. In fairness to Bodin, he was a regular penalty taker.

CROWN . . . in the National Eisteddfod the Crown is awarded for the winning pryddest, which is a long poem that is not written in strict metres.

CRUMLIN VIADUCT . . . Built by T W Kennard for the Newport, Abergavenny and Hereford Railway in 1857. At the time it was Britain's highest viaduct (third highest in the world) at 200 feet (60m) high and nearly 1,600 feet (480m) long. A most elaborate feat, it crossed the Ebbw Valley – all because of the insatiable demand for coal. The strategic importance of Crumlin Viaduct was not unknown to the Germans in World War 2 because photographs of it appeared in books issued to the Luftwaffe. It was unfortunately dismantled in the mid 60s, but not before featuring in the Gregory Peck and Sophia Loren film *Arabesque* (for the hair-raising chase sequence).

CRWTH . . . an ancient type of stringed instrument manufactured and once abundant in Wales. Its popularity died out because of Methodism *c*.1800.

CRYSTAL (David) . . . Holyhead's Professor is the renowned editor of many encyclopedias.

CULVER HOLE on the Gower Peninsula remains a mystery. Was it a medieval pigeon loft? Was it a secret lair for pirates? Part cave, part rocky inlet – why was it virtually bricked up? Is there only one single correct answer?

CURSE . . . in an editorial in The Times in 1866, it was stated: 'The Welsh language is the curse of Wales' (cf Arnold, Matthew).

CWM . . . meaning 'valley', this is a common prefix in Welsh placenames.

CWM BYCHAN . . . in the Rhinog mountains. In 1937, part of *The Drum* starring Raymond Massey and Sabu was filmed on the shores of the lake.

CWM DERI . . . fictional valley, the setting of the popular Welsh language TV soap opera *Pobl Y Cwm*.

CWM HYFRYD . . . a sister colony of Y Wladfa in Patagonia was founded in 1866, about 400 miles (640 km) away at the foot of the Andes.

CWM MERCH GOAT HERD . . . a herd of about forty led by one buck roams the slopes above Afon Merch, a tributary of Afon Glaslyn near Beddgelert. In the spring time rutting period they appear near Cwm Merch Falls, Gwynedd, but Julie Andrews does not serenade them.

CWMBRAN . . . Wales' only 'new town' i.e. as defined by being government-sponsored and purpose-built.

CWMHIR ABBEY . . . a Cistercian place of worship which was once the largest church in Wales. It had a 242 foot (73m) long nave – only three longer ones could be found in Britain, at the cathedral naves of York, Durham and Winchester. The Abbey was somewhat understaffed in the pre-reformation reign of Henry VIII as it had only three monks.

CWM RHONDDA . . . the renowned hymn-tune was written by Dowlais-born John Hughes (1873-1932).

CWRT (Llyn) . . . in Snowdonia at 2,500 feet (750m) it is the highest lake in Wales.

CYMDEITHAS YR IAITH . . . The Welsh Language Society. Passionate body whose worthy aims are to preserve Welsh as a living and working language.

Established in 1962 and inspired by Saunders Lewis' famous 'fate of the language' radio lecture, the society were sadly forced to use tactics such as vandalising road signs to gain recognition. A succession of Welsh Secretaries under consecutive governments refused to meet Society leaders until Ron Davies met chairman Gareth Kiff in 1997.

CYMER . . . recently dubbed 'Little Switzerland', this West Glamorgan town was formerly a blitzed and bleak coal mining area with slag heaps galore. Now it is adorned with beautiful forests.

CYMORTHA . . . Late medieval border magnates added to the lawlessness of the time by forcing the poor to hand over gifts which were used to pay fines. This 'protection racket' was eradicated by Henry VIII on the eve of the Act of Union in 1536.

CYMMRODORION SOCIETY . . . The Honourable Society of Cymmrodorion was founded in 1751 in London by Richard Morris with the aims of uniting London Welshmen in culture and patriotism, fostering Welsh education, publishing and scholarships. The Society's fortunes have waxed and waned. Much prized is the Society's Medal for distinguished service to Welsh Culture.

CYMRAEG CLIR . . . handbook produced by Gwynedd Council to aid people to complete official forms in the Welsh language.

CYMRU . . . The land of the Cymry, (meaning brethren), called Wales in English.

CYMRU AM BYTH . . . motto of the Welsh Guards (Wales Forever). Often seen tattooed on young (and old) Welsh arms in ale houses and scratched on the back of public toilet doors.

CYMRU FYDD . . . founded in 1886 as a Home Rule for Wales movement. A century and thirteen years later the first Welsh Assembly in nearly six hundred years met.

CYNAN . . . Welsh language poet Albert Evans Jones (1895-1970) born at Pwllheli, Gwynedd was thrice winner of the Crown at the National Eisteddfod (1921, 1923 and 1931). He also won the Chair in 1924. Had two spells as Archdruid in the 1950s and 1960s and was knighted in 1969 for services to the cultural life of Wales.

CZECHOSLOVAKIAN . . . is the latest language in which it is possible to read *The Mabinogion* – the romantic tales of heroism and beauty in the misty Dark Ages.

D-DAY . . . the historic WW2 Normandy beach landings were practised on the beaches of Pembrokeshire and watched by Churchill, Eisenhower and Montgomery. Around a third of the ships involved in the D-Day landings sailed from Welsh ports.

D.V.L.A./D.V.L.C . . . Swansea based car and driver licencing authorities.

DAFFODIL (Narcissus pseudnarcissus) together with the Leek is Wales' national emblem.

DAFFY TAFFS . . . the nickname of the Welsh Guards regiment.

DAFYDD . . . Welsh version of the English name David. (Dewi is also translated as David.)

DAFYDD ap Gwilym . . . the 14th Century poet regarded as the best poet Wales ever produced and was a contemporary of Chaucer.

DAFYDD IWAN . . . born 1943 at Brynaman, Carms. Folk-singer, poet, director of record company Sain, chairman of Cymdeithas yr Iaith Gymraeg (1968-1971), former chairman and vice president of Plaid Cymru. Committed to the cause of Welsh nationalism, Dafydd Iwan has influenced many Welsh people by making them more politically aware. It is difficult to suggest what more any patriot could have done to help his country and cause.

DAHL . . . Roald. One of the best-selling writers of children's books and creator of *Charlie & the Chocolate Factory*. Dahl was born of Norwegian stock, in Llandaff, Cardiff and died of leukemia aged 74 in 1990.

DALTON (Timothy) actor who memorably played James Bond in the 80s and early 90s. Born in Colwyn Bay, apparently.

DAMBUSTERS . . . the film used Llyn Efyrnwy (Lake Vyrnwy) in Powys because of its suitable shape and scenic background.

DAM DISASTER . . . Llyn Eigiau dam above the Conwy valley burst open in 1925, and gigantic boulders swept down on the village of Dolgarrog, killing sixteen people.

DAME WALES . . . a cartoon figure which first appeared in *Punch Cymraeg* c.1855. She later appeared in the *Western Mail*.

DAN YR OGOF . . . These Powys caves were discovered in 1912 and have not yet been fully explored. It is the largest cave complex in Western Europe.

DARON – Celtic godess of the oak tree . . . why are there so few placename suffixed Daron in Wales, especially in view of the famed Druidic Oaks which abound across the Principality.

DARRIEN . . . motor cars are built and raced by Team Darrien of Swansea Institute.

DARTMOOR JAIL . . . built by David Alexander who also built South Stack lighthouse at Holyhead on Anglesey.

DAV 1D . . . the cherished number plate of David Emmanuel, the Welsh-born couturier. Princess Di wore his frock for her 1981 wedding.

DAVID . . . Patron Saint of Wales whose feast day is March 1. David was a 5th/6th Century Christian bishop related (according to legend) to King Arthur. St David was responsible for the leek being accepted as the national emblem of Wales. St David is known as Dewi Sant in Welsh, and is the only one of the four British Isles patron saints to actually come from the country he represents. St Andrew (Scotland) was Russian, St George (England) was German and St Patrick (Ireland) was actually born in Wales.

DAVIES (David) (1818-1890). MP and renowned industrialist whose main contribution to the engineering world was the construction of several railways throughout Wales. In conjunction with the engineer Benjamin Piercy (with whom he worked in Wales, he later introduced rail travel to the Mediterranean island of Sardinia. Later still Davies became involved in coal-mining and sank several pits in the South Wales coalfield and developed the docks at Barry for export purposes. He was born at Llandinam, Monmouthshire (*Trefaldwyn*) *BARRY.

DAVIES (Gerald) . . . born Cydweli 1945 One of the all-time greats of Welsh rugby and a lynch-pin in the 'Golden age' side of the 1970s. Davies was blessed with amazing speed, and played for his country forty-six times between 1966-1978, scoring twenty tries from the wing. He was part of the triumphant 1971 British Lions tour of New Zealand.

DAVIES (Harry Parr) . . . Neath born composer of such 20th Century classic songs as *Wish me Good Luck As You Wave Me Goodbye* and *Sing As We Go*. He died in 1955.

DAVIES (Ivor Novello) . . . (1893-1951) Composer, lyricist, actor and film star. He was born in Cardiff and wrote the great WW1 anthem *Keep the Home Fires Burning*, several straight plays and the music for such musicals as *Careless Rapture* (1936), *The Dancing Years* (1939) and *King's Rhapsody* (1949).

DAVIES (John) (born 1938) in the Rhondda. This historian's highly acclaimed major work is *Hanes Cymru* 1990 (which was translated as *A History of Wales* 1993), a superb book the last sentence of which reads 'This book was written in the faith and confidence that the nation in its fulness is yet to be'. He was the first secretary of 'Cymdeithas yr Iaith Gymraeg' in 1967.

DAVIES (Dr John) (*c*.1567-1644) born Llanferres, Denbs. Rector of Mallwyd who helped prepare the 1620 edition of the Welsh Bible. His main claim to fame was as a lexicographer who, in 1632, produced a Welsh-Latin/Latin-Welsh dictionary.

DAVIES (Jonathan) . . . Rugby star who made the grade at Rugby Union, moved successfully north to take up Rugby league, and then swapped codes again to end his career. Won thirty-one WRU caps in two stints which commenced with his 1985 debut.

DAVIES (Lynn) . . . Olympic gold medallist in the 1964 long jump and nicknamed 'Lynn The Leap' henceforth. Born at Nant-y-moel, Glamorgan (*Morgannwg*).

DAVIES (Ron) . . . Labour politician. The former high-flying Secretary of State for Wales whose career hit the buffers somewhat after a much-publicised incident on Clapham Common. Davies had been at the forefront of the campaign for a Welsh Assembly and was in line to become its inaugural leader.

DAVIES (Ryan) (1937-1977) born Glanaman, Carms. Talented and versatile entertainer who died after a heart-attack whilst on holiday in the USA. He had become a household name in Wales after signing a BBC contract in the middle 1960s and memorably starred in the Welsh language TV comedy series *Fo a Fe*.

DAVIES (Russell T) . . . Swansea born scriptwriter who wrote the episode of Coronation Street which saw the Duckworths visiting Las Vegas.

DAVIES (Walford) . . . (1869-1941) a gifted musician from Oswestry, he became Professor of Music at Aberystwyth and succeeded Sir Edward Elgar as Master of the King's Musick in 1934.

DAVIES (Wilfred Mitford) . . . (1895-1966) was an accomplished illustrator of children's books. For years his work appeared in *Cymru'r Plant*.

DAVIES (William) (1814-91). Paleontologist born at Holywell (*Treffynnon*), Flintshire. Esteemed by fellow fossil excavators who recognized Davies' prodigious skills in his work on disinterring the head of the famous Ilford Mammoth in the 1880s.

DAVIES (Windsor) Popular tv character actor who starred in *It Ain't 'Alf Hot Mum* (ten years) and *Never The Twain* (a further seven years).

DAVIS (Fred) . . . the late snooker world champion used to run a hotel in Llandudno.

DEAD POET . . . Ellis Humphrey Evans (1887-1917). 'Hedd Wyn' was a War Poet born at Trawsfynydd and killed in the trenches at the battle of Pilkem Ridge. He was posthumously awarded the chair at the National Eisteddfod in 1917. In the 1990s, a film of his life became the first ever Welsh language movie to be nominated for an Academy Award. *BLACK CHAIR

DEADLY DINNER . . . in 1175, Norman Lord William de Braose invited local Welsh leaders to a banquet at Abergavenny Castle in Gwent – the natives were promptly murdered after they disarmed in readiness for the promised repast.

DEATHBED CONFESSION . . . Richard Lewis (1807-1833) ('Dic Penderyn') . . . was executed for his alleged role in the Merthyr Riots of 1831. He was arrested and tried for the wounding of a soldier, Donald Black, at the Castle Inn in June 1831. Evidence was scant and Dic Penderyn maintained his innocence throughout his trial and subsequent imprisonment, but was executed at Cardiff jail in August. He was buried in his home cemetery at Aberafon. Historical footnote:- In the USA in 1874 Congregational Minister Revd Evan Evans reported that he had received a deathbed confession from a man who claimed to have wounded the soldier Donald Black.

DEATH RAY . . . just one of the inventions of Harry Grindell Matthews of Mynydd-y-Gwair, Clydach near Swansea. His death ray could kill a rat at 21 yards (20 metres). He also pioneered 'talkies' and portable telephones but was too ahead of his time.

DECLARATION of American Independence . . . 1/3 of the signatories were of Welsh descent.

DECHRAU CANU DECHRAU CANMOL . . . Wales' answer to *Songs of Praise*. A popular TV programme of Sunday evenings. After all, Wales is the 'land of the Bible' and 'the land of song'.

DEDWS . . . only in Caernarfon could the mortuary be called Dedws.

DEE (Afon Dyfrdwy) . . . the river whose source is Llyn Tegid (Bala Lake), and whose length is 111 miles (178 km).

DEE (John) (1527-1608) . . . Welsh born astronomer, alchemist and mathematician.

DEFOE (Daniel) . . . the famous author of *Robinson Crusoe*, wrote of the 'impassable heights' of Snowdonia in the 1720s, and many other things that he did not like about the Welsh countryside.

DEGANWY SLATE PORT – a forgotten port connected by rail to Blaenau Ffestiniog in Gwynedd.

DEINIOL . . . Another Welsh Saint whose name is carried by North Wales' oldest cathedral at Bangor.

DEINIOL LIBRARY . . . at Hawarden was founded by W.E. Gladstone in 1894 with thirty thousand of his own books. Later the library received ninety thousand letters, papers and speeches of the founder.

DEINIOLEN . . . the Gwynedd town was originally named Ebeneser and was a thriving quarry town which is now undergoing a regeneration. It has Britain's largest manufacturer of quick-release buckles and harness fittings for high performance cars.

DEMON DRIVER . . . Maureen Rees of Cardiff became an instant celebrity as the 'demon driver from L' in the late 1990s. Her Lada car, Betsy, and her unique driving style won her universal media coverage after the TV series *Driving School*.

DENNIS (Henry) . . . a 19th century Denbighshire entrepreneur who employed ten thousand workers in collieries, brickworks, gas, tramways, lead mines, stone quarries and so on.

DERBY . . . the first Welsh jockey to win the Classic horse race was Geoff Lewis of Talgarth who won in 1971 on the famous Mill Reef.

DERFEL GADARN . . . At Llandderfel (Derfel was a 6th century saint) in Meirionnydd the locals idolised the saint's wooden statue as they believed it could save souls. However, the statue (depicting the saint on horseback) was removed by monastery inspectors in 1536 and taken to London – all part of Henry VIII's attack on anything Papist.

DESERT of WALES . . . is one of the largest wild uncultivated areas of land in Wales and England, which is found to the west of the Elan Valley.

DEVIL'S BRIDGE (Pontarfynach) . . . actually three bridges in a triple decker across a 300 feet (91 metre) deep chasm housing Afon Mynach in Ceredigion. The first bridge was a stone effort built by Cistercian monks in the 12th century; the second dates from 1753 and the most modern was completed in 1901. It's Welsh name was *Pont y Gŵr Drwg*.

DEVIL'S STAIRCASE . . . part of the Abergwesyn pass, with hair-raising hairpin bends and utterly splendid isolation.

DEVOLUTION . . . in the 1979 devolution referendum 80% of Wales voted 'No', although the way the questions were asked, hardly anybody knew what they were voting for or against. *WELSH OFFICE

DEVOTION TO DUTY . . . When Tredegar milkman Trevor Jones was asked to visit Buckingham palace to receive an MBE in the 1990s he declined, insisting that his customers came first!

DEWI DRAGON . . . the feisty, fiery creature who was the official mascot for the 1999 Rugby World Cup.

DEWI SANT . . . a.k.a. St David – the memory of the patron saint of Wales is celebrated on March 1st.

DIC SION DAFYDD . . . a character created by Jac Glan-y-gors in the late 18th century. Dic's knowledge and use of Welsh diminished in proportion to his success on the social ladder. By now Dic Sion Dafydd is synonymous with this type of climber. A similar character in Ireland is called 'Shauneen'.

DIAL A POEM . . . a pioneering venture in Wales in 1970. The poets were gratified to learn that Dai Public was not an utter barbarian in that hundreds of calls were made each week. Sponsored by the Welsh Arts Council, the poems changed weekly and the scheme continued for about 5 years.

DIBDEN (Charles) . . . wrote the light opera *Liberty Hall* which featured the well-known song *The Bells of Aberdyfi* (Clychau Aberdyfi). Some argue that it was written by Maria Jane Williams. However, the song is usually associated with the story of Cantre'r Gwaelod, as the idea of chiming underwater bells helps to enrich the myth.

DIC ABERDARON . . . (RICHARD ROBERT JONES) (1780-1843) is believed to have had more than a mere working knowledge of about thirteen languages. This eccentric who wandered widely throughout North Wales is best known for his Welsh-Hebrew-Greek dictionary which he wrote despite lacking a formal education.

DICKENS (Charles) . . . his novel *The Uncommercial Traveller* is based on the loss of the *Royal Charter* in 1859. As a reporter, Dickens arrived after the event and gleaned material from many locals.

DICTIONARY . . . the Welsh-Hebrew-Greek dictionary of Richard Robert Jones (Dic Aberdaron) is preserved in the museum of St Asaph Cathedral.

DIM MYNEDIAD . . . means 'No Entry'

DINAS DINLLE Award-winning beach on Caernarfon Bay and also home to an airstrip where the first ever RAF Mountain Rescue team was formed.

DINAS ISLAND . . . in Pembrokeshire ceased to be an island about eight thousand years ago due to the vagaries of nature.

DIDDY MEN . . . those famous big-booted-clown-costume-wearing extras to Ken Dodd's throwback to Vaudeville don't all come from Liverpool suburb Knotty Ash, after all. Dodd's father was born in Mold in 1910, so at least half of the Diddy Men must be Welsh.

DISAPPEARED PLACES . . . 15th and 16th century maps and charts of the ever-changing Conwy estuary name Llys Helig, Castell Tremlyd and Penlassoc, places which have long-since disappeared. Were they the same place? Were they just fish weirs built by the monks of Aberconwy? Were they the legendary palace of ancient folklore? The nearest pub overlooking the 'alleged' location is called *The Legend*.

DISAPPEARING ISLAND . . . Mysteriously, the island of Anglesey 'disappeared' in December 1996. Not like a latter day Brigadoon, this was a case of European bureaucratic bungling. In designs for the Euro Bank note Anglesey, (which is 156 sq. miles larger than Malta) was nowhere to be seen.

DISESTABLISHMENT . . . of the Church in Wales. The Act of 1914 was masterminded by that renowned Mancunian born Welshman, David Lloyd George, and saw the Church in Wales becoming independent of its sister the other side of Offa's Dyke. Wales had its own Archbishop in A.G. Edwards of St Asaph. Incidentally, as a result of a certain conflict in Europe (WW1), the act was not actually implemented until 1920.

DISLEY (John) . . . Welshman who founded the London marathon and had earlier won Olympic bronze in the 1952 steeplechase.

DISTILLERY CHAPEL . . . Repairs to Talybont chapel outside Bala involved using the stones of the local former Frongoch distillery – a spirited gesture by the distillers family.

DISTRICT NURSE . . . a late (lamented) TV series starring Nerys Hughes, which lasted until its second series when woeful viewing figues brought a euthansia-style end to the programme.

DIWRNOD SANTES DWYNEN (St Dwynen's Day) is January 25. She is the patron saint of lovers or sweethearts.

DOBSON (Henry Austin) 1840-1921. Accomplished writer of light verse who was educated at Beaumaris.

DOCTOR COCH . . . A renowned monastery inspector Dr Ellis Price (who wore his red university gown, hence the nickname) who used to take his mistress on his tours of duty.

DOCTOR . . . Wales' earliest reference to a doctor is the Roman inscription on a stone in Llangian churchyard in Gwynedd: Meli Medici Fili Martini Iacit' (which loosely translates as 'The doctor's horse has drunk my Martini').

DR WHO . . . the Tardis-travelling TV timelord had a series of adventures on Mynydd Parys, near Amlwch, Anglesey where the aftermath of the coppermining has left a desolate lunar-like landscape.

DOLBADARN . . . and DOLWYDDELAN . . . castles in Gwynedd which were 'homebuilt' i.e. constructed by Welsh princes as opposed to invading conquerors.

DOLE-ON-SEA . . . the ill-judged description of Rhyl by Tory politician Rod Richards.

DOLPHINS . . . the rare bottle-nosed variety now inhabit Cardigan Bay, one of only three areas in the UK that is graced by their presence. Thanks to the Whale & Dolphin Conservation Society, the government has designated Britain's largest bay a 'special area of conservation'.

DOLWYDDELAN . . . Sir Cliff Richard has a country cottage in the North Wales village (population 474 – or 475 when His Cliffship spends a *Summer Holiday*) He is not a frequent visitor.

DONIZETTI . . . the Italian opera writer might have been referring to the mountains of Wales where he describes the 'Liverpool Mountains' in his 1824 opera, *Emilia di Liverpool*.

DOUBLE WEIGHT BOXING CHAMPION . . . In 1927, Frank Moody of Pontypridd was the British Middleweight title holder and the British Lightweight champion – in the same year.

DOUBLE WINNER . . . At the National Eisteddfod at Bangor in 1912, T.H. Parry-Williams became the first poet to win both Crown and Chair.

DOUBLE-DOUBLE WINNER . . . Only three years later, the prolific pen of Parry-Williams landed him the double again!

DOWLAIS . . . was visited by Edward VIII in November 1936. Upon hearing of the helpless plight of the unemployed steelworkers, the then king (and later Duke of Windsor) uttered the oft-repeated words: 'Something must be done'.

DRAFOD Y, (the Discourse) . . . Originally a Patagonian weekly newspaper which was established in 1891 and was at first a wholly Welsh language periodical. After WW1 it began to include Spanish and English articles – needs must where the devil drives – and is still published periodically.

DRAGON . . . In 1807 the Red Dragon was acknowledged as the heraldic Royal badge for Wales. And the Red Dragon flag was acknowledged as Wales' national flag in 1959. Only one other country has a dragon as a national emblem – it's China.

DRAGONS . . . the first appearance of a dragon on Welsh coins was during the reign of Henry VII.

DRIER . . . Wales is drier than Britain's favourite holiday destination, Cornwall.

DROVERS . . . Welsh cattle, sheep and other livestock were shod and driven to English fairs by drovers. From the 15th to 19th centuries they used traditional routes and stopped at inns (The Drovers' Arms naturally). Their return was eagerly awaited as they brought not only gold and silver coins but news, songs, stories, gifts. Drovers were licensed by the government and some became wealthy and even established banks (e.g. in 1799 *Banc Yr Eidion Du* of Llandovery (Black Ox Bank) and *Banc Y Ddafad Ddu* (Black Sheep Bank) at Aberystwyth. The advent of the railways brought about the demise of the drovers in Wales.

DRY DWYFOR . . . the former administrative district in Gwynedd was the last bastion of dry, booze-less, alcohol-free ways on Sundays only, unless you were a member of a licensed club or were signed into a club or . . . The system bristled with anomalies. Fortunately (or otherwise, depending on your disposition) the final referendum in November 1996 showed unequivocally that the great majority wanted Dwyfor to follow the rest of Wales. 24,325 voted for Sunday opening while only 9829 voted against. It must be mentioned that the goal posts and cross bars had been moved since the previous referendum (seven years earlier) in that, due to local government reorganization, voting was not restricted to Dwyforites. Boozers as far away as Abergwyngregyn (near Conwy) and Tywyn (almost mid-Wales) helped change the Dwyfor licensing laws. For the dry lobby the 1996 vote was a lost cause in that the non-Dwyfor areas had one-by-one fallen to the wets and were not likely to think 'we've had enough of wet Sundays – lets go back to shutting the pubs'.

DYNION . . . the sign outside any building remotely resembling a public toilet means 'Men' or 'Gentlemen'. Some conveniences are not convenient at all because of their opening and closing hours. E.g. Pwllheli's close at 5.30 pm.

DYWARCHEN (Llyn y Dywarchen) . . . a floating peat island, first observed by Gerallt Cymro in 1188 between Rhyd-ddu and Nantlle in Snowdonia.

EARHART (Amelia) . . . the renowned aviatrix took off from Trepassey Bay, Newfoundland in 1928. Some 20 hours and 40 minutes later she landed in Burry Port, South Wales becoming the first woman to fly the Atlantic.

EARLIEST HYMN . . . in the Welsh language is 'Gogonedauc argluit, hepich guell' which is contained in *Llyfr Du Caerfyrddin* (Black Book of Carmarthen). It was the first of many thousands.

EDGAR (Elizabeth) of Cardiff. The champion showjumper has won the Queen Elizabeth II Cup a record five times (1977, 79, 81, 82 and 86). Equestrian skills must run in the family as her brother is the not untalented David *Broome.

EDNO . . . Llyn Edno above Nant Gwynant in Gwynedd is home to cannibal trout – observed by Charles Kingsley.

EDWARD I . . . King who treated the Welsh roughly. His forte was conquering, torturing, maiming and killing. Also built a few castles.

EDWARD II . . . born 1284 at Caernarfon, he was the first heir to the English throne to be given the title Prince of Wales. A recent edition of the *Hutchinson Encyclopedia* lists Edward II as one of only two 'famous' people of Gwynedd . . . surely through lack of space. The other is T.E. Lawrence (of Arabia).

EDWARDS (A.G.) . . . Wales' first Archbishop of the newly created Church in Wales, he was enthroned at St Asaph in 1920.

EDWARDS (Dorothy) (1903-34). Novelist who was regarded as one of the best of her age who had struck a new note in English Literature, writing a collection of short stories called *Rhapsody* in 1927, and *Winter Sonata* in novel form a year later. She was a fervent Welsh Nationalist although unable to speak the language. Born at Ogmore Vale in Glamorgan, she committed suicide.

EDWARDS (Gareth) . . . Former captain on *Question of Sport*. Also quite good at Rugby and, we believe, was once the youngest captain of Wales. In 1999 Edwards was voted the best rugby footballer of all time.

EDWARDS (Huw) . . . the Bridgend-born, Llanelli-raised Six O'Clock News anchorman, following the great Welsh tradition of John *Humphrys and Martin Lewis as news presenters.

EDWARDS (Ifan ab Owen) . . . (1895-1970) of Llanuwchlyn, Bala, Gwynedd. In 1922 he founded *Urdd Gobaith Cymru* (Welsh League of Youth) which, eighty years later is still gaining strength and doing more for young people and their language than any other similar movement in the world. He succeeded his father O.M. *Edwards as editor of *Cymru'r Plant* a children's magazine, and invited readers to join Urdd Gobaith Cymru. Another Sir Ifan (he was knighted in 1947) success was his association with the first Welsh medium primary school at Aberystwyth in 1939.

EDWARDS (Gwilym Meredith) . . . (1918-1999) born Rhosllanerchrugog, Wrexham) Enjoyed a sixty year acting career on stage and screen, appearing in over seventy films including *A Run For Your Money* and *The Cruel Sea*. He was also a staunch patriot.

EDWARDS (Owen Morgan) (1858-1920) . . . born Coed-y-pry, Llanuwchllyn, Gwynedd. At Oxford University he was one of the founders of *Cymdeithas Dafydd ap Gwilym*, a Society which helped foster Welsh culture. 'O.M.' (as he was affectionately known) strove to make the Welsh more aware of the inestimable value of their own history, language and culture. To further people's knowledge of their country and nationhood, he produced Welsh language books on the history and traditions of Wales. As Chief Inspector of Schools after 1907 he saw the need for (a) Welsh language education, and (b) Welsh language publishing for children – his *Cymru'r Plant* was published between 1892 – 1920. At its peak it sold twelve thousand copies per month. His invaluable work for the language (comparable to that of Thomas *Gee, the Denbigh publisher) was continued by his son, Sir Ifan ab Owen *Edwards who founded the *Urdd* movement in 1922.

EDWARDS (Thomas) (1848-1927). Independent minister who emigrated to the USA in 1870, where he became one of the most successful ministers with probably the largest church in the country at that time.

EISTEDDFOD – any of a number of cultural festivals held in Wales, which are dedicated to the bardic arts of literature and music. The first record of the word possibly comes from such an event in Aberteifi in 1176, under the patronage of Rhys ap Gruffudd (Yr Arglwydd Rhys). The principal Eisteddfodau are the International Eisteddfod held annually at Llangollen which attracts competitors from all over the globe – Luciano Pavarotti appeared in 1956 as a competitor in his father's choir – and the Welsh National Eisteddfod which takes place at different venues every August. Since its inception the National Eisteddfod of Wales has been held annually except for two years 1914 and 1940.

ELAN . . . the valley and dam 4 miles south-west of Rhaeadr, where Barnes Wallis helped perfect his 'bouncing bomb' technique which proved so successful for the WW2 Dambusters.

ELECTION . . . When is an election not an election? In the 1830 general election there were no contested seats in Wales.

ELECTRICITY 1 . . . Dinorwig's 'Electric Mountain' is a pumped storage power station in Llanberis at the foot of Snowdon. Over three million tons of slate were hollowed out of Mynydd Elidir and £450 million spent on the ten year project (commenced 1974). Full capacity can be reached in a mere ten seconds and Dinorwig's generators provide a 'safety net' for all of the UK.

ELECTRICITY 2 . . . Wales' first underground pit-lighting appeared in two pits in 1882, at Risca and Pontypridd.

ELECTRICITY PYLONS . . . there are more in Snowdonia than in any other UK National Park.

ELEPHANT BOY . . . one of the earliest major films to be shot on location in Wales. Starring Sabu ,it was filmed in and around Harlech in Gwynedd whose rugged landscape was briefly transposed as India in 1937.

ELGAR (Sir Edward) . . . the great composer was inspired to write his *Introduction & Allegro* while on a cliff-top walk at Tresaith, Ceredigion (near Llangrannog) as he heard a choir rehearsing on the beach. He also completed *The Apostles* at a friends house in Betws-y-coed in July 1903. In addition, his own house in Hereford was called 'Plas Gwyn'.

ELLIS (Nesta Wyn) . . . Wales' foremost psychic and author.

ELLIS (Osian) . . . the internationally acclaimed solo and orchestral harpist who comes from Denbigh.

ELTON JOHN . . . the singer (was born Reg Dwight) . . . Geoffrey Dwight, his half brother lives in Ruthin, North Wales.

ELVIS . . . The Bishop of Munster who baptized St David. St Elvis is a parish near Haverfordwest. As Elvis Presley's (Preseli's) parents Gladys and Vernon had Welsh(ish) names, can we then claim Welsh descent for The King? Don't get All Shook Up about it. It's only a theory.

ELWY Valley . . . in Denbighshire immortalised by Gerald Manley Hopkins in the poem *In the Valley of the Elwy*.

EMIGRATION . . . The brave and hardy souls who struck out from their Welsh homeland, risking life and limb on a journey into the unknown . . . At the end of the 19th century it is recorded that some 100,000 expats were living in the USA with a further 12,000 in Australia and Canada.

EMMANUEL . . . a poem of 22,000 lines, penned by William Rees (Gwilym Hiraethog) (1802-1883 – that's his lifespan not the length of time it took to write!). It is the longest poem in the Welsh language.

EMMANUEL (Ivor) born Pontrhydyfen. A singer, he hosted and starred in the popular Sunday TV programme *Land of Song* (1958-1965). He took early retirement in 1981 and lives in Benaldamena, Spain.

EMPORIA . . . a Welsh settlement in Kansas established in the 1870s.

EMYN . . . the Welsh word for hymn.

ENCYCLOPEDIA BRITANNICA . . . in its infinite wisdom for many editions listed Wales under the heading. 'For Wales, see England'.

Yr ENFYS . . . the bilingual quarterly publication of Welsh expatriates worldwide

ENGLISHMAN WHO WENT UP A HILL BUT CAME DOWN A MOUNTAIN . . . the 1995 movie starring Hugh Grant and filmed on location in mid Wales.

ENLLI . . . (Bardsey Island) which was a place of pilgrimage in early Christian times. The island lies off the tip of the Llŷn Peninsula and is said to be the burial place of twenty thousand saints. As Enlli's area is four hundred and forty four acres, then there are forty-five saints per acre. A football field measures approximately one acre, so one half of the field would house twenty-two saints. Bless my soul. If all the players in a soccer match are crammed in one half of the pitch then the long-ball game is finished! In medieval times three pilgrimages to Enlli were equivalent to one pilgrimage to Rome. During inclement weather, pilgrims stayed at Y Gegin Fawr (The Big Kitchen) in Aberdaron on the mainland waiting for safer weather to make the crossing. The island once had a thriving community and it's own 'king'.

EPYNT . . . Your Country Needs A Firing Range. Between 1939 and 1940 fifty-four families of Mynydd Epynt were re-housed so that the area could be used for military target practice.

EQUALS . . . the mathematical symbol = was first used by a Welshman, Robert Recorde.

EQUITY . . . Gwynedd has more Equity members and resting actors than Hollywood, due to the burgeoning film industry. Acting is a growth occupation.

ERDDIG HALL . . . the mansion near Wrexham was found to be in a two hundred year old timewarp when acquired by the National Trust in 1972.

ERIN-G-BRAGH . . . the first vessel used on the Liverpool to North Wales route in 1821. It took six hours to reach Bangor. Wooden paddle steamers used to travel between Merseyside and the North Wales ports of Llandudno and Menai Bridge.

ETHNIC SOCIETY . . . the oldest ethnic society in America is 'The Welsh Society of Philadelphia' founded in 1729.

EVANS (Caradoc) . . . the writer of a 1920s satire *Taffy*, which was booed by a predominantly London Welsh theatre audience on its opening night in 1923. This was not surprising since the play was about the greed of the London Welsh.

EVANS (Edward) (1823-1878). A musician from Llanidloes who, it is claimed, became the first conductor in Wales to undertake a performance of Handel's *Messiah* with an orchestra.

EVANS (Einion) . . . writer, actor, playwright, appeared in the radio series *Welsh Rarebit*.

EVANS . . . (Sir Geraint) Baritone singer born in 1922 at Cilfynydd near Pontypridd who made his operatic Covent Garden debut in 1948. Knighted in the early 70s, he was the first singer to be knighted by QEII. He retired from the stage in 1984 and died in 1992.

EVANS (Gwynfor) . . . born 1912. The first ever Plaid Cymru MP to be elected. Educated at Aberystwyth and Oxford university, he first won a seat at Westminster in 1966. Famously went on hunger-strike in support of equal recognition of the Welsh language and a Welsh language televison channel. It is one of the few occasions that the Thatcher government gave in to pressure.

EVANS (Thomas John) (1863-1932). A journalist born in Ceredigion who founded the periodical *The London Welshman and Kelt* which was a bilingual newspaper which ran for two decades until a paper shortage during WW1 forced its closure. It reappeared between the wars as *Y Ddolen* and following WW2 as *Y Dinesydd*. Following 1959 it again became *The London Welshman* and continues to appear occasionally.

EVE OF ST JOHN . . . A 1921 play by the later eminent Welsh dramatist Saunders Lewis. His first work, and his only play in English, was considered a failure by the author.

EVEREST . . . (Sir George) born in Crickhowell in the Usk valley. His position as Surveyor General of India meant he was able to have the world's highest mountain renamed. Known as Chomolunga (meaning Goddess, mother of the world) it was crassly renamed Everest.

EVEREST EXPEDITION 1953 . . . The tallest mountain in the world was finally successfully scaled in this year. Members of the expedition trained in Snowdonia and their names are written on the ceiling of the Pen-y-gwryd Inn in Nant Gwynant.

EVICTION . . . About one hundred and forty families in the Cilmeri and Capel-y-babell areas of Brecon were given marching orders by the government in 1939, as the area was needed for military training. Sixty years later the area is still owned by the M.O.D.

EXCALIBUR . . . the mighty sword of King Arthur sank in Llyn Ogwen,

Snowdonia. It might have been retrievable at the time of sinking, but probably impossible now as due to centuries of silting, the lake is now only 10 feet (3m) deep. Its proper name, according to the earliest sources which were Welsh, is Caledfwlch.

EXECUTION . . . The last execution in Wales took place in Swansea Gaol in 1958.

EXPLOSIVES . . . During WW1 five thousand tonnes of TNT were stored in Dan yr Ogof caves, which are now a haunt of cavers and a Site of Special Scientific Interest.

EXPORTS . . . Wales' main export has long been human beings – men, women and families.

FAW . . . The Football Association of Wales was founded at Wrexham in 1876. The aeroplane carrying the Welsh squad and committee of the FAW to the Sweden World Cup Finals in 1958 was overbooked – some players were forced to remain on the runway whilst the officials took off on the junket. Wales has not qualified for any major finals since. I wonder why?

FUW . . . (Farmers Union of Wales) . . . the organisation founded in 1955 by Welsh farmers who were dissatisfied with the NFU. The organisation has its HQ at Aberystwyth.

FAILURE . . . Why did the S.P.C.K. (Society for Promoting Christian Knowledge) persist in trying to teach literacy to the Welsh in the English language?

FAIRBOURNE & BARMOUTH STEAM RAILWAY . . . of the 'great little trains of Wales' this is the 'greatest' and the 'littlest' . . . the narrow gauge of this track is only 15 inches (38cm).

FALKLAND'S HERO . . . Simon Weston OBE, the former Welsh guardsman who suffered horrific burns during the 1982 Falklands War and now works for charity and runs Weston Spirit helping youngsters, was born in the Rhymni Valley in 1961.

FAMOUS FRED . . . this pop singing cat who has clawed his was to a BAFTA award was in 1999 nominated for an Oscar for animation. Produced for S4C by Joanna Quinn, Famous Fred's voice in the film is that of Lenny Henry.

FANTHORNE (Revd Lionel) . . . a humble assistant priest at St German's Church in Adamstown, Cardiff and actually the world's most prolific author with two hundred books published since 1952 (mostly science fiction and mystery). Clearly a clerical cleric.

FARR . . . (Tommy) (1913-1988) . . . The Tonypandy born boxer who in August 1937 was only a whisker away from beating the great 'Brown Bomber' Joe Louis in a Madison Square gardens bout for the World Heavyweight Title. Louis was out-punched but Farr was out-pointed. Farr was one of eight children whose father was an Irish bare-knuckle fighter and miner. Farr boxed on until he was forty. N.B. His post-Louis-Contest broadcast from ringside was 'Hello, Tonypandy . . . I done my best'.

FAST BOAT . . . the Dublin Swift is Irish Ferries £25 million super fast ferry plying between Holyhead on Anglesey and Dublin. It carries two hundred cars and eight hundred passengers and is named after the Irish writer Jonathan Swift.

FED . . . The South Wales Miners Federation. Founded in 1898 and soon had 100,000 members.

FEMINISM . . . Alice Grey Jones (1852-1943) a feminist writer of Llanllyfni, Gwynedd, founded the North Wales Women's Temperance League.

FENTON (Richard) . . . (1747-1821) author of the 1811 *Historical Tour Through Pembrokeshire* – much quoted by later writers.

FENTON (Samuel) . . . built Fishguard pier to secure the burgeoning pilchard fishing industry, as opposed to being a pier for enjoyment. *AMERICAN WAR OF INDEPENDENCE

FERNS . . . these are very ancient plants – some are millions of years old. Of the six thousand species only forty are found in Wales.

FERRAR (Robert) (died in 1555). Protestant martyr burnt at the stake on the instruction of Queen Mary during the Counter-Reformation. Born in Yorkshire he was bishop of St David's from 1548. He was burned in the market square at Carmarthen after being charged with heresy, and his refusal to recant.

FERRY SERVICE . . . In 1959 the Abermenai ferry service over the Menai Strait from Caernarfon ceased after seven hundred years.

FERTILIZER . . . Charles, Prince of Wales, on a rare visit to Cymru to paint Carreg Cennen Castle, was mistaken by a landowner for a fertilizer salesman.

FIBUA . . . Wales has one of just five in the UK. Owned by the Ministry of Defence, who acquired the land (30 acres) near Brecon in 1939, a Fibua is a *Fighting in Built Up Areas* training village. The actual village was built in 1980. *EVICTIONS

FINE REWARD . . . Owain Glyndŵr's two thousand supporters in Anglesey were fined by the English king. The collector, Robert Parys, was rewarded with a mountain, Mynydd Trysglwyn, which became Parys Mountain (famous for it's copper). *ANGLESEY PENNIES

FFESTINIOG RAILWAY . . . the slate-carrying railway made history in 1865 when it was allowed to carry passengers. Prior to this no narrow gauge lines (less than 4' 8¹/2" or 141.6cm) were permitted to carry passengers.

FFLAT HUW PUW . . . a famous Welsh sea shanty about the ship of Liverpool sea captain Huw Pugh (1795-1865) . . . by J Glyn Davis. The song, well-loved to this day, tells the story of Pugh's vessel, a 60 ton flat named Ann, which traded between Runcorn, Liverpool, Caernarfon and Porth Dinllaen. She sank in Cardigan Bay off St Tudwal's islands in 1858 *en route* to Barmouth (*Y Bermo*).

FFLINT . . . the first borough in Wales to receive a Royal Charter (1284).

FFLINT CASTLE . . . the first Edwardian castle to be built. It was built hurriedly and within a week of commencement in 1277 the overseeing masterbuilder, James of St George, had over two thousand ditchers working on the foundations including three hundred who had been drafted in from Lincoln. The walls of the donjon or keep are the thickest castle walls in Britain at 23 feet (7 metres) thick.

FFLINTSHIRE . . . once had two hundred coal pits.

FFYNNON CASEG . . . off the A5 between Bethesda and Capel Curig. Wild ponies headed there to give birth in spring – it is said.

FILM COMMISSION . . . the North Wales Film Commission was established in 1998 to help producers find locations. The film *First Knight* helped inject £2.6 million into the local economy in only a ten day shoot.

FILMS . . . Wales, with its stunning scenery, is regularly used for location film making.

FISHERMANS' TALES . . . at Llantrisant on the river Usk in 1781 the largest salmon ever caught in Wales was hooked and weighed 68 pounds 8 oz (31.2 kg).

FIRBANK (Thomas) . . . A Canadian who bought Dyffryn Mymbyr farm on the slopes of Glyder Fach in Gwynedd. He became a best-selling author in 1940 with the book *I Bought a Mountain* describing farming 2,400 acres with thirteen hundred sheep in the 1930s.

FIRE . . . In October 1989 a fire began at a tyre dump near Knighton in Powys and, although initially brought under control, it has smouldered ever since and, at the time of going to press, was heading for a place in the Guinness Book of Records.

FIRST ASCENT OF SNOWDON . . . this is recorded as being in 1639 when London chemist and investigator climbed to the summit collecting samples of plant life.

FIRST BOOK . . . William Gambold (1672-1728) was born in Aberteifi and his *Grammar of the Welsh Language* (1727) was one of the first English language books to be printed in Wales.

FIRST BOWLS CLUB . . . in Wales opened in Abergavenny in 1860.

FIRST FEMALE DOCTOR . . . in 1885 Frances Hoggan became Wales' first female medical doctor.

FIRST GOLF COURSE . . . the first in Wales was established at Tenby in 1888.

FIRST HYMN BOOK . . . the first in Welsh was *Grawnsyppiau Canaan* which was published in Liverpool in 1795.

FIRST KNIGHT . . . the 1995 film starring Sean Connery, Richard Gere and Julia Ormond is an adaptation of the story of King Arthur. It was filmed on location, near Trawsfynydd amongst others, in Gwynedd.

FIRST SCHOOLS INSPECTOR . . . Sir Owen Morgan Edwards (1858-1920). A man of letters, he notably became the first chief inspector of schools under the newly introduced Welsh Education Department in 1907 and is regarded as one of the saviours of the Welsh language.

FIRST MINER TO BECOME AN MP . . .This was William Abraham (Mabon) (1842-1922). A native of Cwmafon, Glamorgan became the first miner MP in 1884 and in 1898 became the first president of the South Wales Miners Federation. Abraham caused laughter in the House of Commons when he spoke Welsh. The laughter soon subsided when he coolly explained that he was reciting the Lord's Prayer.

FIRST NUMBER ONE . . . the first Welsh artist to achieve a number one hit record was Shirley Bassey. Her *As I Love You* hit the top spot in 1959.

FIRST RAILWAY RAILS . . . Penydarren to Quaker's Yard was the route of the world's first railway locomotive pioneered by Richard Trevithick in 1804 (long before the Liverpool – Manchester railway of 1819)!

FIRST SCHOOL . . . the Guinness Book of Records states that Britain's first school was a Christian college at Llanilltud Fawr which dated back to around 500 AD and was attended by St David, St Patrick and St Gildas.

FIRST WELSH PRIME MINISTER . . . David Lloyd George became PM on December 7 1916.

FIRST WELSH FEMALE MP . . . In 1929 Lady Megan Lloyd George (daughter of David Lloyd George) became the Liberal MP for Anglesey.

FISH . . . the migratory sea-trout, the sewin, is found nowhere else in Britain except Wales.

FISH STONE . . . The Crickhowell Fish Stone which stands at 18 feet high is the tallest standing stone in Wales.

FISHGUARD . . . (Abergwaun). Mid-Wales port with a ferry link to Rosslare in the Republic of Ireland.

FIVE TO THREE . . . irreverent football fanzine 1987-1992 and 1996 (one-off). Witty, often vulgar, amateur produced football magazine based in Pwllheli, Gwynedd. Consistently praised, often slated. Originals, mostly collectors items including autographed copies are a rarity and fetch astronomical prices. Most sought after issues (1987 1, 2 & 3) fetch up to £35 in London – issue one was only 25p at the time.

FJORD . . . The Great Orme (Gogarth) at Llandudno became a fjord in 1958 when Kirk Douglas and Tony Curtis starred in the film *The Vikings*. This was quite apt as the Vikings had gone there, about 1000 years earlier. Orme in the Viking language means sea dragon.

FLAG . . . The Welsh national flag (Y Ddraig Goch – the red Dragon)is belived to be the oldest flag of any country in the world as it has remained unchanged for 1000 years. *DRAGON

FLAG WAVING . . . and flag wearing is the latest big thing . . . even lorry drivers have the Welsh flag draped across the back of the cab.

FLAG DAY . . . the first Flag day held in the UK was at Pontypool in 1914.

FLAT HOLM ISLAND . . . in the Bristol Channel was used in 1884 to isolate or accommodate suspected cholera sufferers.

FLORA . . . 71% of British flora can be found in Wales.

FLORIDA . . . there is a Lake Wales near the tourist resort of Orlando, Florida.

FLUELLYN . . . appears in Shakespeare's *Henry V* where his forceful character typifies Henry's attitude to the strong Welsh element in the armies versus France.

FLUTE . . . the earliest musical instrument known in Wales. A piece of an ancient flute was found at *Pen yr Wrlodd* cairn in the 1990s.

FOGHORN . . . the one on Ynys Enlli (Bardsey Island) was installed in 1878.

FOLLETT (Ken) . . . the Cardiff born author of world renown. *Eye of The Needle* was his eleventh novel and it won an 'Edgar' award. The film version was a Hollywood extravaganza featuring Donald Sutherland. Follett is one of only two dozen Welsh people to gain a mention in *International Who's Who*.

FOOT (Michael) . . . Labour politician and speaker of renown. Possibly best known for his personal 1983 election result where he won a 70% majority in his constituency poll – the biggest ever Labour majority. That general election however, was a disaster for then party leader Foot, as Labour were trounced. Michael Foot had his surgery address at 10 Morgan Street, Tredegar – the only number 10 he ever got into!

FOOTBALL . . . the earliest account of a soccer match held in Wales dates to about 1734, to an event on Anglesey that attracted a crowd of around five hundred spectators. The Football Association of Wales was founded at Wrexham in 1876. The heaviest defeat inflicted on the Wales national team was an 1878 9-0 drubbing by Scotland.

FORESTRY COMMISSION . . . a quango often accused of afforesting 10% of Wales.

FORT BELAN and FORTWILLIAMSBURG on the Menai Strait were built by Lord Newborough during the Napoleonic Wars. His lordship, fearing a French invasion, ensured his own privately paid militia manned the forts.

FORD (Trevor) . . . famous Wales international footballer who at one time in the 1950s was the most expensive player in the professional game.

FORTY-FIRST CHILD . . . on the tombstone of Nicholas Hookes in St Mary's churchyard, Conwy, it states that Hookes died in 1637 and was the forty-first child of his father. The tombstone further reveals that Hookes himself fathered twenty-seven.

FRANCIS (Dick) . . . the former National Hunt jockey-turned-author was born at Lawrenny, Tenby in 1920.

FRANCIS (George Grant) (1814-1882) . . . Swansea born businessman who worked relentlessly on many local improvement schemes. He helped to found the Royal Institution of South Wales in 1835.

FRANKLIN (Benjamin) . . . who helped create the American Constitution, but moved in the same London circles as free-thinking Welshmen including Richard Price (1723-91) of Llangeinor, Glamorgan and David Williams (1738-1816) of Caerphilly, Glam. These prominent Welsh political thinkers influenced the American constitution and Price later refused the offer of American citizenship.

FREE WALES ARMY . . . formed in 1967 to oppose the 1969 Investiture of

Prince Charles as Prince of Wales. Led by Julian Caio Evans a farmer and horse-trader.

FRENCH (Dawn) . . . the cherubic and chubby comedienne (*Vicar of Dibley, French & Saunders, Comic Strip* etc, etc) was born in Holyhead.

FRENCH DETECTIVE . . . Welsh actor Rupert Davies played sleuth Maigret in Simenon's detective TV series in the 1960s.

FRENCH LEAVE . . . In 1998 whilst North Wales tourism operators were bemoaning the poor holiday season at home, the Wales Tourist Board's Chief Executive was on holiday. Mr French was on leave in Spain.

FRIENDSHIP . . . the first sea plane to cross the Atlantic landed in Burry Port (see *EARHART, Amelia).

FROM RUSSIA WITH LOVE . . . the early James Bond blockbuster featured scenes that were shot on location in Wales.

FRONCYSYLLTE . . . Labour politician John 'Two Jags' Prescott once attended primary school in this town near Wrexham. He was presumably then known as 'Two Bikes.'

FROST (Bill) (1848-1935). A pioneer of aviation from Saundersfoot who built a prototype flying machine in 1896 (seven years before the Wright Brothers). Bill Frost's contraption remained airbourne for around ten seconds.

FROST (John) (1784-1877) . . . Chartist campaigner for social justice who in 1839 led an angry army of six hundred armed men (with nearly twenty thousand unarmed protestors) against government forces at Newport. The Chartist aims included votes for all men over 21, payment of MPs and annual parliamentary elections. The revolt was quashed with the loss of twenty Chartist lives. Frost was sentenced to death, but was reprieved at the 11th hour and transported to Australia. He received a full pardon in 1856 and returned to his native Newport.

FUNERAL . . . the best attended funeral in Wales was that of boxer Jim Driscoll in 1925, when over one hundred thousand people lined the route of the procession. *GENTLEMAN JIM DRISCOLL

FURNICULAR TRAMWAYS . . . there are only three in the World and one runs up the Great Orme in Llandudno. Opened in 1902, it remains the longest cable-hauled tramway in Britain.

GANNETS . . . Wales' only gannet colony is on Grassholm Island twelve miles off the Pembrokeshire shoreline. There are an estimated thirty thousand pairs. Each bird has an average wing span of $5^1/2$ feet (1.7 metres). That's around a third of a million feet of wings and mucho guano.

GAVELKIND . . . a traditional Welsh form of land law in which a father's land was shared between the sons. Henry VIII's Act of Union abolished gavelkind, which was replaced by the English system of primogeniture under which the first son became the sole inheritor.

GEE (Thomas) . . . (1815-98) Denbighshire publisher and Methodist preacher who founded Gwasg Gee (press) and became the first chairman of Denbighshire County Council. His best known publications include the ten volume *Y Gwyddoniadur Cymreig* (a Welsh encyclopedia) which took 25 years to collate, and *Y Faner* (1857), a Welsh weekly paper.

GELERT . . . legendary hound whose tale was created for the amusement of gullible tourists. The nursery of Prince Llywelyn's infant son was found in disarray with fresh blood smeared all round. Jumping to the conclusion that his once trusted hound, Gelert, had attacked his heir, Prince Llywelyn slew the dog only to discover the dead body of a wolf nearby. In horror the true picture became clear – in protecting the baby, Gelert had killed the wolf. The dog is said to be buried in Snowdonia at Beddgelert (Gelert's Grave). Gelert was, not surprisingly, an Irish wolfhound as opposed to a Chihuahua.

GELERT . . . the horse! In the late 1990s pupils at the village school in Beddgelert were eagerly awaiting the delivery of the new school tee-shirts – the school traditionally carries the imagined image of Gelert the dog in their logo. Unfortunately, the manufacturers had replaced the dog with a horse! Neigh! Neigh! Neigh!

GEOFFREY OF MONMOUTH . . . archdeacon of Llandaf Cathedral who helped immortalise the story of King Arthur in his twelve volume work *Historia Regum Britanniae circa* 1135 in which he traced the history of *British* kings back to Brutus (the mythical great grandson of Aeneas.)

GEIRIONYDD (Llyn) . . . near Llanrwst covers an area of some 45 acres. In the past locals believed it to be poisoned.

GENERAL STRIKE . . . of 1926. Disillusionment with the Fed (South Wales Miner's Federation), which was heavily involved in the failed General Strike, led to the defection of one hundred and thirty-six thousand members of the Fed. Many joined the newly established South Wales Miners Industrial Union and the Fed's membership hit a new low level of only seventy-three thousand.

GENTLEMAN JIM DRISCOLL (1881-1925) of Cardiff. A boxing champion, also known as 'Peerless Jim', he served his apprenticeship in sideshow boxing booths where he would dispatch some fifteen or twenty opponents a day. He later became British and European featherweight champion winning all but ten of sixty-nine fights (losing only three) and won a Lonsdale Belt outright. His Cardiff funeral in January 1925 was akin to a state occasion in that reports refer to one hundred thousand people lining the route for the mile-long funeral procession. In 1997 a statue of 'Peerless Jim' was erected in Cardiff's Bute Street at a cost of some £25,000.

GERALD CAMBRENSIS (a.k.a. Giraldus Cambrensis, a.k.a. Gerallt Gymro, a.k.a. Gerald the Welshman). (1148-1223) born Manorbier, Pembs. A scholarly writer of eleven books who strove for a Welsh archbishopric with status equal to Canterbury. In 1188 Gerallt accompanied Archbishop Baldwin on a recruiting drive in parts of Wales for men to join a crusade to the Holy Land. Gerallt described this tour in the minutest details – probably the first travel books to be written.

GERMAN ROCK STAR . . . Ulrich John Rott the former lead guitarist with German heavy metal rock band The Scorpions is the owner of two Welsh mansions. Plas Tan-y-Bwlch, Aberystwyth and, since August 1999, Plas Glynllifon near Caernarfon are his. He hopes to breed eagles and re-introduce them to Eryri.

GIBSON (John) . . . Conwy-born sculptor (1790-1866) who was the first British sculptor to use colour. He became a member of the Royal Academy in 1838 and in 1850 he famously sculpted Queen Victoria.

GIGGS (Ryan) . . . funny how he's quite often 'injured' when a friendly Welsh international looms, but is 'fit again' when Manchester United have their next match. At the age of 17 he became the youngest player to appear for Wales and in 1996 he became the forty-third BBC Welsh Sports Personality of the Year.

GILL (A.A) . . . Scottish-born journalist, columnist and author who launched several insulting attacks on Wales, and the Welsh in the 1990s, his barbed baiting earning him the accolade of being a master-baiter of the Welsh nation.

GINGER BANDITS . . . Gwylliaid Cochion Mawddwy were a gang of 16th century bandits who terrorised Meirionnydd. Eighty of their number (all red-heads) were hanged on the orders of Judge Lewis Owen *circa* 1555. Mysteriously the judge was murdered at Dugoed *en route* from Welshpool to his Dolgellau home. The first written reference to these *Ginger Bandits* was in Thomas Pennant's *Tours of Wales* over two hundred years after the events supposedly occurred.

GIRLIE MAGS . . . publisher of The Sunday Sport (and girlie top-shelf magazines), David Sullivan was born in Penarth in 1949. He is the fifty-first richest man in Britain (1998 figures) and the second richest Welshman. He has a stake in Birmingham City football club.

GLADIATORS . . . The Via Julia (Roman Road) to Caerleone, which runs through Celtic Manor's one thousand acres and Coldra Woods golf course, has a training area for Roman gladiators preserved on the course.

GLADSTONE (William Ewart): The Grand Old Man of Victorian politics whose home was at Hawarden in Fflintshire. He formed four Liberal governments and memorably boobed, when at the Mold National Eisteddfod in 1873 he referred to the Welsh language as being a 'venerable relic of the past'. Note: It was under a Gladstone-led government that public houses in Wales were closed under the 1881 Sunday Closing Act.

GLAMORGAN . . . the 1992 edition of the *Hutchinson Encyclopedia* lists no 'famous people' for the county. Gwynedd has a meagre two albeit an English king (Edward II) and a war hero (Lawrence of Arabia) whilst Gwent boasts a mighty three. By the 1999 edition, the format of Hutchinson had changed.

GLAMORGANSHIRE GOLF CLUB . . . founded at Penarth in 1890, was the birthplace of golf's Stableford system of scoring.

GLAW . . . Welsh word for rain. Not often seen so not often used.

GLOBAL WARMING . . . John Houghton of Dyserth produced scientific evidence for the global warming theory which led to international agreements on controlling output levels of Carbon Monoxide.

GLODDFA GANOL – Once the largest slate mine in the world located at Blaenau Ffestiniog in Gwynedd. It closed as a tourist attraction in 1998 but continues to operate as a commercial quarry.

GLYDERAU . . . range of mountains in Snowdonia which boasts five peaks soaring above the magical '3000 foot' barrier – only fourteen peaks in Wales exceed this height.

GLYNDŴR (Owain) Welsh leader of the 15th Century who sought to free Wales from English control. He defeated Henry IV three times but was eventually defeated and Wales retaken in 1413. Three years later, and after a covert guerilla campaign against the English, Glyndŵr disappeared. Shakespeare wrote well of him (*MEIBION GLYNDŴR)

GOD BLESS THE PRINCE OF WALES . . . the song (words by George Linley, tune by Brinley Richards) was first sung in February 1863 by Sims Reeves (not Jim Reeves!) a Swansea tenor.

GOG. a North Walian who comes from the Gogledd (North).

GOLD 1 . . . mined in Wales by the Romans at Dalaucothi, transported to London and on to the imperial mint at Lyons, France.

GOLD 2 . . . The Dolgellau area of Gwynedd rich in former gold mines. The 'golden years' were c.1900 when twenty-five mines flourished basking in the glory that followed the 'royal' seal of approval in 1893, when gold from St David's mine was used for the wedding ring of the future George V and Princess Mary. The Welsh tradition was followd by the royal wedding rings of the Queen Mother, Elizabeth II, Princes Charles and Princess Diana and Prince Andrew and Sarah Ferguson. Recent history shows it to be a waste of good gold.

GOLF . . . the world's most influential golf course designer is Welshman Robert Trent Jones Snr, who has worked on over six hundred course developments, for example the recent Celtic Manor courses at Caerleon.

GOLF CAPTAIN . . . In 1934 the Prince of Wales (later King Edward VIII, albeit briefly) was the captain of the Royal St David's Golf Club in Harlech.

GOOSE STEPS . . . Welsh drovers walked geese through a mixture of tar and grit, which protected their feet before they goose-stepped to market. Then the railways came.

GORKY'S ZYGOTIC MYNCI . . . another Welsh pop group that has taken the music scene by storm.

GORSEDD Y BEIRDD . . . there are only three non-Welsh speaking members of this august body, namely The Queen, The Duke of Edinburgh and the Queen Mother.

GOSCOMBE (John) (1869-1952) Cardiff born sculptor who famously sculpted the heads of Lloyd George and T E Ellis, Evan James and James James. John Goscombe has a memorial in Ynysangharad Park in Pontypridd.

GOWER (David) . . . the former England cricket captain is not Welsh – despite his name.

GOWER (Iris) . . . Authoress described as 'the Catherine Cookson of Swansea' with a string of best-selling books set in the Mumbles area.

GOWER PENINSULA . . . 73 square miles of wonderful scenic beauty. In 1956 it became Britain's first Area of Outstanding Natural Beauty . . . followed in 1957 by 60 square miles of the Llŷn coastline)

GOWER GOLD . . . for many years Spanish gold coins were found on Rhosili sands after very stormy weather. Records show that the 'golden years' were 1807 and 1833.

GO WEST! . . . *Y Gwladgarwr* published in Aberdare (1858-1882) was a periodical urging emigration, especially to America.

GRACE (Chris) MBE . . . S4C's head of animation.

GRACE (Dr W.G.) . . . the cricketing legend was born *circa* 1848 in Gloucestershire and began his famous career with South Wales Cricket Club (founded 1859). In 1864 he scored 170 in an innings, aged just 16 years. Grace later scored innumerable centuries for the England and Gloucestershire teams.

GRADIENTS . . . The Dowlais – Cardiff line presented coal-hauling steam trains with an uphill task. The toughest section was a seven mile stretch with a 1 in 40 gradient which needed four (not just three) locomotives. This line had the two highest railway stations in Britain at Cwmbargoed (1250 feet [384m] above sea level) and Rhymni Bridge (1100 feet [330m] . . .)

GRAND SLAM . . . in Rugby Union's annual Five Nations Championship this phrase describes the rare occasions when one nation defeats all of the others in a season. In 1978 (o.k. it's a long way back!) Wales completed their third Grand Slam season of the decade having won it in 1971 and again in 1976.

GRAND SLAM AWARD WINNERS . . . in 1976 the entire Welsh squad of Grand Slam winners became Welsh Sports Personality of the year under the leadership of Merfyn Davies

GRANT (Russell) . . . the jolly rotund TV astrologer was born in Middlesex but his grandmother was Cardiff-bred through and through, which makes him 100% Welsh as a rugby or soccer player.

GRASSHOLM . . . the island, 12 miles (19 km) off the Dyfed coast is the site of the world's largest gannet colony with over 30,000 pairs of gannets and an estimated total bird population of over 100,000.

GRAVES (Robert) . . . the author of the poem *Welsh Incident* refers to sea caves 'at Criccieth yonder'.

GRAY (Thomas) (1847-1924). Mining engineer born in Durham who lived at Margam in Glamorgan where he invented the 'Gray Safety Lamp' for miners.

GREAT ORME GOATS . . . are all descendents of a pair given to Queen Victoria.

GREEN, GREEN GRASS OF HOME . . . one of Tom Jones' biggest hits of the 1960s and always heard at every Karaoke Night in every pub in Wales along with Tom's other mega-hit *Delilah*.

GREGYNOG HALL . . . five miles (8 km) north of Newtown, Montgomeryshire. In 1960 Lady Bountiful, Miss Margaret Davies (grand-daughter of David Davies of Llandinam) gave the hall and seven hundred and fifty acres to the University of Wales as a conference and study centre.

GREGYNOG PRESS . . . Gwendoline (1882-1951) and her sister Margaret Davies (1884-1961), grand-daughters of the great industrialist David Davies of Llandinam founded the press in 1923. Famously, the press only published forty-two titles but these were beautifully produced and of superb quality. The sisters also collected French Impressionist paintings. In the mid 1970s the press was revived as Gwasg Gregynog by the University of Wales.

GREAT TRAIN ROBBERS . . . they hid out, albeit briefly, in Hay-on-Wye.

GREATEST BRITISH FILMS . . . in September 1999 the British Film Institute released a list of the Top 100 British Films on the 20th century. Many had a Welsh connection. *Lawrence of Arabia* (in at no. 3), *Don't Look Now'* (no. 8 and starring Wales resident Julie Christie), *Saturday Night and Sunday Morning* (no. 14 featuring Rachel Roberts), Henry V (no. 18 about Monmouth's most famous son), *Dr Zhivago* (no. 27, Julie Christie, again), *Zulu* (no 31), *Tom Jones* (no. 51 – ok, ok, it's got nothing at all to do with the singer!) *This Sporting Life* (no. 52 with Rachel Roberts again.) *The Cruel Sea* (no. 75 starring Stanley Baker) and *Carry on Up The Khyber* (no 99. filmed on location in Wales).

GREENER . . . Wales is becoming greener. Our generation has stopped two centuries of rape and desecration of the landscapes, so come and see How Green Are Our Valleys!

GREN . . . the celebrated cartoonist of the South Wales Echo.

GRENVILLE (Charles Francis) (1749-1809) . . . the founder of the port of Milford Haven. In 1790 his uncle Sir William Hamilton obtained a private parliamentary act to enable him to develop land in Carmarthenshire for quays, docks and piers along with a market and arterial roads etc. Hamilton was British Ambassador to the Neapolitan court and Greville oversaw the Milford Haven development in his absence. Hamilton's wife was Lady Hamilton, the mistress of Admiral Nelson, who had a hand in raising Nelson's Column.

GRESFORD COLLIERY . . . Nr Wrexham. When it closed in 1974 there were only two remaining coal mines in North Wales.

GRESFORD COLLIERY DISASTER . . . 261 died there in 1934.

GREY (Tanni) . . . one of the world's best wheelchair athletes who has won gold medals at every distance from 100 metres to marathon. Thrice-times winner of the London marathon, Tanni was born in Cardiff.

GRIFFITH (Hugh) – late Anglesey born actor who won an Oscar for his portrayal of an Arab leader in *Ben Hur* in 1959.

GRIFFITHS (James) . . . (1890-1975) the first ever Secretary of State for Wales. Former miner who became an MP in 1936. In 1964 under the Harold Wilson

Labour administration, the Welsh Office was created with Griffiths as Secretary of State.

GRIFFITHS (Robert) (1805-1883). Denbighshire born inventor who developed a method of screw propulsion for seagoing craft.

The GROES INN . . . in 1573, this still thriving establishment in the Conwy valley became the first licensed house in Wales.

GRUFFUDD (Ioan) . . . the Cardiff born, RADA trained actor of film, TV and stage. Played fellow Welshman Harold Lowe in the movie *Titanic* (coming back on a lifeboat and finding the frozen and floating (yet still breathing) heroine.

GUEST (Lady Charlotte) Lincolnshire born wife of Sir Josiah who bore him ten children and took over the running of the Dowlais steelworks on his death. Having mastered the Welsh language, she famously translated *Pedair Cainc y Mabinogi* in a three volume work, changing the name to *The Mabinogion* in the process Died 1895.

GUEST (Sir Josiah John) (1785-1852) . . . One of the fathers of the Industrial Revolution in South Wales. Under his ownership the Dowlais steelworks of Merthyr Tudful grew to become the world's biggest. He eventually became Merthyr's first MP (1832).

GUILD OF ST GEORGE . . . John Ruskin, the writer and social reformer established this guild at Barmouth (*Y Bermo*) where his experiment in social living occupied a number of cottages in the mid 19th century.

GUILD OF GLYNDŴR . . . founded in August 1999 to protest as a group against anything anti-Welsh. The Guild is based in Leeds!

GULF STREAM . . . the warm ocean current which flows from the Gulf of Mexico and contribues to the mild, warmer winter climate of the Welsh Croeso. Have you ever counted the palm trees in North Wales?

GUTO NYTH-BRÂN . . . (*Griffith MORGAN) . . .

GWALCHMAI . . . the first Anglesey village to use electricity. These days it is merely a 30 mph inconvénience for truckers on the Holyhead ferry port run along the A5.

GWALIA . . . the make of the first motor vans produced in Wales, in Cardiff in 1922.

GWASG GOMER . . . the biggest and busiest book publisher in Wales with around one hundred and twenty titles appearing per annum. The press began in 1982.

GWENLLIAN (Princess) . . . born Abergwyngregyn, Bangor in 1282. The only daughter and sole heir of the last prince of Wales, Llywelyn ap Gruffudd, was kidnapped and banished by Edward I to Sempringham convent in Lincolnshire where she died in 1337. In 1996 the Princess Gwenllian Society was founded to perpetuate her memory.

GWENN (Edmund) . . . London born actor of a Welsh family who won Best Supporting Actor Oscar in 1947 for *Miracle on 34th Street*. Admired as one of Britain's finest character actors. Gwenn died in 1959.

GWEITHIWR, Y . . . Established in Merthyr Tudful in 1814, it was the first workers' newspaper written in the Welsh language.

GWERIN . . . the 'ordinary, common people' as opposed to the '*crachach' have long been acknowleged as 'halen y ddaear' (salt of the earth), but these days American Express cards, personalised number plates, mobile phones, snappy business suits, sun tans from ski holidays, designer labels and Ray Ban sun shades are nibbling away at this classy idea!

GWIR . . . 'Y gwir yn erbyn y byd' (the truth against the world) is the motto of *Gorsedd y Beirdd Ynys Prydain*.

GWLAD Y GÂN . . . The Land of Song, a.k.a. Cymru, a.k.a. Wales.

GWYNANT (Llyn) the Snowdonian lake which covers eighteen acres is believed to be bottomless, as is also Llyn Cau on the southern slopes of Cadair Idris.

GWYNFRYN (Hywel) Celebrated Welsh TV and radio star. The equivalent of Terry Wogan, but with his own hair.

GWYNEDDIGION SOCIETY . . . was founded in London in 1771 to foster the Welsh language and culture. Two conditions of membership were fluency in the language and a love of harp music.

GWYNIAD . . . A rare ice age fish found in Llyn Tegid, Bala, not to be confused with the monster Tegi who also lives in the lake. The gwyniad is also found in Scotland and called the powan, and in the Lake District where it is called schelly.

HAFOD & HENDRE . . . In mountainous areas of Europe, farming people moved house seasonally between lowland and highland pastures. This practie is known as transhumance. In Wales, the summer home was called *hafod*, while the better-built lowland winter home was called *hendre*. The Royal family do something similar between Buck House and Balmoral.

HALL (Benjamin) (1778-1817). Born at Llandaf. He became the first great industrialist to enter politics in opposition to the interests of the landed gentry. He was elected MP for Glamorgan in 1814 having served as Member in two English constituencies since 1806.

HANGING . . . Wales' last public hanging was in Swansea in 1866 when Robert Coe was executed.

HANSOM . . . he of Hansom cab fame also designed the gaol at Beaumaris, Anglesey and Bodelwyddan Castle.

HANRATTY (James) . . . the murderer hanged in 1962, partly because of doubt about his claim to have been in Rhyl on August 28 1961. Campaigners have worked to earn him a posthumous pardon but have so far failed in their efforts. Do you remember seeing him seeking lodgings on that date? He was not Welsh, we hasten to add. His only connection with Wales is the Rhyl connection, which he unfortunately failed to establish.

HARDIE (James Keir) . . . the first ever labour MP was elected to represent Merthyr Tudful in 1900.

HARLECH CASTLE . . . built in MFI quick-speed fashion between 1285 and 1290 on a 200 foot (60m) crag above the water's edge, this was the piece-de-resistance of impregnability and has never been 'taken' by an enemy. Okay, they could starve you out as Owain Glyndŵr did with Henry IV, which was reciprocated by the Mortimer family (including Glyndŵr's daughter and grandchildren), and again by Dafydd ap Einion during the Wars of the Roses. In 1647, incumbents at Harlech Castle – namely Royalists – surrendered to a faction of Oliver Cromwell's New Model Army led by Colonel John Jones – brother in-law of Cromwell himself. *JONES (Colonel John)

HARLECH TELEVISION . . . the original name for the TV company HTV, which celebrated its 30th birthday in 1998. When HTV won the franchise from TWW in 1968, they were backed by Hollywood legends Richard Burton and Stanley Baker, and the team was led by renowned broadcaster Wynford Vaughan-Thomas under the chairmanship of Lord Harlech, formerly British Ambassador in Washington. The studios of Harlech Television were in Cardiff.

HARLEQUIN THEATRE . . . at Rhos-on-Sea (*Llandrillo-yn-Rhos*), Conwy is Britain's only purpose-built puppet theatre.

HARPS . . . Wales' traditional musical instrument.

HARRIS (Frank) . . . the famous biographer of Shakespeare and Oscar Wilde, and author of the contentious autobiography *My Life and Loves* which was banned in the UK and USA for over 40 years because of the sexual nature of the content, attended Ruabon Grammar School.

HARRIS (Hywel) . . . (1714-1773) of Trefeca, Brecs. Was an organiser of the Methodist Revival in Wales, a religious movement which shook the nation. Tireless and passionate, Harris often preached three hour sermons in all weathers to vast congregations. His mission was to save souls.

HARRIS (Rolf) . . . apparently of Welsh extraction. Is that why he spends his time huffing and puffing behind a tied down kangaroo – sport?

HARRISON (John) . . . the alias of Elizabethan puritan preacher John Penry, chosen as it was a translation of his Welsh name (John ap Henry) into the English version 'John son of Harry'.

HARVEY-JONES (Sir John) . . . the big-business expert is a quarter Welsh, or as he would doubtless put it, 25% Welsh.

HAUL . . . is the Welsh word for sun which always shines on the Gower and Llŷn Peninsulas.

HAY-ON-WYE . . . the second hand book capital. With ten miles of bookshelves, more than two million books and thirty two book shops, approximately. The brainchild of Richard *Booth.

HEADLESS SKELETON . . . In September 1846 the Revd Wellington Starr, a

Northamptonshire vicar, arrived in North Wales on a walking holiday. One evening he decided to embark on a moonlight ascent of Snowdon. In July 1847 his headless skeleton was found – without a wristwatch. Had he been robbed and murdered? Then a guide claimed to have found the missing watch which somewhat negated the murder suspicions, but some questions remain unanswered. Could the watch have survived a Welsh mountain winter? Experts said no. Why did analysis of the skeleton eradicate any suspicions of a fall? Why did the coroner record a verdict of death by misadventure? Was it murder? Was there a cover up to protect Welsh tourism?

HEADS OF THE VALLEYS ROAD . . . the A465. Does South Wales have any other roads of note? Surely, the most-oft-mentioned road in Wales.

HEARST (William Randolph) . . . the US press mogul (on whom it is said Orson Welles modeled the classic *Citizen Kane*) had a home at St Donats Castle in the Vale of Glamorgan. The property is now home to the international Atlantic College school.

HEAVEN . . . Welsh is the language of heaven.

HEAVILY BOMBED . . . Swansea was the most heavily bombed place in Wales during WW2

HEDDIW . . . is Welsh for today.

HEDDLU . . . means the boys in blue, the cops, the fuzz, Y Glas . . . etc., etc., etc.

HEDD WYN . . . *EVANS, (Ellis Humphrey)'

HELICOPTER RESCUE . . . RAF Valley on Anglesey is the home of the SARTU, the helicopter Search And Rescue Training Unit for pilots, navigators and winchmen.

HELUESTRA . . . the remains of a boat off Rhosili on the Gower peninsula (just blackened wooden stumps). The craft ran aground in 1887.

HEN GYMRU LAWEN . . . (Merry Old Wales) Before the constricting restrictions of Puritanism and Methodism, the Welsh enjoyed a carefree existence with much merry-making in taverns, fairs and markets playing harmless games and listening to balladeers, harpists, anterliwts and story-tellers. They came to rue the day that non-conformists ruled the day!

HENGWRT MANUSCRIPTS . . . The finest library collection of Welsh manuscripts which were collected by the antiquary Robert Vaughan (*c*.1592-1667) at Llanelltyd near Dolgellau in the 17th century.

HEN WLAD FY NHADAU . . . (Land of My Fathers) National anthem of Wales. Written by father and son Evan and James James in 1856.

HENRY II wrote to the Byzantine Emperor: 'The Welsh are a wild people who cannot be tamed' *circa* 1150.

HENRY IV . . . in the Shakespeare play (Part 1) act 3 scene one, the line 'Now I perceive the devil understands Welsh' is uttered. So much for the language of heaven!

HENRY V . . . born in Monmouth Castle in 1387 and immortalised by Shakespeare, who ensured that the monarch and Fluellyn capitalised on their imagined Celtic roots. Henry V's victory over the French at Agincourt in 1415 was attributed to the skills of Welsh longbowmen.

HENRY VII . . . Henry Tudor was born in Pembroke Castle and lived in Wales until he was 14. During the next fourteen years, no fewer than thirty-five bards wrote verses promising the return of Henry Tudor from exile as the deliverer of the Welsh. In 1485 he defeated Richard III at Bosworth and became King of England, but the long awaited 'deliverer' did not deliver.

HENRY (Graham) . . . the charismatic 'honorary Welshman' (actually a New Zealander) who re-invented the habit of winning for the Welsh national rugby fifteen.

HERBERT (George) (1593-1633) . . . poet of Welsh stock from a rich land-owning family. He became MP for Montomery and wrote as a contemporary of John Donne but, as he rejoiced in personal agonies and unworthiness, it is fitting that he is regarded as far inferior to Donne.

HERBERT (Sir William) (died in 1593) . . . Educationalist whose speech in parliament in 1584 (a tirade against Mary Queen of Scots) was the first such speech to be recorded by a Welsh member.

HERITAGE COAST . . . over 40% of Wales' 750 mile (1200 km) coastline is 'Heritage Coast'. Introduced in 1973, the original five areas have trebelled.

HERITAGE SITES (World Heritage Sites) . . . Are there four in Wales or is there only one? 'The castles and walled towns of Edward 1 in Gwynedd' is the official name, but as these include Conwy, Caernarfon, Beaumaris and Harlech, there are actually four distinct World Heritage Sites are there not?

HERITAGE SITES 2 . . . Wales has two on the short list for consideration in the future. 1 – Pontcysyllte (Aqueduct) near Wrexham and 2 – Blaenafon's early industrial landscape near Pontypool.

HESELTINE (Michael) . . . the wealthy Conservative politician, born in Swansea, hides his Welshness well. However, at his daughter's wedding the tune *Myfanwy* was played as the wedding march. Cymru am byth, Tarzan!

HESS (Rudolph) . . . Hitler's deputy was at one time jailed at Maindiff Military Hospital in Abergavenny where he tried to commit suicide in February 1945. Abergavenny does have that effect on some people!

HIGH FLYER . . . Wales' first Aviation Certificate was issued to Victor Hewitt at Rhyl in 1910. Vic flew a Bleriot Monoplane.

HIGHEST PUB IN WALES . . . is the Sportsman's Arms on the Denbigh Moors which stands 1,547 feet [476m] above sea level. It was first licensed as the Bryn Trillyn in 1829 but changed name in 1870.

HIGHEST POINTS SCORER . . . Welsh Rugby hero, Neil Jenkins holds the world record for points scored.

HIGHEST ROAD IN WALES . . . is the road over Bwlch y Groes near Bala, which climbs to a height of 1,791 feet [551m].

HIGHWAY MAN . . . in May 1535, coach and horse passengers in Oxfordshire were held up and robbed by no ordinary bandit. He was Abbot Salisbury of Valle Crucis near Llangollen who should have been contemplating in his monastic cell – obviously the good Abbot was fed up with Holy Orders and his vows, especially the vow of poverty!

HILL (The) in 1854 George Borrow disparagingly referred to Mount Snowdon as 'The Hill'.

HIRAETH . . . Welsh word meaning longing for home or nostalgia for childhood.

HIRED THUG . . . John Jones (1811-c.1858) was a Rebecca Rioter who was transported to Tasmania in 1844. A constant offender and lawbreaker, he was known by the nickname 'Shoni Sgubor Fawr'. Hazy evidence exists about his formative years but it is certain that he did serve in the forces before becoming a bare-knuckle prize-fighter. He memorably fought a bout with John Nash, the Cyfarthfa champion, at the opening of the Taff Vale railway line to Merthyr. By 1843 he was frequently being brought before magistrates on drunk and disorderly charges. He was engaged by the Rebecca Rioters and was paid a few shillings each night for the destruction of turnpikes. In August 1843 he was arrested after a drunken rampage through Pontyberem which incorporated an incident with a gun – he had shot at someone. Subsequently tried and sentenced (not for the destruction of turnpikes, but for the gun incident) he laughed when the judge sentenced him to prison and transportation. Whilst in Carmarthen jail he revealed the names of many fellow Rebecca Rioters. In 1847 Jones arrived in Tasmania and was a persistent offender and trouble-maker who, when he was not pilfering potatoes, was drunk and disorderly. For his incalcitrance he received further periods of imprisonment, including bouts of solitary confinement. Shoni Sgubor Fawr was unrepentant. After his death (the whereabouts and cause of which are not known) a contemporary described him as being 'a half-witted inebriate ruffian.' Join the club!

HIRFAEN GWYDDOG . . . Wales' earliest mentioned boundary stone. Referred to in the *Book of St Chad*, the 15 foot (4.6m) monolith stands near Ffaldybrenin on the Ceredigion-Carmarthenshire boundary.

HISLOP (Ian) . . . editor of satirical magazine *Private Eye* and team captain on TV's *Have I Got News For You* was born in The Mumbles, Gower. He left aged 5 months, which has nothing to with Paula Yates's infamous description of him being 'the spawn of the devil'.

HITLER . . . Lord Howard de Walden of Chirk Castle (John Osmael Scott-Ellis) nearly killed Adolf Hitler in Munich in 1931. Whilst driving a car, he knocked over the jay-walking, goose-stepping politician who, as we know, unfortunately made a complete recovery. Rumours about Herr Hitler undergoing surgery to remove a testicle damaged in the accident have not been substantiated. In fact it's a load of balls.

HOAXER . . . Iolo Morganwg coined hundreds of proverbs which he passed up as ancient and authentic. They were included in *The Myvyrian Archaiology* of 1801. *MORGANNWG (Iolo)

HÔB (Yr) . . . the Welsh version of Hope, the Flintshire town.

HODGE (Sir Julian) . . . The sixth richest man in Wales. Born in 1904 his family settled in Pontllanfraith in 1909. He established a financial services business in Wales, including his own Julian Hodge Bank in Cardiff.

HOLT, Wrexham . . . has a claim to fame in that H.G. Wells (of *War of The Worlds* fame) once taught at Holt academy. In his *Experiment in Autobiography* Wells tells of his Holt period.

HOLY GRAIL . . . The wooden cup used by Jesus Christ at the Last Supper was brought to Britain by Joseph of Arimithea who built the first British church at Glastonbury. The Holy Grail, with its magical healing powers, was then kept at Strata Florida monastery until Henry VIII's dissolution in 1536. Then??? mystery. Somehow, by magic, the Holy Grail got to Nanteos Mansion near Aberystwyth. The Nanteos Cup is apparently safe in the vault of a Welsh bank, while another three Holy Grails are owned by three different European Churches.

HOLYHEAD (Caergybi) . . . Anglesey's largest town which is a container and passenger ferry port connecting mainland UK with Dublin in the Irish Republic.

HOLLY FERN . . . a rare breed of fern found only in the Arfon district of Gwynedd. It was first discovered *circa* 1682 by Edward Lhuyd.

HOLYWELL (Treffynnon). . . In Flints. St Winifrid's well, fed by a spring with healing properties, still attracts pilgrims who bathe in the shrine, which is known as 'the Lourdes of Wales'. Famous pilgrims from days of yore include Henry V, Margaret Beaufort (mother of Henry VII) and James II. *The Miracles of Wales* of 1820 refers to scores of infirm people who discarded crutches and skipped home after a visit to Holywell.

HOMFRAY . . . ironmaster family from Penydarren, Merthyr.

HOOSON I.D. . . . (Isaac Daniel) Welsh language poet of renown (1880-1948). Born at Rhosllanerchrugog. His work naturally lends itself to public recitation and includes *Wil, Barti Ddu* and *Guto Nyth-Brân.*

HOPKIN (Mary) . . . The Pontardawe schoolgirl who won on *Opportunity Knocks* TV programme; taken under the wing of Paul McCartney she was signed to the new Beatles Apple label. Her initial hit *Those Were The Days* replaced her mentors's acknowledged classic *Hey Jude* at the the top of the charts and stayed there for six weeks. A few other chart hits followed until she fell away from the spotlight.

HOPKINS (Sir Anthony) . . . Oscar-winning actor who was born in South Wales in 1937. His most notable film roles include the Oscar winning role of Hannibal Lecter in the spine-chilling *Silence of The Lambs*. Almost equally famous as a stage performer, Hopkins specialised in historical and Shakespearean roles.

HOPPER (Thomas) . . . he designed Windsor Castle for George IV and was also commissioned to erect Penrhyn Castle (1827-1840), outside Bangor, for Lord Penrhyn. He also worked for the wealthy Talbot family of Margam.

HORSES . . . animals in Penrhyn castle received an annual pension of £45, compared to the quarrymen's pittance of a wage.

HOT SUMMER . . . the hottest recorded summer temperature in Wales, of 124 degrees Fahrenheit (51.1°C) in Cardiff in 1911. Presumably the weather had been arranged by Lloyd George as it coincided with the Investiture of the Prince of Wales.

HOUDINI . . . the great escapologist was a Welsh man!. When two cross-strait ferry boats sank in the Menai Strait, on both occasions there was a sole survivor – amazingly both were called Hugh Williams.

HOUSTON (Donald) . . . (died 1991) this actor was brought up in Tonypandy and made his big screen debut in *The Blue Lagoon* (1949) He also appeared in *A Run for Your Money, Where Eagles Dare, Sea Wolves* and *The Longest Day.*

HOUSTON (Glyn) . . . thespian brother of Donald Houston who hit the screen in *The Blue Lamp* (precursor of Dixon of Dock Green). Glyn appeared in many other films including *Bulldog Breed* and *The Waiting Game.*

HOVERCRAFT . . . In July 1962 the world's first commercial hovercraft service was started between Rhyl and Wallasey, Merseyside.

HOWARD (Michael) . . . the former Home Secretary hails from Llanelli.

HOW GREEN WAS MY VALLEY . . . This 1939 work by Richard Llewellyn (1906-1983) is the best known novel by an Anglo-Welsh writer. An instant best-seller, it became an Oscar winning film (partly shot on location in Wales) for Walter Pidgeon and Maureen O'Hara in 1940. By now the book has been translated into twenty-four languages and has sold ten million copies worldwide. There is however considerable doubt about Richard Llewellyn's claims to ever having lived in the South Wales valleys as a child.

HOWE (Sir Geoffrey). the eminent Conservative politician (formerly a Chancellor of the Exchequer and Foreign Secretary) was born in Port Talbot.

HOWELL (Thomas) (died c.1540). Monmouthshire born philanthropist whose will provided dowries for spinsters of his family. Some three hundred years after his death, two schools were set up in his name by the Drapers Company, one at Llandaf and the other at Denbigh. In 1997 the Denbigh school faced closure but a concerted effort by concerned parties earned a reprieve.

HOWELLS (Jack), in 1962 he won an Oscar for the short documentary *Dylan* about 'the' Dylan – Mr Thomas.

HUET (Thomas) . . . A Biblical translator who, in 1567, translated the book of Revelations for the Welsh version of the New Testament.

HUGHES (Charles Evans) . . . (1862-1948) . . . American born of a Welsh immigrant family (from Brynteg, Anglesey). Regarded as one of the greatest jurists and statesmen of all time. He served as a New York lawyer and became governor in 1906. Ten years later he narrowly lost the Presidential election by twenty-three electoral votes and a mere half million popular votes. He later served as Secretary of State and Supreme Court Chief Justice.

HUGHES (Mark) . . . born 1965. The footballer-cum-Wales manager who is nicknamed 'Sparky'.

HUGHES (Nerys) . . . actress best known for her role in *The Liver Birds*. Also featured in the Half Man Half Biscuit song *I Hate Nerys Hughes*, the lyric of which was no more than those four words screamed with a passion.

HUMPHRYS (John). Born 1943, in Cardiff. Journalist, broadcaster and TV presenter. He has been a tenacious questioner of politicians on Radio 4's *Today* and was voted the sixty-seventh sexiest man in Britain in a 1998 poll.

HUMPHREYS (Emyr) . . . born 1919 at Prestatyn, Flints. A novelist, poet and dramatist. In 1952 he won the Somerset Maugham Award for *Hear and Forgive* and, six years later the Hawthornden Prize for *A Toy Epic*. He has written twenty-one novels, four volumes of verse, short stories and also a Welsh language TV drama. He is also the author of the excellent historical interpretation, *The Taliesin Tradition*.

HUNDRED YEAR OLD COUNCILLOR . . . Dr William George (brother of David Lloyd George) attended meetings of Caernarfonshire County Council after his 100th birthday.

HUNLLEF ARTHUR . . . a long poem (21,000 lines, actually) by Bobi Jones (born 1928) (Professor Robert Maynard Jones).

HWYL . . . a Welsh language comic by D J Williams (1886-1950) of Corris, which was launched in 1949.

HYDER . . . Wales' largest public company.

HYDRO ELECTRICITY . . . the first generated in Wales was at Cwm Dyli on the side of Snowdon.

HYMNS . . . William Williams of Pantycelyn who is regarded as the finest Welsh language poet of the 18th Century wrote over 1,000 hymns. He was born into a wealthy Llanymddyfri farming family in 1717 and died in 1791.

HYWEL Y FWYELL . . . or Hywel ap Gruffudd who died in 1381. A mighty medieval gladiator who was the best decorated Welsh professional soldier of all time. He pole-axed his battle rivals with his pole-axe at Crecy (where he was knighted for gallantry on the field of battle) and Poitiers (where he captured the French King John). In 'retirement' he was awarded the title of Constable of Criccieth Castle in 1359. In 1969 Lord Snowdon was awarded a similar post (with Caernarfon Castle) for his 'bravery' in marrying Princess Margaret.

HYWEL DDA . . . (Hywel the Good) a.k.a. Hywel ap Cadell (died *circa* 950) is the only Welsh leader to earn the flattering soubriquet 'Dda'. He had authority over most of Wales and is acknowledged as a law-giver, as he codified Welsh laws which lasted until 1536. Public property, consumer protection, trading standards, women's lib are not 20th century phenomena. They are enshrined in the Laws of Hywel Dda. Scales of fines, compensation and punishments were stated clearly. Even cats had a warranty: 'Whoever shall sell a cat, let him guarantee it is free from caterwauling every moon, and it do not devour its kittens, and that it has ears, eyes, teeth and claws and that it is a good mouser'. No pussyfooting around with Hywel Dda then.

ICE SKATING RINK . . . the one at the Deeside Leisure Centre near Queensferry is the National Centre of Ice Sports in Wales and has been the training base for many British skating champions including Steve Cousins.

ICELAND . . . If Rhiannedd, the wife of Malcolm Walker Iceland's chief executive, had not suggested 'Iceland' in 1970, then this insertion under 'I' could have been under 'P' for Penguin or remained under 'I' but been listed as Igloo or Icicle. However, that's all in the past, or in the ice-age even. The North Wales frozen food retailing giant has snowballed since 1970 and has nearly eight hundred stores throughout the UK. The Iceland HQ is at Queensferry, Flintshire.

ICH DIEN . . . The motto of the Prince of Wales and the Royal Welsh Fusiliers.

IF . . . If Charles Windsor's father had not married the then Princess Elizabeth, Charles would not have enjoyed the title Prince of Wales. If Phil the Greek (born Corfu) had not changed his name to Mountbatten, Charles would have been Charles Schleswig-Holstein-Sonderburg-Glucksburg or Charlie 4 Hyphens to his chums.

IFANS (Rhys) . . . North Wales born, Guildhall-trained movie and tv star who appeared in *Twin Town* and the 1999 monster hit *Notting Hill* alongside Hugh Grant and Julia Roberts.

IMMERSION . . . St Myllin established a church and holy well at Llanfyllin in Powys *circa* 600AD. He was the first to use immersion for baptism.

IMMIGRANTS' NEWSPAPER . . . *Y Drych* was a Welsh language newspaper for Welsh immigrants to the USA, founded in 1851 in New York it then moved its home base to Milwaukee – surely nothing to do with the booze Milwaukee produced? It ceased to be all-Welsh in the 1930s and is now published in St Paul, Minneapolis by Mary Morris Mergenthal.

IMPOSTOR EVANS (Mary) (1735-1789). Known as *Y Fantell Wen* (Whitemantle) she duped followers into believing that she was betrothed to Jesus Christ, and led a long procession of guests to her 'marriage' in Ffestiniog church. She was the beneficiary of many wedding gifts! The sect, who held ceremonies on the mountains around Ffestiniog, spread throughout the Meirionnydd area. Mary, who had been born on Anglesey, insisted to the cult members that she would never die and consequently her corpse lay unburied for a considerable time when she actually did die. Her followers insisted on keeping scraps of her clothing after the funeral but the sect, who were regarded as harmless (but very gullible), soon died out.

INDEED TO GOODNESS . . . is the first English language expression which Welsh infants learn. This is inevitable because it is of course the only English expression ever uttered by their parents, uncles, aunts, grandparents and great grandparents.

INFAMOUS WRECKERS . . . the Wreckers of Crigyll lured 18th century ships on the rocks near Rhosneigr, Anglesey. For their crimes they were hanged after a trial at Beaumaris.

INLAND SEA-BIRDS . . . there is still a cormorant breeding ground at Craig y Deryn in the Dysynni Valley of southern Snowdonia, several centuries after the last time that the valley was anywhere near the sea.

INNES (J.D. (James Dickson) (1887-1914) born Llanelli, Carms. A landscape painter, friend of Augustus John, who painted the Arennig Valley near Bala and also many European scenes.

INSPIRATION . . . Wales, according to the Wales Tourist Board's award winning slogan is 'the land of inspiration'.

INSULTS . . . *Gill AA.

INVASION . . . Picture the scene . . . date: August 7, 1485 . . . venue: Dale near Milford Haven . . . Event: the chosen landing place for Hari Tudor (*Henry VII) and his army of 4,000 French and exiled Lancastrians. It took two weeks but he eventually defeated the forces of Richard III (the famous crook-backed Yorkist and latterly King of England) and founded the Tudor dynasty from which our beloved parasites of today claim lineage – albeit with a lot of German, Dutch and Greek injections inbetween. . . .

INVESTITURE . . . July 1, 1969 saw the Investiture of Charles, Prince of Wales at Caernarfon Castle. He became the 23rd Prince of Wales in a spectacle which broke TV viewing records with five hundred million glued to the box. One of the benefits of this bit of theatricality is that Charles' uncle, Anthony Armstrong-Jones (Lord Snowdon) was appointed Constable of Caernarfon Castle, which helped Cofis and indeed most Gogs to sleep more soundly in their beds. One of the lighter moments of this bit of solemnity was when the Mayor of Caernarfon (Ivor Bowen (I.B.) Griffith proferred his hand to the Prince and said 'I.B. Griffith' to which the prince quipped 'I be Charles'. Who said he was aloof, dry and starchy?

INN OF THE SIXTH HAPPINESS . . . Hollywood blockbuster movie of 1958 starring Ingrid Bergman, based on the true story of nurse Gladys Aylward and her missionary position in wartime China. Filmed on location in North Wales at Nanmor near Beddgelert. Dozens of locals were employed as extras, as well as hundreds of children from the Chinese communities of Merseyside and Manchester.

INVESTMENT . . . Wales is currently enjoying more investment from foreign countries than other parts of Europe.

IOLO MORGANWG . . . 'born Edward Williams (1747-1826) at Llancarfan, Glamorgan. He was a gifted bard, story-teller, hymn-writer and antiquary and hoaxer who claimed he'd 'found' ancient manuscripts which gave authority to his own inventive genius. Iolo Morganwg felt that the Eisteddfod system needed more pomp and ceremony and he devised *Gorsedd Beirdd Ynys Prydain* (Assembly of the Bards of the British Isles) in 1792 on Primrose Hill in London. It was first incorporated into the National Eisteddfod at the 1819 Eisteddfod held at the Ivy Bush hotel, Carmarthen, which could be described as the first 'modern Eisteddfod' as it featured the ceremony of robes, the sword of peace, the horn of plenty, trumpets, three orders of bards in white, blue and green robes, and mini stone circles. This was a great contribution to the Welsh language and culture as Gorsedd membership is Wales' own honours system.

ISLE OF MAN CONNECTION . . . the 150 year old link was broken in 1982 when the last steam boat left Llandudno for the island. *The Manxman* a grand old lady, avoided the scrap yard and enjoys 'sail on' parts in movies, e.g. include *Chariots of Fire*.

IRISH FERRIES . . . on their Holyhead to Dublin route the biggest super-ferry in Northern Europe *The Isle of Inishmore* carries 2,330 passengers, 856 cars and 122 freight units.

IRISH MAIL . . . this Euston to Holyhead mail train was the world's first named train – the Royal Scotsman, Orient Express etc came later.

IRISH TUNNEL. 1999 saw talk of a tunnel linking Wales with Ireland, from Holyhead to Dublin. It would further reduce the ninety-nine minute fast ferry crossing to a mere forty-five minutes. The fifty-six mile project would cost £14 billion and would be the world's longest tunnel.

IRON . . . Henry Cort's *Welsh Method* innovation in 1874 involved stirring or *puddling* molten iron which somehow enabled a fifteen fold increase in production.

IRON COFFIN . . . John Wilkinson (died 1821) was the Ironmaster whose foundry perfected the art of making perfectly straight barrels for war time cannon, thus reducing the casualty rate amongst cannon operators and increasing the mortality rate for enemies. (*Bersham). Wilkinson was buried in an iron coffin.

IRON ROLLING MILL . . . the first iron rolling mill in the USA was built at Sharon, Pennsylvania in 1817 by Welsh exile David Morgan of Pontypool.

ITALIAN JOB . . . Castles don't grow on trees. The Edward I-constructed castles in North Wales cost three quarters of a million pounds (loadsamoney in those days) – he borrowed the filthy lucre off the Italian bankers Riccardi of Lucca in Tuscany.

ITALY . . . the Italian newspaper *Corriere della Sera* has often misinformed its readers about some of the basics concerning Wales and the Welsh. Apparently, readers of this highly respected tome have lately been informed that the capital of Wales is Birmingham, that Dylan Thomas was a famous English poet and that Welsh is a dialect of English. So now we know that the capital of Italy is Berlin, that Michaelangelo painted the Forth Bridge and that pasta is a medieval dance in two-four time.

IVORITES (ORDER OF TRUE) . . . a friendly society with the furtherance of the Welsh language as one of its objectives. Founded in 1836 at Wrexham, its headquarters later moved to Carmarthen and hundreds of lodges were established in South Wales.

J4O . . . a type of children's pedal car began production in Pontllan-ffraith in 1949. Thirty two thousand were made.

JACKS . . . Name given to Swansea residents by their Cardiffian cousins.

JACK DANIELS . . . we are led to believe that a Ceredigion-born distiller emigrated to America and carried on the family tradition of producing whisky – it would be nice to learn that this was, in fact, true.

JACKDAW . . . for centuries this description has been reserved for the inhabitants of Conwy who were born within the massive town walls.

JACKSON (Colin) – OBE nifty Olympic medal winner in the 110 metre hurdles – was born in Cardiff in 1967. By 1999 he was the most succesful Welsh athlete ever.

JACOB (Sarah) (1857-1869) . . . 'The Welsh Fasting Girl'. Born in Carmarthenshire. After an illness in 1867 she fell unconscious and did not wake for over a month. After this she refused all food except for very small amounts of milk. By October of 1867, it is said that she refused all food and drink and lived for a further one hundred and thirteen weeks. News of this strange fasting brought countless visitors bearing gifts to the family home at Llanfihangel-yr-arth including many eminent medical practitioners perplexed by the phenomenon. After her death, her parents were accused of not feeding her and were sent to trial, and were jailed. The medical practitioners and religious leaders, who showed more interest in how long she could last without food than in her well-being, got off scot free.

JACOBITES . . . the Tory sympathisers who supported the exiled Stuarts in the early 18th century had fancy names for societies. South Wales saw the Society of Sea Sergeants established in 1725, and North Wales saw the Circle of the White Rose established 1710.

JAGUARS . . . Legacy, near Wrexham has more Jaguar cars than any other similar sized town in the UK – but not because the locals are well-heeled. The various jags are in a car dismantler's yard.

JAMES (David John) . . . (1887-1967). Born Pontrhydfendigaid, Ceredigion. Welsh philanthropist who is best known as the sponsor of the well-known Pontrhydfendigaid Eisteddfod, which offers valuable prizes.

JAMES (Evan) (1809-1878) . . . author of the words to the Welsh National anthem Hen Wlad Fy Nhadau. His son James, composed the tune.

JAMES (Jesse) . . . the grandfather of the famous (infamous) wild-west outlaw was William James (1754-1805), who was born in Pembrokeshire.

JAMES (Leighton) . . . brought glory to Welsh soccer in 1977. His winning penalty goal at Wembley, against an England side featuring Peter Shilton, Mike Channon, Kevin Keegan and a host of others, broke twenty-two years of English victories over Wales.

JAMES (Ronnie) . . . (1918-1977) On September 4 1946 over 40,000 people crammed into Ninian Park Cardiff to watch local boy Ronnie, the British lightheavyweight Boxing Champion lose his World Championship bout to Ike Williams of the USA. This was the biggest ever crowd at the ground.

JAPAN . . . The Japanese navy corvette *Hei Yei* was built at Pembroke Dock in 1877.

JARVIS VALLEY . . . Dylan Thomas' fictitious location in some of his early stories.

JEEFREYS (Judge George) . . . presided over the infamous *Bloody Assizes* of 1685, when hundreds of followers of the Duke of Monmouth were tried after a failed rebellion. Prosecutors duped prisoners into pleading guilty, informing them that mercy would be shown. However, Judge Jeffreys sentenced more than three hundred people to death and ordered that around eight hundred and fifty rebels should be shipped overseas to penal colonies. Born at Acton Park near Wrexham, the judge died in the Tower of London after falling out with his peers.

JEFFERSON (Thomas) . . . the former American President who was the first signatory of the Declaration of American independence had ancestors from Llanberis in Snowdonia.

JENKINS (Revd Eli) . . . 'Praise God! We are a musical nation' said the *Under Milk Wood* man when he hears Polly Garter singing.

JENKINS (Ffion) otherwise known as Mrs William Hague or 'Jolly' Jenkins because of her funloving nature. Teacher, singer and instrumentalist – she sang in the National Youth Choir of Wales, played clarinet in the National

Youth Orchestra of Wales, and taught William the words (not just the title) of the Welsh National anthem. (*REDWOOD)

JENKINS (Joseph) (1856-1962) . . . born Pont-Rhyd-Y-Groes, Ceredigion. Well-known author of popular books for young readers e.g. *Dai y Dderwen* (1926) *Robin y Pysgotwr* (1926), are both about mischievous boys.

JENKINS (Rachel) . . . One of Patagonia's most influential Welsh settlers who realised the value of irrigation and argued that canals had to be built to channel water from the Chubut river. She is commemorated with a large monument in Port Madryn in the province of Patagonia in Argentina.

JENKINS (Roy) . . . Abercynon born politician. Became Lord Jenkins of Hillhead and President of the European Community after helping form the SDP. He earlier legalised abortion and homosexuality as a Labour Home Secretary.

JET SKI LAKE . . . Aberafon town is home to the only heated freshwater jet-ski lake in Europe.

JOAN (Siwan) . . . the wife of Llywelyn Fawr (The Great) who lived in a castle at Abergwyngregyn, Bangor after she had an adulterous affair with William de Braose (grandson of the Ogre of Abergavenny) whom Llywelyn subsequently hanged – well-hung willy?

JOHN ap JOHN (*c.*1625-1697) . . . born at Trefor Isaf, Ruabon, Denbs. Wales' first Quaker evangelist. A street preacher – often jailed, he was one of the few to face the music rather than fleeing to Pennsylvania.

JOHN (Augustus) (1878-1961) . . . born Tenby. A renowned artist who studied at Slade School in London and became leader of a set of Bohemian painters. John is famous for his brilliant portraits of the rich and famous, including George Bernard Shaw, T.E. Lawrence, W.B. Yeats and Dylan Thomas.

JOHN (Barry) . . . World class rugby fly-half who retired at the age of 27. He scored 188 points on the 1971 British Lions tour of New Zealand, on which he was dubbed *the King*.

JOHNS (Glynis) . . . Welsh born daughter of film actor Mervyn Johns. By the age of 17 she'd starred in seven films. Later a Tony Award winner.

JOHNS (Mervyn) . . . (1899-1992) film actor born in Pembroke Dock. He starred in the 1951 film *Valley of Song* and appeared in dozens of other movies in over fifty years of acting.

JOHNSON (Amy) . . . the famous aviatrix took off from Pendine (Pentywyn) Sands in 1933 on her record breaking Atlantic flight. (*EARHART, Amelia)

JOHNSON (Dr Samuel) (1709-1784) . . . During one of his visits, this learned lexicographer complained that there was nothing to delight the eye of the imagination for the traveller. Was he blind, or just paving the way for A.A. Gill?

JOKES . . . Is there a grain of truth in Welsh legends? One legend is that a 'Cardi' once bought a round of drinks. Another is that a small group of Llanelli rugby supporters once applauded a try scored by their opponents.

JONES – the most common Welsh surname (since the Act of Union) as you might assume. Strangely, the letter 'J' is not strictly part of the alphabet of the Welsh language.

JONES (Abel) (1830-1901) . . . Llanrwst born singer regarded as the 'prince of the ballad singers' who travelled the country. He only had one eye and died in the Llanrwst workhouse.

JONES (Aled) . . . Former boy soprano from Anglesey who had a number of hit records in the UK, most notably *Walking In The Air* which reached the top five in 1985. The song featured in classic animation film *The Snowman*.

JONES (Alice Gray) (1852-1943) . . . born Llanllyfni, Gwynedd. Writer who launched the feminist magazine *Y Gymraes* in 1896 (it lasted until 1919). She was also one of the founders of the North Wales Women's Temperance League.

JONES (Bobi) . . . Properly Robert Maynard Jones a writer so prolific that he penned a twenty-one thousand line poem in 1986 called *Hunllef Arthur*.

JONES (Clay) . . . a popular Welsh born expert on *Gardener's Question Time* sadly himself pushing up daisies since 1996.

JONES (Dai) . . . born Llanilar. Popular, smiling TV presenter and interviewer, a gifted singer, writer and public speaker. His book *Fi Dai Sy' 'Ma* broke

Gwasg Gwynedd's sales record. As only 1% in Britain speak and read Welsh, the sales were approximately the equivalent of selling 600,000 (six hundred thousand) English books in a single week.

JONES (Daniel) (1811-1861). Mormon missionary. Born in Abergele. He became a convert to Mormonism after his emigration to the USA. He was with the Mormon leader and prophet Joseph Smith on the night that the latter was assassinated in June 1844.

JONES (Edward) (died 1586) . . . conspirator. Born in Denbighshire. Involved in the Babington's Plot to overthrow Queen Elizabeth 1 so as to install Mary Queen of Scots on the English throne. Co-conspirator of Robert Salusbury.

JONES (Elwyn) . . . (1923-1982) born Cwmaman, Glam. Writer and TV playwright who created *Softly Softly* and the character of Inspector Barlow. He also wrote *The Ripper File* in 1975.

JONES (Ernest) Welsh born psychoanalyst (1879-1958). Was a personal friend and colleague of Sigmund Freud, and introduced psychoanalysis to both the UK and USA. Later became professor of psychiatry at Toronto.

JONES (Griff Rhys) . . . Cardiff born (in 1953) comedian who memorably appeared in *Not The Nine O'clock News* in the 1980s, and latterly several series with Mel Smith. Griff Rhys Jones moved to south-eastern England as a babe-in-arms.

JONES (Dame Gwyneth) . . . born Pontnewydd, Gwent in 1936. A soprano with an international career who has made award winning performances at Berlin, Bayreuth, Covent Garden, Paris, Tokyo and Lisbon. Audiences worldwide have been enthralled by her Wagnerian roles. She became a CBE in 1976 and an OBE in 1986.

JONES (Hugh Robert) (1894-1930) . . . The 'founder' of the Welsh Nationalist Party. Born in Deiniolen, Caernarfon. He initially worked in the slate quarries until ill-health forced him to leave. After a spell working in Liverpool, he returned to Deiniolen as secretary of the village Co-operative Society until he went to Manchester to serve as a clerk in the Society's main office. He later became a commercial traveller for a Merseyside based company and traversed up and down Wales, which enabled him to spread the political views he had developed. In 1921 he formed the Home Rule association which became the Welsh Nationalist Party in 1925. (*Plaid Cymru)

JONES (John) . . . all twenty-seven of them who appear in the *Oxford Companion to the Literature of Wales.*

JONES (John) (1790-1855) . . . printer. Born in Glan Conwy. He published *Yr Amserau* (The Times!) which became the first Welsh language newspaper to prosper and grow.

JONES (John Gwilym) (1904-1988) . . . born Groeslon, Gwynedd. Dramatist, novelist and playwright recognised along with Saunders Lewis as the greatest Welsh dramatist of the 20th century.

JONES (John Puleston) (1862-1925) . . . devised a Braille system for the Welsh language.

JONES (Colonel John) . . . of Maes y Garnedd one of the fifty-nine signatories of the death warrant of King Charles I. At the Restoration he was tried as a regicide and executed. (*HARLECH CASTLE)

JONES (John) Jac Glan-y-gors (1766-1821) born Cerrigydrudion, Denbs. A poet, pamphleteer against oppression, drover, London inn-keeper, President of the Gwyneddigion Society and founder of the Cymreigyddion Society.

JONES (Jonah) . . . born in Durham of Welsh descent. A sculptor who settled near Porthmadog. A novelist and writer of guide books as well as the biography of Clough Williams-Ellis.

JONES (Kelly) . . . lead-singer, guitarist and song-writer with the group Stereophonics. Apparently used to sell fruit and veg on a stall at Aberdare market.

JONES (Ken) OBE . . . As a Welsh international rugby player he won forty-four caps and toured with the British Lions in 1950. He was a Welsh champion sprinter and long-jumper. At the 1948 Olympics he won a silver medal in the 4x100 relay, in 1954 he captained Britain in the European Games, and in 1958, he managed Wales in the Empire Games in Cardiff.

JONES (Lewis) (1836-1904) . . . a pioneer of the Welsh exodus to Patagonia. For a short while he was the governor of Patagonia and was the only Welshman to have been appointed to this post by the Argentine government. Born at Caernarfon, he visited Patagonia in 1862 and on returning over-exaggerated the virtues of the area to such an extent that people were clamouring to emigrate. The first emigrants were greatly disappointed when they arrived and turned against Jones, who left to work in Buenos Aries as a printer. However, when he heard that the emigrants were planning to leave Patagonia, he hurried back and talked them into remaining.

JONES (Mari) . . . sixteen year old girl who walked nearly thirty miles to Bala to ask for a Bible in 1800. A plaque commemorating this epic journey stands on a memorial in Bryn-crug.

JONES (Michael Daniel) . . . (1822-1898) born Llanuwchllyn, Meirionnydd. After an unsuccessful attempt in America, where the English language was being adopted by settlers from different parts of Europe, he organised the founding of the Welsh settlement in Patagonia as a second homeland for Welsh immigrants.

JONES, RICHARD LEWIS (Dic Jones) . . . born Ceredigion in 1934. A prolific poet who won no fewer than five Bardic chairs at Urdd Eisteddfodau as a youngster. In 1966 he won the Chair at the National Eisteddfod and, ten years later, was controversially disqualified from the competition for a breach of the rules. Dic Jones has published several volumes of his work, is a regular magazine columnist, and is one of the 20th century's finest exponents of poetry.

JONES (Steve) . . . Wales' greatest distance runner who won marathons in London, New York, Chicago and Toronto. In 1984 at Chicago, he created a new World Record of only 2 hours, 8 minutes and 5 seconds.

JONES (Terry) . . . Comic writer and performer who formed part of the Monty Python team. Born in Colwyn Bay.

JONES (Tom) . . . Powerful singer whose career has spanned three decades and spawned hits such as *It's Not Unusual, Green Green Grass of Home* and *Boy From Nowhere*. Born in Pontypridd.

JONES (Vincent) . . . Welsh international footballer, and some time captain of the team, born in England. Made his name by putting the squeeze on Paul Gascgoine. Latterly turned to the silver screen and made a widely-praised debut in the film *Lock, Stock & Two Smoking Barrels* in which he plays a South London hardman.

JONES (William R.) . . . Scots born US philanthropist Andrew Carnegie, who developed the Pittsburg iron and steel industries, needed a right-hand man. It was Welsh born William R. Jones who played this role.

JOSEPHSON (Brian) . . . Wales' only science Nobel prize winner was educated at Cardiff High School. He won the prize in 1973 and his field is low-temperature physics which plays an important part in computer technology, so they say.

JULIAN CALENDAR . . . John Dee (1527-1608) was the Surrey-born astronomer, alchemist, mathematician, geographer and spy, who claimed descent from Rhodri Mawr, and was consulted by Queen Elizabeth I about reforming the Julian calendar.

ST JULIETTA'S Church . . . This place of worship at Capel Curig is the smallest church in Snowdonia.

K . . . has ceased to be a Welsh letter, OK.

KAISER WILHELM . . . the German king during WW1. He once visited Llandrindod Wells to take the waters.

KANE (Vincent) . . . the television personality who received a special BAFTA Cymru Award in 1998, in recognition of his outstanding service to Welsh broadcasting.

KARRIE (Peter) . . . This star of *Phantom of The Opera* and *Les Miserables* in London's West End was born in Bridgend.

KEENOR (Fred) (1892-1972) . . . footballer. Captained Cardiff to their FA Cup final win in 1927. He played three hundred and sixty-nine games for Cardiff and won thirty-two Welsh caps in midfield.

KEEP THE HOMES FIRES BURNING . . . an example of 1970s and 1980s 'black humour', as in 'charred humour' when the so-called 'arson campaign' was in the limelight. The BBC TV comedy show *Not The Nine O'Clock News* ended one episode with a play on the then current coal advertisement: *Come home to a real fire – buy a cottage in Wales'*.

KEEP WALES TIDY . . . The Welsh language version is 'Cadw Cymru'n Daclus'. This means **you**.

KEEPER OF THE GREAT SEAL . . . John Williams, Conwy's most famous son, became Lord Keeper to James I. Later, under Charles I, he was made Archbishop of York.

KELLOG'S . . . The cereal manufacturers. A recent query in one of the national newspapers asked whether the trademark of the crowing cockerel used on Kellogg's corn flakes was used because the word for cockerel in Welsh is 'Ceiliog' which looks and sounds a bit like 'Kellogg'. Rather disappointingly the answer was 'No.'

KELLOW DRILL . . .'invention of Moses Kellow (1862-1943) the last manager of the Croesor Slate Quarry in Snowdonia. It greatly reduced the time taken to bore holes in slate. Prior to its invention it took ten hours to drill a $7^1/2$ foot (2.25m) hole. Using the water-powered, dust-free drill took only one and a half minutes – four hundred times quicker. Moses Kellow also invented pumps to displace water which collected in slate mines.

KELP . . . fish found in certain parts of beautiful Cardigan Bay.

KELSEY (Jack) . . . sometime Arsenal goalkeeper and Welsh international soccer star. Included here merely to bolster the rather scant listings under the letter 'K'.

KEMBLE (Charles) (1775-1854) . . . actor. Born at Brecon he was the founder of a renowned dynasty of actors and actresses, which included daughter Sarah Siddons.

KILBRANDON REPORT . . . of 1973 recommended that Wales should have a national assembly. Obviously didn't say when since it took a further twenty-six years to materialize.

KILNS . . . quicklime was added to sweeten the acid soil in many parts of Wales which lead to a proliferation of lime kilns across the principality.

KILTS . . . When Emma Day married Kirk Hill in Llanddewi, Swansea in 1998 the groom and his attendants were the first to wear the St David tartan kilts designed by Cardiff company Welsh Regalia. The tartan kilt comprises red, green and white – the traditional colours of Wales.

KILVERT (Francis) . . . author of Kilvert's Diary, a detailed record of village life in Clyro near Hay-on-Wye in the 19th Century. Kilvert was a curate there from 1865-1872 and kept the diary for ten years from 1867. Only three of twenty-two diaries survive and were published in 1938, filmed in 1960 and, by the year 2000, have been re, re, re-printed.

KIMCHI . . . spicy garlic cabbage, the favourite national dish of Korea (and South Wales if the WDA's overtures to Korean investment bears fruit).

KINDERGARTEN . . . Robert Owen of Newton, Montgomery established Britain's first at his model factory in Scotland.

KING OF BARDSEY (Brenin Enlli) . . . This beautiful peaceful island off the Llŷn Peninsula enjoyed special 'kingdom' status. In 1820 Lady Newborough, who owned Ynys Enili crowned John Williams as King. The tradition died in 1927 on the demise of Love Pritchard. In 1999 Bryn Terfel, already a 'king' in his own right, was offered the crown. He said he was too busy.

KINMEL . . . in 1919 Canadian soldiers who had served in WW1 were barracked at Kinmel near Rhyl as they awaited transport to ferry them back home. Upset by the length of the wait and the primitive conditions, the soldiers grew agitated and violence erupted. The uprising was eventually quelled by the police and troops.

KINNOCK (Glenys) . . . Member of the European parliament and wife of Neil.

KINNOCK (Neil) . . . politician and former leader of the Labour Party who was elected to the post in 1983 as the then youngest ever leader of the party. He led Labour through many policy changes and through two unsuccessful General Elections before stepping down in 1992. Under his leadership Labour's popularity rose substantially, but not enough to overthrow the Conservative government of the time. Kinnock is generally accepted as a fine orator, and perhaps 'the best Prime Minister we never had'.

KIRBY (Esme) . . . In 1968 she co-founded the Snowdonia National Park Society.

KITE (Red Kite) . . . the bird of prey re-introduced to northern England in the summer of 1999 after centuries of absence from the region was never away from Russia, the Baltic States, Afghanistan, Pakistan, The Canary islands, northwest Africa . . . and Wales. Called *barcud* in Welsh

KLONDIKE . . . Dolgellau was Wales' answer to the Klondike when there was a gold-rush in the area in the 19th century.

KNIGHT (Bernard) . . . born in Cardiff in 1931 this barrister and doctor uses the pseudonym of Bernard Picton to write crime fiction and historical novels on Welsh topics. He is professor of Forensic Pathology at the Wales National School of Medicine.

KNITTING . . . a scarf measuring twenty-two miles (35.4km) long and nine inches (23 cm) wide was paraded at the Bala National Eisteddfod in 1997. Knitters from all corners of the world contributed sections of the monster which was later turned into blankets for the charity Oxfam.

KOESTLER (Arthur) the writer spent a few years living in Blaenau Ffestiniog following WW2.

KOLLAKIS (Lou) . . . Barry shipping magnate who is the joint third richest man in Wales.

KOREAN INVESTMENT . . . the Welsh Development Agency built a massive factory for the Korean Forklift truck giants, Hall Euro Enterprises, in 1997 at a cost of £18.6 million.

KREMLIN . . . Emlyn was a South Wales Trade Union official who was regarded as being so left-wing he was nicknamed 'Emlyn Kremlin', naturally.

KWIK SAVE . . . the first Kwik Save store was opened in Prestatyn in 1965. The founder was Albert Gubay of Rhyl, who used a £7,000 loan.

KYALAMI . . . Welsh racing driver Tom Pryce (the son of a Rhuthun policeman) was killed in an horrific 100 mph (160 kph) crash at the Kyalami race circuit in the South African Grand Prix. He was 27 years old.

KYNNIVER LLITH A BANN ('So many lessons and excerpts'.) Printed in 1551, this book by William Salesbury contained his translation of the Epistles and Gospels in Welsh, which showed the need for a Welsh Bible.

LABOUR MAYOR . . . Enoch Morrel who became mayor of Merthyr Tudful in 1905 was the first Labour party mayor in Wales.

LADAS . . . a Snowdon Mountain Railway locomotive derailed on its first journey to the summit, causing the death of the landlord of the Padarn Villa Hotel in 1896 – the first and last fatality on the line.

LADIES OF LLANGOLLEN (The). Namely Lady Eleanor Butler and Miss Sarah Ponsonby who eloped from Ireland and lived together at Plas Newydd in the Vale of Llangollen in the early 19thC. They were immortalised in poem by their friend Anna Seward and were written a sonnet by William *Wordsworth.

LADY-IN-WAITING . . . Blanche Parry (*circa* 1508-1590) of Breconshire was Lady-in-Waiting to Queen Elizabeth I. She was later promoted to the position of 'Chief Gentlewoman of the Queen's most honorable privy chamber and keeper of her majesty's jewels', which was a gem of a job for a humble Welsh lass.

LAKES . . . there are over two hundred and fifty in the Snowdonia National Park, which perhaps makes it more of a Lake District than the Lake District. Some of Snowdonia's lakes have not even been given the dignity of a name – shocking, even winds (tornados) get given a name and are then forgotten. Are the Welsh a lake-lustre nation in this respect? The deepest lake in Snowdonia is Llyn Cowlyd at two hundred and twenty two feet (66.6m), the shallowest Llyn Ogwen at only ten feet (3m), and the largest is Llyn Tegid at Bala.

LAND OF MY FATHERS . . . a book written by the first Plaid Cymru MP, Gwynfor Evans. Dylan Thomas once said: 'My father can keep it'.

LAND OF SONG 1 . . . Wales has the image but, in some forty-five years of the record charts, artists from Wales have only managed around a dozen number one hits, and Shakin' Stevens had four of them!

LAND OF SONG 2 . . . a very popular long-running TV programme hosted by Ivor Emmanuel between 1958 and 1965. Ivor, like Richard Burton, hailed from Pontrhydyfen, but had a better singing voice.

LANDSKER . . . an imaginary demarcation line dividing English and Welsh Pembrokeshire. To the North the population are predominantly Welsh and to the South . . . the little England beyond Wales where the Welsh were removed to be succeeded by Anglo Saxons and then Flemish immigrants.

LANGUAGES – there are 6,000 living languages worldwide, according to Professor David Crystal of Holyhead. One of the oldest is Welsh.

LARGEST ESTATE . . . In 1994 the sixth Marquess of Bute left an estate worth £130 million – the largest ever British will.

LARGEST ISLAND . . . Anglesey is the largest island in England and Wales – twice the size of the Isle of Wight, but with half the head of population.

LARGEST MARKET . . . Pwllheli on the Llŷn Peninsula boasts the largest open air market in Wales with (at the height of the tourist season) around two hundred stalls.

LARGEST PORT . . . in Wales is Milford Haven.

LARGEST SAND DUNES . . . the Llanddwyn Sands on Anglesey are the largest expanse of sand dunes in western Britain.

LAST DAYS OF DOLWYN, The . . . A 1949 film about a village due to be flooded to create a new reservoir. Directed by Emlyn Williams it won a prize at the Venice Film Festival.

LAST INVASION . . . set aside the Falklands War, the last invasion of Britain was in February 1797 when about fourteen hundred French men landed at Carreg Gwastad near Fishguard. The local militia aided by local ladies (who donned their red capes and black hats to give the impression of numerical superiority) soon forced the invaders to surrender. Jemima Nicholas, a local Amazon, captured a dozen drunken despoilers and earned herself the title 'The Welsh Heroine' according to her tombstone in Fishguard.

LAST QC . . . Sir Samuel Thomas Evans (1818-1905) Born at Skewen, Glamorgan. A politician and judge who was the last man to become a QC during the reign of Queen Victoria.

LAST HORSEDRAWN TRAM . . . to operate in Britain ran from Pwllheli to Llanbedrog on the Llŷn peninsula. It last ran in 1927.

LAST LIGHTHOUSE . . . the last one in Britain in private ownership was on The Skerries (Ynys y Moelrhoniaid) off Anglesey, which was sold to Trinity House in 1840 for nearly half a million pounds.

LAWRENCE OF ARABIA – World War One war hero T.E. Lawrence, whose life was portrayed on the big screen by Peter O'Toole. He was born in 1888 at Tremadog, near Porthmadog. In 1914 he joined military intelligence and was actively involved in the Arab Revolt against the Turks and the taking of Aqaba and Damascus. His account of this period *Revolt in the Desert* was known in its unabridged form as the *Seven Pillars of Wisdom* and is recognised as a classic of the genre of war literature. Later, Sir Winston Churchill was to describe the book as one of the 'greatest books ever written in the English language'. Lawrence became so famous that he suffered a breakdown and, in a bid to regain anonymity, he changed his name to J H Ross and enlisted in the RAF. He then changed his name to T.E. Shaw and joined the Royal Tank Corps and, later, the RAF again. He retired in 1935 and was tragically killed in a motorbike accident near his Dorset home at Clouds Hill.

LAWS OF HYWEL DDA . . . served Wales for six centuries. An insight into medieval society is given in the scale of values attached to different things. One penny was the value of a hen, a suckling lamb, kid or piglet. Two pennies was the value of a plough or a goose, twenty four pence was the value of a male hawk and one hundred and twenty pence was the worth of an oak tree.

LAVER BREAD . . . supposedly 'the national dish' which consists of the rather nauseous sounding cooked red seaweed. The seaweed is gathered off rocks, washed, boiled for hours until thick, mixed with oatmeal, made into cakes and fried in home cured bacon fat. Laverbread is still sold door to door – but not on my doorstep.

LEARNER DRIVERS . . . ten-a-penny everywhere (although lessons cost considerably more than a penny these days). Tourists should be made aware that novice motorists in Wales are allowed to display a 'D' plate on their vehicle (D = Dysgwr = Learner = L plate) thanks to the belated equality that the Welsh language has been afforded.

LEAST USED TELEPHONE KIOSK IN WALES . . . this is at Tan-yr-allt in Dyffryn Nantlle in Gwynedd.

LEE (John) . . . born London, he was a war time evacuee in South Wales. The former owner of Shepperton Studios, he has supplied cameras and lighting for nearly four thousand films. He scouts for film locations especially in South and North Wales.

LEE (Rowland) . . . the President of the Council of Wales between 1534 and 1543, he was under orders to restore order to Wales and the Marches. Despite hanging around five thousand people and using other strong-arm tactics, lawlessness reigned.

LEEK . . . Along with the daffodil, the leek (*Allium porrum*) is a national emblem of Wales. In Shakespeare's Henry V, replying to Fluellyn's remarks that the king is sporting a leek on St David's Day, the king observes: 'I wear it for a memorable honour for I am a Welshman you know, good countryman'. The leek is traditionally eaten on St David's Day by the Welch Regiment's youngest recruit.

LEGENDS . . . Like every other nation, the history of the Welsh is steeped in myth and legend. A lot of them (Gelert et al) are totally fictitious created for the interest of the gullible tourist. This means you!

LEISURE CENTRES . . . There are more leisure centres per capita on Anglesey than in any other area in the UK.

LEPER'S WINDOW . . . In St Michael's Church at Llanfihangel-y-Pennant, Snowdonia. Presumably lepers were encouraged not to attend services, but were allowed to observe them from outside.

LERPWL (Liverpool) . . . long considered the 'Capital of North Wales'.

LETTERS . . . David Green a Pembrokeshire solicitor and author has had around one hundred and forty letters published in The Times. In 1972 he had twelve published and his shortest to date was: 'Sir, 'Yes' which made the May 31, 1993 edition.

LEWIS (Alun) 1915-44 . . . South Wales born poet who was killed in Burma during WW2. Whilst the most famous 'War Poets' are linked with WW1, Lewis could quite legitimately be regarded as being of this genre.

LEWIS (Dr David) . . . of Abergavenny. Became the first principal of Jesus College, Oxford.

LEWIS (Morland) . . . Welsh painter who favoured scenes of the Tywi estuary.

LEWIS (Saunders) (1893-1985) . . . one of the founders of Plaid Cymru and an extremely influential figure in politics in Wales. Lewis had a deeply felt interest in Wales and, predominantly, the Welsh language. He was sentenced to a spell in Wormwood Scrubs after the 1936 bombing school fire. In 1962 Saunders Lewis delivered the BBC Wales Annual Lecture on the subject *'Tynged yr laith'* (the state of the language) and single-handedly influenced the formation of Cymdeithas yr laith Gymraeg without whom there would be no Welsh TV, no Welsh/bilingual official forms and paperwork, and no official recognition for the language.

LIBEL . . . the Denbigh-born Artemus Jones, a future county court judge, was personally involved in a libel case of the 1900s which led directly to the now universal declaration on all fictitious publications of the disclaimer that any resemblance to a living person was unintentional. Briefly, a *Sunday Chronicle* writer penned a tale about a fictional 'Artemus Jones' and his sexual habits. The later Sir Thomas Artemus Jones QC was not amused. He sued and he won.

LICENSING . . . in 1881 the public houses of Wales were shut on a Sunday; in fact every Sunday, fifty-two weeks of the year. This remained the case for eighty years until, at the beginning of the later-dubbed Swinging Sixties, parliament introduced a referendum for the drinkers or abstainers of the Principality. Held every seventh year from 1961 until 1996, each referendum saw various districts fall to the 'wet' lobby. The former district of Dwyfor (which covers the Llŷn Peninsula) was the last bastion of a 'dry' Sunday.

LIFEBOAT . . . a BBC drama set in West Wales which sank after only one series. Its author was Lynda la Plante who had better success with the series *Prime Suspect*.

LIFEBOATS . . . Wales has thirty-one lifeboat stations, all under the RNLI, a registered charity that was founded in 1824.

LIFEBOAT V.C . . . Dick Evans of Moelfre, Anglesey is one of the all-time greats. Two epic rescues earned him two gold medals (the RNLI equivalent of the Victoria Cross). The Moelfre Lifeboat coxswain and his crew made the two legendary rescues in 1959 and 1966 – truly a legend in his own lifeboat.

LIFE SAVER . . . Welsh squire Dafydd Gam saved the life of Henry V at the Battle of Agincourt.

LIGHT . . . the light in North Wales is comparable to the Mediterranean, it has been said, which partly accounts for the burgeoning film industry in the North.

LIGHTHOUSE . . . St Anne's Head (Milford Haven) in 1662 saw Wales' first lighthouse.

LION IN WINTER, The . . . film of 1968 starring Katherine Hepburn was partly shot on location at Pembroke Castle, which stood in for France.

LLOYDS BANK . . . was first opened in Birmingham in 1765, founded by Samuel Lloyd II a Quaker from Dolobran near Meifod, Powys.

LINCOLN (Abraham) . . . the lineage of the American statesman can be traced to the hamlet of Ysbyty Ifan in Conwy.

LINE DANCING . . . In August 1999 a new British and European record was set at Rhyl when two thousand and sixty lined up – yeeehaagh!

LITTLE BIBLE . . . *Y Beibl Bach* was the term used for the first cheap Welsh Bible of 1630. It cost five shillings.

LITTLE ENGLAND BEYOND WALES . . . a title bestowed on the town of Chepstow as well as the area to the south of the Landsker in Penfro (Pembrokeshire).

LITTLE MOSCOW . . . the Rhondda village of Maerdy, noted for its militancy. Its miners were among the last to return to work after the collapse on the General Strike in 1926. In 1990 Maerdy was the last pit in the Rhondda to close.

LITTLE TRAINS . . . there are a number of Great Little Trains in Wales. The narrow gauge lines that sprang up to carry slate from the mines to the coast now thrive as tourist attractions.

'LITTLE WHITE BULL' . . . A mistake by entertainer Tommy Steele that, for some inexplicable reason, became a money-spinning hit. Was this a reference to the Dinefwr Herd of rare Welsh cattle?

LIVERPOOL MAYOR . . . In Tudor times Dafydd ap Gruffydd was twice mayor of Liverpool – 1503 and 1515. He settled there as one of Henry VII's tax collectors.

LIVERPOOL MOUNTAINS . . . Donizetti, in *Emilia di Liverpool* his opera referred to 'Liverpool mountains'. This was not poetic licence. It was Italian ignorance.

LOAD OF BULL . . . At a Dolgellau sale in 1997 a Welsh Black Bull bred at

Nebo, Llanrwst, was sold for 9,500 guineas. This was a record price. His name, just for the record, was 'Graig Goch Capten 12'.

LOCATION HUNTER . . . In 1999 Gwynedd Council launched this service for prospective film makers, which includes details and photographs of hundreds of possible film locations across the county.

LONDON WATER . . . Sir Hugh Myddleton of Chirk, who died in 1631, brought London its fresh water supply, His forty mile long aqueduct, *New River* stretched from Ware springs in Hertfordshire to Clerk's Well (Clerkenwell) and was built in 1609-1613. Wales is still deeply involved in supplying England with water.

LONDON WELSH . . . Wales has a very important historical and contemporary relationship with London. On the cultural side, the National Eisteddfodau of 1859 and 1909 were actually held in London, while London Welshmen formed the Gwyneddigion Society in 1779. In sport, there is the London Welsh Rugby Club.

LONELY PLANET . . . A recent edition of this publication, aimed at independent youthful travellers, was somewhat reticent about Wales' beauty and charm. In fact Wales was compressed into a few pages and described as 'England's unloved back yard.'

LONG BOW SHOOTING . . . see Crecy, Poitiers etc. It lives on in the Greenwood Centre near Caernarfon, where it is just one of the attractions on offer.

LONG DISTANCE RUNNER . . . Griffith Morgan (1700-1737) or *Guto Nythbrân* was a renowned cross-country runner from Llanwynno, Glamorgan. Much of his actual life is steeped in legendary exploits that he is said to have undertaken. Some say he died after winning a race against a horse. What is certain is that he did drop dead after completing a 12 mile (19km) run from Newport to Bedwas in fifty-three minutes. (An average of a mile (1.6km) every 4.41 minutes which was a phenomenal achievement.)

LONGEST GOLF HOLE . . . Chirk golf course has the longest golf hole in Britain at 664 yards.

LONGEVITY . . . George Lyttleton (1709-1773) MP toured Wales (like every other toff) and wrote an account *A Gentleman's Tour Through Monmouthsire and*

Wales. In Ffestiniog he heard of a farmer who died aged 106 and whose three wives bore him upwards of forty children. His youngest son was eighty-one years younger than his eldest, and eight hundred people descended from his body attended his funeral.

LOOK YOU . . . the basic utterance of caravan site owners and their sons in North Wales – according to Coronation Street script writers who set a series of episodes in Conwy in 1999 and depicted the locals as South Walians!

LORD HAW HAW . . . the WW2 traitor (real name William Joyce) who broadcast on the radio on behalf of the Third Reich, lived for a while at Coed-y-bleiddiau near Maentwrog, Snowdonia. He maintained that the German army HQ in Wales would have been Plas Tan-y-bwlch (the Snowdonia National Park study centre), and that Adolf Hitler would also have had a summer residence in Snowdonia.

LORD MAYOR OF LONDON . . . Sir David Treharne Evans (1849-1907). Welsh born (at Llantrisant) local government councillor who became Lord Mayor of London in 1891 – the first man from the principality to hold that post for over seventy years.

LOST PORT . . . Aberamffra in Gwynedd off the A486 Barmouth to Dolgellau road, is a lost port. In the 17th century it played an important role in wool exporting.

LOTTERY. . . 1997 statistics showed that Anglesey was lucky. Whilst the rest of Wales averaged one jackpot per 44,776 people, Anglesey's average was one per 22,000 – island of dreams.

LOVE NEST . . . Before their association became public knowledge, Prince Charles and Camilla Parker-Bowles dallied in Glyn Celyn mansion in Powys.

LOVE SPOONS . . . (Llwyau Caru). Carved from a single piece of wood to a random pattern, the intention was to show the recipient the affection and art of the creator.

LUCKY GOLDSTAR . . . In 1996 the L.G. Group, the South Korean-based electronics giant boasted that the £1.4 billion investment at Newport would create six thousand direct jobs and fourteen thousand knock-on jobs.

LUNATIC ASYLUM . . . the North Wales town of Denbigh once housed one of the largest lunatic asylums in the country.

LUXURY BRINE . . . Holyhead's Station Hotel (now demolished) once offered the ultimate in luxury to passengers *en route* to Ireland. Guests' baths had three taps – the third one offering sea water.

LLAIS LAFUR . . . launched in 1898, it was the first Welsh language Socialist newspaper.

LLAN . . . A very common place name prefix. There are over five hundred placenames prefixed *Llan* in the principality.

LLANBADRIG . . . the church in Cemaes Bay is the only one in Wales that is dedicated to St Patrick, the patron saint of Ireland (who was Welsh)!

LLANBEDROG . . . village on the Llŷn Peninsula, which is home to Oriel Plas Glyn-y-Weddw Art Gallery.

LLANBERIS . . . in Snowdonia is the home of the world's only National Slate Museum.

LLANDARCY . . . is one of the few Welsh towns with a *llan* prefix named after a modern 20th century person.

LLANDEILO . . . the bridge arching 365 feet (110m) across Afon Tywi is Wales' longest single-span stone bridge.

LLANDDULAS . . . Renowned novelist Evelyn Waugh unhappily taught at a Llanddulas prep School in 1925.

LLANDRINDOD WELLS . . . in Powys is a purpose-built Victorian Spa town. The biggest spa in Wales, it boasted a saline spring and sulphur water which cured gout and rheumatism while the magnesium in the 'waters' helped cure digestive problems and TB etc. The Pump House Hotel and the railway arrived after 1865.

LLANDUDNO . . . self-styled 'queen of the Welsh Resorts' or 'Naples of The North' A former Bronze Age copper mining centre it has one of the oldest copper mines in Europe, dating back four thousand years and was worked for about one thousand years in tunnels up to 200 feet (60m) below ground.

LLANDUDNO PIER . . . the first pier was built in 1858 and was 2,295 feet (688m) long but very short lived, as it was demolished by a storm within a year. Construction of the second (present) pier began in 1876. It was built of sterner stuff and resisted the suffragettes' attempt to burn it in 1914.

LLANDUDNO (Cape Town) . . . South Africa has a Llandudno, which is a tourist town to the south of Cape Town. However, it does not benefit from the Gulf Stream.

LLANDWROG AIRFIELD . . . In April 1942, within a year of opening as an airfield, RAF Llandwrog's Senior Medical Officer established a small search and rescue group to deal with aircrashes in the Snowdonian mountains. In the first six months they saved twelve airmen and retrieved thirty-five fatalities. The M.O. George Graham, was awarded the M.B.E for services to mountain rescue.

LLANFAIR P.G. . . . the Anglesey town with one of the longest placenames in the world. The name was invented in the 1870s by a Menai Bridge draper Thomas Hughes.

LLANGAMARCH WELLS . . . the water was rich in barium which was good for heart ailments.

LLANRHAEADR YM MOCHNANT . . . in Denbighshire. William Morgan became vicar here in 1578 and within nine years he translated the Bible into Welsh, a monumental task even for a Cambridge scholar who had studied Latin, Greek and Hebrew, the original languages of the Bible.

LLANWRTYD WELLS . . . a spa on Afon Irfon offered 19th Century tourists 'the waters' which had a high sulphur content, the local well water was ideal for curing anaemia.

LLANYBYDDER – monthly horse sales take place at this town near Llanbedr Pont Stephan on the last Thursday of each month.

LLANYMYNECH GOLF CLUB . . . near Oswestry saw Ian Woosnam's introduction to golf. It lies on the border between England and Wales, and partly on Offa's Dyke. The fourth tee is in Wales and the 4th green in England. There are views for fifty miles (80km) from parts of the course.

LLAREGGUB . . . Despite Dylan Thomas' backward spelling, Fishguard, Mumbles, New Quay, Ferryside and Laugharne all claim to be the true Llareggub.

LLECHWEDD SLATE CAVERNS . . . a major tourist attraction in Blaenau Ffestiniog, Gwynedd which opened in 1972 and has since won ALL the major tourism awards.

LLEWELYN (Dai) . . . party-loving socialite who once said: 'I am a dark, hairy-chested Welsh goat. I am genetically programmed to mate with blondes'. Quite!

LLEWELYN (Sir Harry . . .)Won the first British showjumping gold medal at the 1952 Helsinki Games. He won it only fifteen minutes before the closing ceremony.

LLEWELYN (John Dilwyn) . . . Swansea's pioneering photographer was the first to capture motion on film. This major success won him the silver medal in the 1855 Paris Exhibition.

LLEWELLYN (Roddy) . . . born Abergavenny in 1948. His close friendship with Princess Margaret, especially their holiday snaps (which were not taken by Tony 'The Camera' Armstrong Jones) on Mustique, didn't help her marriage.

LLIGWY BURIAL CHAMBER . . . Near Moelfre in Anglesey is one of the largest Neolithic tombs in Britain. It measures 18 x l5ft (5.4m x 13.7m) and has a 28 tonne cap stone. The chamber dates to around 3000 BC.

LLOEGR . . . a strange land inhabited by even stranger inbred people. Some call it by the name 'England' which translates as 'Aggressive, conniving, sneaky neighbours'. We jest.

LLOYD GEORGE . . . Statesman. 1863-1945. Although he was born in Manchester, David George spent much of his boyhood in the picturesque Dwyfor village of Llanystumdwy where he was raised by his mother and his uncle, Richard Lloyd. The future political leader added his uncle's name later as a mark of respect. David Lloyd George was a qualified solicitor who entered parliament in 1890. He represented the Caernarfon Boroughs for fifty-five years. During the Boer War, Lloyd George became recognised as a gifted orator and his rise through the ranks of the then Liberal party is well-documented. He was President of the Board of Trade and introduced the Merchant Shipping Act of 1906, the 1907 Patents Act, and also established the Port of London Authority in 1908. Under the Premiership of Herbert Asquith, Lloyd George was the Chancellor of the Exchequer who introduced the so-called People's Budget of 1909 and the 1911 National Insurance Act. The House of Lords were against the 1909 budget and the wrangling that followed eventually led to a reduction in the powers of the Upper Chamber. However prevalent in the 1990s, political scandal is not a new thing. In 1912 it was revealed that Lloyd George had bought shares in Marconi, who were the company that the government planned to use to found a national wireless chain, but the scandal left him unscathed. During WW1 Lloyd George served as Minister of Munitions before becoming War Secretary in 1916. A confusing period of political infighting ended abruptly in December when Asquith resigned the Premiership and Lloyd George, supported by the Conservatives, formed a coalition government as Prime Minister. After the War, Lloyd George's government won an overwhelming majority in the General Election of 1918. In the early 1920s the political situation in Ireland and a military skirmish between British troops and the Turks led to the Conservatives withdrawing their support for the coalition, and Lloyd George resigned in 1922. Lloyd George's private life was also under scrutiny. A married man – he lived openly with his secretary Frances Stevenson. The couple were married in the 1940s after the death of his first wife. However, despite the blemishes, history has judged that David Lloyd George was one of the most brilliant British statesmen of the 20th Century.

LLWYBR CYHOEDDUS . . . might sound like a painful medical affliction but is, in fact, the Welsh for public footpath.

LLYN CERRIG BACH . . . a dozen ornate swords, slave-gang chains, chariot fittings – in fact, one hundred and forty-four artefacts, all pre-Christian, were discovered in the Anglesey lake in 1943. Were they thrown in by the Druids in an attempt to secure the aid of the gods against the Roman invaders?

LLYWELYN AP GRUFFYDD . . . (The Last). He was the grandson of Llywelyn Fawr and became King of Wales in 1246. He aided the English barons in their revolt against Henry 111 and led the Welsh in battle against Edward 1. He was killed at Cilmeri near Builth Wells in 1282, when Wales lost her independence.

LLYWELYN FAWR (The Great) . . . born *circa* 1173 Llywelyn Ap Iorwerth was a Welsh Prince who drove the English from North Wales in 1212, took the garrison town of Shrewsbury, and united the parts of Wales which were not under Norman occupation. In a non-military sense, he most famously helped gain recognition of Welsh rights in the Magna Carta in 1215. He died in 1240.

McGOOHAN (Patrick) . . . Actor of renown who spent a good deal of time in Meirionnydd during the 1960s – he had to as he was starring in the now-cult TV series *The Prisoner* filmed at Portmeirion.

McCARTHY (John) . . . the famous Beirut hostage spent a period of recuperation in a Brecon Beacons cottage having been freed by his Lebanese captors.

McLEAN (David) . . . the massive North Wales construction company.

MABINOGION . . . A collection of medieval myths known in Welsh as *Pedair Cainc y Mabinogi*. The word *Mabinogi* roughly translates as 'legend' or 'fable'. It is accepted as the greatest Welsh contribution to European literature and is now believed to have been written by one author of genius during the second half of the 11th century. It mainly survived through *Llyfr Gwyn Rhydderch* (*c.*1350) and *Llyfr Coch Hergest* (*c.*1400).

MacDONALD (Julien) . . . Merthyr Tudful-bred fashion designer who achieved instant fame having created THAT see-through backless dress for model/actress Emma Noble, which she almost wore at the 1998 BAFTA Awards. His creations have also adorned the bodies of Madonna, Cher, Whitney Houston and Nicole Kidman, amongst others.

MACKENZIE (Millicent) . . . in 1918 she became Wales first female parliamentary candidate (unsuccessful).

MADOC (Philip) . . . born Merthyr Tudful. Actor star of *Last of The Mohicans*, *Lloyd George* and *Fortunes of War*. More recently he appeared as Trotsky in *Nina* and in the bilingual *Yr Heliwr/A Mind To Kill*. Madoc can speak six languages.

MADOG ap OWAIN GWYNEDD . . . his epic voyage is commemorated on a plaque in a garden, near the 17th fairway of Rhos-on-Sea golf club.

MADOG MYTH . . . Did Prince Madog discover American three hundred years before Columbus? Did he teach Welsh to the Mandan indian tribe? Evidence is scant . . . but how do we explain the pre-Columbian stone fort, identical in design to Dolwyddelen castle (Madog's birthplace), that was built not far from Madog's purported landing place in Mobile?

MADOCKS (William Alexander) (1773-1828) . . . born Fron Yw, Denbs. He built Tremadog and Porthmadog which he hoped would be on the London – Ireland road. His land-reclamation project involved building a mile long cob across Traeth Mawr on the Glaslyn delta.

MACHYNLLETH . . . Machynlleth was seat of power of Owain Glyndŵr, the 15th Century Welsh leader who called the first Welsh parliament here after his spring 1404 success against English rule.

MAGGIE BONT . . . a jocular inoffensive nickname coined in 1958 for Princess Margaret on her engagement to Anthony Armstrong-Jones, whose parents owned a second home (albeit a stately one) in Bontnewydd, Caernarfon. After the marriage, he became Lord Snowdon and she remained Maggie Bont.

MAGIC LANTERN THEATRE . . . the first one in Britain was opened in Monmouth

MAGIC OF WALES . . . is a shop in Florida's Epcot Centre.

MAIL ORDER . . . the Royal Welsh Warehouse in Newtown was launched in 1861, becoming the first ever mail-order business.

MALE VOICE CHOIRS . . . It was a universally acknowledged truth that all Welshmen could sing and most were members of at least one choir, the chapel choir, the miners choir or the village choir.

MAN WHO NEVER WAS . . . When Glyndwr Michael of Aberbargoed died in January 1943, his body was kept in dry ice for three months. In April he became Captain W.H.N. Martin, Royal Marines. A brief case containing top secret information was chained to his arm and he was dumped at sea off Spain to be discovered by the Germans so as to help them believe that secret allied plan was to land a wartime invasion in Greece. This gave the allied invasion of Sicily, the real target, a better chance of success. On a more personal note Glyndwr, aged 34 and with no family connections, had committed suicide.

MANCHESTER . . . The Anglican church in 1838 failed in an attempt to amalgamate the Bangor and St Asaph dioceses. The purpose behind the devilish scheme was to use St Asaph's revenues to prop up an intended new diocese in Manchester. Charming!

MANIC STREET PREACHERS . . . from Blackwood in Gwent. The band was voted the biggest band in the world in the 1998 awards hosted by music magazine 'Q'. The three-piece group comprising James Dean Bradfield, Sean Moore and Nicky Wire managed to overcome the drawback of the loss of co-founder Richey Edwards (who vanished in 1995 and has not been seen since) to release powerful rock anthems in the late 1990s and, along with a clutch of other bands, helped bring fresh Welsh talent to the attention of UK record companies.

MANOD . . . former slate quarry at Blaenau Ffestiniog. Remarkably adapted with an air-conditioning system during WW2 to house the art treasures of the nation! During the Blitz the cabinet decided London was not safe for the priceless collections of many galleries and, after a suggestion by National Gallery Director Sir Kenneth Clarke, Manod Quarry was chosen as the secret hiding place for at least nineteen Rembrandt paintings, works by Gainsborough, Titian, da Vinci and van Dyck, several exhibits from the Tate Gallery, priceless antiques and more. One rumour was that even the Crown Jewels were moved to North Wales. Obviously no one knew how long the war would last and the lease on Manod Quarry was negotiated for over forty years! And after 1945, throughout the 50s, 60s, 70s and up until 1981, two men were employed to maintain the cavern shelter in readiness for the outbreak of another war when the treasures of the nation might again have to be moved to Snowdonia; or was the quarry earmarked as an underground centre for a government forced to flee London due to an imminent nuclear strike? Was the quarry set aside and maintained for decades in readiness to act as a nuclear shelter for dignitaries such as the Royal family? We shall probably never know.

MAP . . . The first map of Wales was published by Abraham Ortelius of Antwerp in 1573. The information was provided by Humphry Llwyd.

MAP MAN . . . Humphry Llwyd of Denbigh was a 16th century antiquary famous for his maps of England and Wales showing the succession of major towns and cities from Roman times, and giving their names in Latin, Welsh and English.

MARBLE CHURCH . . . This edifice at Bodelwyddan, Denbs was built using local stone in 1856. Its 202 foot (61m) spire towering above the A55 North Wales coast road adds to its presence.

MARCHES . . . The area of the Wales-England border.

MARGAM PARK . . . in West Glamorgan has one of the world's largest hedge mazes.

MARI LWYD . . . well known folk custom associated with the Christmas and New Year period when revellers carrying a decorated horse skull visited houses, especially in south-eastern Wales, and challenged the occupants to competitions of verse and wit. The winners were invited in for food and drink.

MARIAN MARTYRS . . . Not a pop group but those who chose to die for the new Protestant faith in the bloody reign of Mary 1. William Nichol of Haverfordwest was one of the only three Welsh Marian Martyrs, and was burned at the stake in 1558.

MARI'R FANTELL WEN (Mary of the White Veil) *IMPOSTER EVANS

MARKET HALL . . . the only surviving black & white half-timbered market hall in Wales is at Llanidloes, Powys.

MARKS (Howard) . . . born Kenfig Hill, Bridgend c.1944. Oxford-educated global traveller in beneficial herbs (tried and tested over 8,000 years) worth about £1 billion who was hooked on the use of aliases (forty-three at the last count). His autobiography *Mr Nice* details his adventures involving travel, arrest in Majorca, extradition battle, and early release from America's toughest prison seven years into a twenty-five year sentence. Now a columnist for *Loaded* men's magazine. He contested an East Anglian seat in the 1997 General Election, campaigning for drug law reform.

MARLAIS . . . Dylan Thomas' middle name.

MARQUAND (Richard) . . . Cardiff born movie director of such films as *Return of the Jedi* and *Jagged Edge*.

MARQUESS OF ANGLESEY . . . the first Marquess, despite being a uniped, lived until the age of 86 and produced eighteen heirs and seventy-three grandchildren – she liked a man in uniform.

MARTHA'R MYNYDD (Mountain Martha) . . . an impostor who lived in the late 18th Century in a mountain cottage at Llanllyfni near Caernarfon. She persuaded many villagers that she had become friendly with a wealthy clan called *the Invisibles* and in particular a gentleman called 'Mr Ingram' and his daughter 'Miss Ingram' who allegedly lived in an invisible mansion on the mountainside near Martha's cottage. The Ingrams preached to gatherings held at the cottage in the middle of the night where collections were taken for their Invisible sect. It does not take much detective work to realise that Miss Ingram was Martha, whilst her father took the role of Mr Ingram, and that they were benefiting from the gullible nature of the locals who crowded into the small cottage in pitch blackness to hear the preaching of the Invisibles. On one occasion it was common knowledge that Martha had burned her foot during the day and, during that night's prayers meeting, one doubting local took it upon himself to stand on the foot of 'Miss Ingram' as the congregation gathered in the darkness. Folklore tells that it was Martha's voice which cried out in pain. Despite this seemingly obvious uncovering of the deceit, it was the non-believer who was forced to flee the area by angry adherents of the Invisibles. However, doubts began to set in and eventually Martha herself even joined the Methodist church.

MARY . . . The first royal yacht of Charles II which was wrecked off the Skerries (north of Anglesey) in March 1675 whilst on a trip from Dublin to Chester. Nearly forty survivors of the wreck were rescued from the islands after three days. The ship had been presented to Charles in 1660 by the city of Amsterdam whilst the monarch was in exile in Holland. The vessel was designed to navigate Dutch canals rather than the treacherous waters of the Irish Sea – as was discovered fifteen years later. The wreck was discovered in 1971.

MASAI WARRIOR . . . Lyn Davies of Connah's Quay married warrior Jocob Lekupuny in Mombassa, Kenya. The marriage made the UK national press and, as her groom had no visa to live in the UK, she became an African War bride and went back to visit him in his Masai homeland, only to observe her beloved courting yet another Shirley Valentine.

MATTHEWS (Cerys) . . . born 1969. Llanelli. The lead singer of Catatonia.

MAUSOLEUM . . . Squire R.J. Lloyd Price of Rhiwlas, Bala (born 1843) built the family mausoleum using the proceeds of a big win on the gee gees. Bendigo, the horse, is thanked on a commemorative stone.

MAWR . . . the Welsh word for big.

MAXIM Magazine . . . According to a *Nightmare Holidays* survey in the magazine in the late 1990s, Wales was equal fourth most unpopular place in the world to take a break.

MAYNARD (Matthew) . . . cricketer born in Lancashire who moved to Menai Bridge (*Porthaethwy*) on Anglesey aged eight. As captain of Glamorgan during the 1996 season, he scored the county's fastest ever one-day century off 58 balls, and over the season scored 1,610 runs.

MEIBION GLYNDŴR . . . The number of MI5 agents involved in bringing Sion Aubrey Roberts to court on firebombing charges was thirty-nine. Llangefni-based, he admitted membership of Meibion Glyndŵr and was sentenced to twelve years in gaol – but was released early.

MELLY (George) . . . the jazz performer has a house on the banks of the River Usk and can often be seen indulging his passion for fishing.

MENAI BRIDGE (Pont-y-Borth) . . . built by Thomas Telford to take the A5 across the Menai Strait to Anglesey. It was not the first suspension bridge in the world but it was the longest for a few years.

MENAI STRAIT . . . long stretch of fast flowing water which separates mainland Wales from Anglesey. In 1985 it almost became the country's first Marine Nature Reserve.

MEN OF HARLECH . . . this popular march-tune was inspired by the story of the bravery of Dafydd ab Einion's men during the Wars of the Roses. Starvation forced them to surrender Harlech Castle, but Dafydd was allowed to march out leading his men.

MENSA . . . In 1996 Chantelle Coleman a then three year old girl from St Athan, Cardiff became the world's youngest Mensa member.

MEREDITH (Billy) . . . Chirk-born footballer known as the 'Welsh Wizard.' played successfully for both Manchester clubs in the early 20thC, helped form a union for professional footballers until a bribery scandal ruined his career. Played for his country at the age of 49.

MERLIN . . . the most famous person to have emerged from Carmarthenshire.

MERLIN MOVIE . . . Yet another success for the Caernarfon based North Wales Film Commission. The film, made for American TV, included locations for ancient British scenes such as Llyn Gwynant, Capel Curig, Blaenau Ffestiniog and Harlech, all of them in Gwynedd.

MERLIN'S OAK . . . once stood in Carmarthen but . . . still a piece is kept in the town's civic centre in a glass case.

MERMAIDS . . . Cardigan Bay, the beautiful sweep of Celtic coast with sandy beaches and rock strewn shallows stretching down from the tip of Llŷn to St David's Head near Fishguard, abounds with mermaids. They are not just legendary.

MERTHYR RIOTS . . . At its height the Merthyr Rising of 1831 was an armed insurrection by the working class, who had a variety of grievances. Crowds of thousands confronted soldiers, shots were fired, around twenty rioters were killed, and over seventy wounded. Punishments were severe. Many were gaoled, four were transported and Dic Penderyn was hanged.

MERTHYR TUDFUL . . . In the first census of 1801, Merthyr's population was 7,500. It was Wales' biggest town followed by Swansea (6,000) and Wrexham (4000). Merthyr is claiming World Heritage status because, during the industrial revolution, it was the 'iron capital' of the world – by 1850 the largest ironworks on earth were at Cyfarthfa and Dowlais. Merthyr's technical improvements in steel add to this claim.

MERTHYR TYDL . . . is how the telephone directory once (in the late 1970s) spelled the name. This was a slur on the monarchy as Merthyr Tudful calls itself the 'Queen of the Valleys'.

METEORITE . . . the largest one to hit Wales weighed 25 ounces (707 grins) and landed in Beddgelert, Snowdonia in 1949.

METHODISM . . . The apathy of the 18th century Anglican church guaranteed the success of the Methodist movement in Wales. Methodism provided active, enthusiastic preachers whose hell-fire sermons could save souls. Methodist hymn-writers realised the power of music. Salvation could be achieved through religious experiences and congregations needed Welsh language preaching. Many powerful preachers reduced congregations to tears of joy and Hwyl; hysteria gripped many, who jumped up and down in utter exuberance and declared that they were converted.

METHODIST MARTYR . . . William Seaward, a preacher, starved himself to death at Hay-on-Wye in 1742 – the first Methodist Martyr in Wales.

METHODIST NEWSPAPER . . . Y *Drysorfa Ysbrydol* (The Spiritual Treasury) was launched in 1799 and ran for six issues before folding in 1801.

METHODIST POPE . . . John Elias born Abererch, Gwynedd in 1774 was a preacher who became known as the Methodist Pope.

MICHAEL (Alun) . . . born 1943. Not everyone agrees with TV inquisitor-cum-tormentor Jeremy Torquemarde Paxman's description of Alun Michael as 'Blair's poodle'.

MIFFED . . . Wrexham's bid for city status caused embarrassment to the city of Bangor when a national newspaper article mentioned that while south Wales boasted two cities, north Wales had none and needed one.

MILK SUPPLIER . . . the largest independent milk supplier in North Wales is South Caernarfon Creameries at Y Ffôr, Llŷn. It also produces more than five and a half thousand tonnes of cheese a year.

MILLAND (Ray) . . . Neath-born Oscar winner. (The first Welsh-born winner of an Academy Award). The film was 1945's *The Lost Weekend* in which he played a doomed alcoholic writer. He was born in 1907 and given the moniker Reginald Truscott Jones – would he have ever made the grade had he not changed the name? Milland succumbed to cancer in 1986.

MILLENNIUM STADIUM . . . in Cardiff. The UK's newest sports stadium (1999) has a roof weighing eight thousand tonnes, sixteen bars, seven hundred toilets and seven thousand four hundred tonnes of turf. It is mooted that when Wembley Stadium is out of action during refurbishment, the English FA will hold the FA Cup Final at the jewel in Cardiff's crown – the final has never been played outside England before.

MIMOSA . . . the vessel which carried the first Welsh settlers to Patagonia in 1865.

MINES ACT . . . the law of 1842 which prohibited the employment of women and children undergrounds was often ignored in South Wales.

MINOGUE (Danni and Kylie) . . . Aussie actress/singer sisters whose mother Carol was born in Maesteg and emigrated in 1955.

MINORITY LANGUAGES . . . there are 35 in Europe. Welsh is one of them.

MINT . . . in 1637 a mint was established at Aberystwyth producing a range of silver coins. It was short-lived. (*ROYAL MINT)

MISS WALES . . . Helen Morgan of Barry remains the only Miss Wales beauty queen to go on to become Miss World (1974). She controversially 'resigned' after it later transpired that she was an unmarried mother.

MISS WALES' BRISTOL COMPETITION . . . In 1980, the organisers of the Miss Wales competition staged it in Bristol.

MISSILE RANGE . . . Aberporth, on Cardigan Bay is the home of an RAF missile range which extends into the bay, and shipping are warned to keep clear!

MISSING ROCK STAR . . . Richey Edwards, a member of the rock group Manic Street Preachers disappeared from a London hotel on February 1 1995. He has not been heard from or seen since. (*MANIC STREET PREACHERS)

MISSIONARY . . . Morgan John Rhys (1760-1804) born Llanbradach, Glam established a Welsh settlement called Cambria in Pennsylvania and named its capital Beulah. A Baptist minister, he tried to convert the native Indians and published *The Western Sky* newspaper. As was often the case, it was a short-lived settlement.

MOBILE PHONE . . . inventor Harry Grindell Matthews actually gave Queen Mary a demonstration of a prototype mobile phone in 1912.

MOBSTER . . . Llewellyn Morris Humphreys was born into a strict Welsh Methodist family, and became one of the USA's most notorious and successful criminals who worked with the infamous Al Capone. Known in underworld circles as 'Murray The Hump', he became America's Public Enemy Number One when Capone was jailed for tax evasion in 1933. 'The Hump's' parents were Ann Wigley and Brian Humphries who were married at Llanidloes Methodist Chapel. Ann Wigley is a distant relative of the Plaid Cymru politician Dafydd Wigley. Who said that politicians were all crooks?

MOBY DICK . . . a whale and a book and a film. The film was shot in Fishguard Harbour in 1956, and starred Gregory Peck, Richard Basehart and Leo Genn.

MOEL FAMAU . . . is the favourite mountain of Welsh exiles in Liverpool.

MONEY . . . The village of Mounton near Chepstow was kept busy from 1727 to 1876 manufacturing special paper, which was used for pound notes and larger denominations for the Bank of England.

MONEY BAGS . . . Sir William Rearden Smith, the treasurer of the museum fund of the National Museum of Wales (it wouldn't have been John Jones would it?), was concerned at the slow pace of fund raising and the fast pace of construction costs. In 1925 he casually asked to see the books which showed an overdraft of £21,000 and then, even more casually, wrote a cheque for that sum. A museum gallery bears his name.

MONMOUTH . . . Until local government reorganisation in 1974 Monmouth had not always been acknowledged as a Welsh county. In '74 it was renamed Gwent and declared to be in Wales. Following further tinkering in 1996, it again became Monmouth/Mynwy, but remained in Wales.

MONMOUTH (Duke of) . . . He also behaved like an illegitimate, rebelling against the king in 1685. His mother, Lucy Walter, because of her close relationship with the future Charles II, was known as Lucy Regina (you can't speak clearer than that!).

MONOPOLY . . . A Welsh version of Waddington's finest game was launched in July 1999, with Portmeirion as the equivalent of Mayfair, and other sites like the National Stadium and Caernarfon Castle featuring around the board.

MONSTER . . . Llyn Cau on Cadair Idris in southern Snowdonia is apparently home to a monster which seized a swimmer in the 18th century.

MONSTER MOLLUSCS . . . Shrimps measuring 4 inches (10 cm) were found in August 1999 off St Tudwal's Islands near Abersoch on the Llŷn Peninsula. Further evidence of the gulf stream warming the Welsh coastline.

MONTGOMERY CANAL . . . The first UK canal to benefit from National Lottery cash. Originally built to carry coal, limestone and agricultural goods, its new cargo will be tourists.

MONTGOMERYSHIRE SOCIETY . . . Founded in London in 1927, its aim was ' . . . the promotion of friendly intercourse among Montgomeryshire folk' in the capital.

MOONLIGHT CLIMB . . . In 1791 Worsdworth climbed Snowdon by moonlight and included this experience in *The Prelude*.

MORGAN (Cliff) born Trebanog, Rhondda 1930. A former rugby great who moved into broadcasting and became a captain on *A Question of Sport*.

MORGAN (Sir Henry) (*c*.1635-1688) . . . Glamorgan-born pirate who was kidnapped as a child and shipped from Bristol to the West Indies. As an adult he led a band of buccaneers in raids on Dutch and Spanish settlements in the Caribbean and in Central America. Most infamously remembered for the sacking of Panama in 1671. He was arrested and brought to London in 1672 by way of appeasing the Spanish, but when hostilities restarted in 1674, Morgan was knighted. He died holding the office of Deputy Governor of Jamaica.

MORGAN (Rhodri) (born 1939) . . . The politician was once asked by Jeremy Paxman whether he would stand as leader of the Welsh Assembly. Morgan's reply was, 'Does a one-legged duck swim in circles?' The as-ever unruffled Paxman commented that he assumed Morgan's reply was 'Welsh for yes'.

MORGAN (Steve) . . . (born 1955). He grew up in Colwyn Bay, and owns Redrow, the Wales-based construction company, which has made him Wales' second richest man.

MORGAN (Bishop William) (1545-1604) . . . translated the Bible into Welsh in 1588 whilst vicar of Llanrhaeadr-ym-Mochnant. This ensured the survival of the Welsh language as it unified various local dialects and created a standard version of the language. Contrast the Welsh and English versions of the Bible – the English one of James I took a team of fifty writers to complete; Bishop Morgan went solo. He was born at Tŷ Mawr in the Conwy valley, which is now a National trust owned property and naturally houses a display of Welsh Bibles.

MORMON MISSIONARY . . . the first Welsh-speaking Mormon missionary was Dan Jones who was so successful in his proselytising that Wales had the largest Mormon congregation in Britain by 1855. 'Captain' Dan Jones began his work in 1845. Many hundreds of Welsh Mormons emigrated to Salt Lake City.

MORMON CHAPEL . . . Wales' oldest was the front part of Abergele's Bull Hotel.

MORRIS (Geraint) . . . the top TV producer who created *Casualty* is Welsh.

MORRIS (Jan) . . . (born 1928) One of Wales' best known travel writers was previously called James Morris. Her autobiography is entitled *Conundrum*. Regarded by many as the world's finest travel writer.

MORTAL KOMBAT . . . the movie of 1995 features scenes filmed in Wales at Dinorwig Quarry and Anglesey's Mynydd Parys.

MOSQUE . . . The Noor-el-Islam Mosque in Cardiff was established in 1947.

MOST ASCENTS OF SNOWDON . . . Raymond Foulkes of Llanberis has been to the summit over 25,000 times. After all, he did spend 34 years as a driver on the Snowdon Mountain Railway so it's not surprising really!

MOST DECORATED SOLDIER . . . Wales most decorated hero remains CSM John Williams of the South Wales Borderers who served during WW1. He won a DCM, MM and bar to MM before, in 1918, he single-handedly took a German machine gun position capturing fifteen enemy soldiers. For this he was awarded the Victoria Cross. By December of 1918 Williams had also been awarded the Croix De Guerre (the French Victoria Cross). He was subsequenly wounded and returned to his native Ebbw Vale. Died in March 1953.

MOST NORTHERLY PUB . . . in Wales is in Cemaes on the isle of Anglesey.

MOSTYN (Lord) . . . his family benefit from the enclosure acts to grab the land on which they developed Llandudno, which was previously a small mining village on the Orme. By 1856 Lord Mostyn had built accommodation for eight thousand visitors, who flocked to the town after the opening of the railway in 1849.

MOT . . . not all sheepdogs in Wales are called Mot. In fact it was only 92.7% at the last census.

MOTOR CYCLES . . . production of Wales' first motorcycles (555cc), made by Powell Brothers of Wrexham, began in 1920.

MOTORWAY TUNNELS . . . the first to open in the UK were at Brynglas, Newport in 1967.

MOUNTON . . . Nr Chepstow, is known for its paper milling, making paper for bank notes between 1727 and 1876. (*MONEY)

MUDIAD AMDDIFFYN CYMRU . . . (Movement for the defence of Wales). A republican, anti-water-stealing by the English protest group that caused explosions in the 1960s.

MULBERRY HARBOURS . . . In 1943, nine hundred men began mysterious work in Conwy – building sections of the Mulberry harbours that were eventually used in the D-Day landings.

MULTI PRIZE WINNER . . . John Owen Williams (Pedrog) (1853-1932) was an orphan brought up by his aunt at Llanbedrog in Llŷn. He became a non-conformist minister, poet, writer and archdruid (1928-32), and won more eisteddfod poetry prizes than anyone.

MULTIPLE SAINTS . . . Llanpumsaint and Llantrisant are places with connections with more than one saint. The former has five while that latter a mere three.

MUMBLES RAILWAY . . . was established in 1804 and carried its first passengers three years later. The five mile track from Swansea to Oystermouth was the world's first public railway. It closed in 1960 – presumably having had foresight of the Beeching Axe.

MUSTARD GAS . . . Britain's main WW2 production factory for mustard gas was at Rhydymwyn, Mold, Flints. The eighty-six acre site had large subterranean caves, and was still causing controversy in the locality as recently as the 1990, because of the possibility of contamination.

MUTATIONS . . . 'Y Treigliadur' published in 1993, by D.G. Lewis is a guide to Welsh language mutations.

MWNT . . . in Dyfed, the 'jewel of Cardigan Bay' is a beautiful sandy bay on a Heritage Coast in National Trust land.

MYFANWY . . . one of Wales' best known tunes, composed by Dr Joseph Parry.

MYSTIC MEG OF THE 17th CENTURY . . . Arise Evans (1607-60) He had visions and dreams most notably about what the future held for the then King Charles 1 (soon to be overthrown in the English Civil War). After the restoration, he was able to cure an abnormal growth on his own nose by simply rubbing it on the hand of Charles 11 as the monarch walked in St James's Park. Born in the parish of Llangelynin.

MYTH . . . many acknowledge as fact the story that Edward I promised the Welsh a prince who could speak no English, as he was presented to the people as a baby. This story was first recorded in 1584 i.e. three hundred years later, akin to modern writers writing hearsay about the Great Fire of London!

NAIN . . . the Welsh word for grandmother.

NAMES . . . Beaumaris residents are called Bimarensians; Cardiffians hail from Cardiff; Cardis are from Cardiganshire (if the transport is free!); Pontypriddians are from Pontypridd; Caernarfon has Cofis; Maglonians are from Machynlleth; and Pwllheli has gentlemen and ladies.

NAME CHANGE . . . in the mid 16th century William Middleton adopted a Welsh version of his name i.e. Gwilym Ganoldref (Ganol = Middle; dref = town).

NANT . . . meaning spring. It is a fairly common placename prefix.

NANT GWRTHEYRN . . . or Y Nant as it is known in Llŷn, is the home of the world's only permanent Welsh language residential centre. It is a truly magical place.

NANTES . . . the French town which is twinned with Cardiff.

NANTEOS . . . the mansion near Aberystwyth has a music room which inspired the composer Wagner to write Parsifal. The room is the only example of Rococo architecture in the country, whilst the mansion itself was reputedly once the home of the Holy Grail.

NANTGARW PORCELAIN . . . six miles north of Cardiff, production of the well-known soft-paste porcelain, was brief but the quality was second only to Sevres.

NANTGLYN, Denbighshire . . . has an ancient Yew tree. (*YEW TREE)

NAPOLEON . . . thanks to the 19th century French leader, Wales was visited by notable English aristocrats and tourists. With the Napoleonic Wars raging the Grand Tour of Europe brigade became the Celtic Grand Tour gang. Thanks Boney!

NASH (John) (1752-1835). Architect. Born at Aberteifi, Ceredigion he designed the county jail and later became world famous for his work in Regent's Park, London.

NASH (Richard) (1674-1761) born Swansea. Known as 'Beau Nash' he made the city of Bath an 'A list' destination.

NATIONAL BOTANICAL GARDENS of WALES . . . at Middleton Hall, Llanarthne, Carms. Scheduled to open in May 2000 at a cost of £44 million. On a five hundred acre site with a great glasshouse measuring 100 x 60 metres as a centre piece – the world's largest single span glasshouse. The Welsh gardens make Kew Gardens look like a hanging basket!

NATIONAL EISTEDDFOD . . . At Bala, Gwynedd in 1997 the attendance record was broken with one hundred and seventy-three thousand people enjoying the festival. The Bala eisteddfod cost £1,771, 596 and it made a profit of only £6,227.

NATIONAL GALLERY . . . At least two thousand paintings from the National Gallery in London were moved to a North Wales slate quarry during WW2 to avoid potential destruction from the Luftwaffe. (*MANOD)

NATIONAL LIBRARY OF WALES . . . at Aberystwyth. Opened in 1937 (although established about twenty years earlier). It contains many rare books and manuscripts including whole libraries e.g., the *Peniarth Manuscripts* including *Llyfr Du Caerfyrddin* (the Black Book of Carmarthen) and *Y Llyfr Du o'r Waun* (the Black Book of Chirk) which contains the earliest version of the laws of Hywel Dda. It was the first of five British National Libraries (the other four are at London, Edinburgh, Oxford and Cambridge) which are entitled to receive a copy of the eighty-thousand or so new publications per annum. This is a legal requirement under the 1911 Copyright Law.

NATIONAL MUSEUM OF WALES . . . opened in April 1927 in Cathay's Park, Cardiff. The museum now encompasses eleven sites throughout Wales. Lack of funding delayed its opening by about twenty years as the Royal Charter was granted in 1907. (*MONEY BAGS)

NATIONAL PARKS . . . there are eleven in Britain and 10% of Wales and England falls within recognised National park boundaries. See details of individual National parks in Wales – Brecon Beacons, Pembrokeshire Coast and Snowdonia.

NATIONAL TRUST . . . Dinas Olau near Barmouth (*Y Bermo*) was given to the National Trust in 1895, and was the first National Trust-owned property in the UK. By 1999 one hundred thousand acres in Wales including one hundred and thirty miles of coastline were in the hands of the Trust.

NATIONAL YOUTH ORCHESTRA OF WALES . . . consists of a select band of only one hundred and ten, whose places are funded by the twenty-two unitary local authorities.

NATIONAL YOUTH THEATRE OF WALES . . . founded in 1976 and similarly funded (see above), this even more select crew of just sixty attend a summer residential course.

NATIONAL WINNER . . . In Wales these words refer to eisteddfodic success rather than victory in the Grand National steeplechase.

NATIVE PLANTS . . . Wales has fifteen hundred native plants.

NATURE RESERVE . . . the first in Wales was Cwm Idwal, established in 1945.

NAZI LIKE . . . was the NME (New Musical Express) description of fans of the group Stereophonics, who waved the Welsh flag whilst the band strutted their stuff at an August 1999 gig.

NAZI NERVE GAS . . . Tabun was a deadly nerve gas developed in Nazi Germany in the late 1930s. It was never used during WW2 but in 1945 seventy-one thousand bombs were confiscated. They were stored at the disused airfield of RAF Llandwrog in Gwynedd and, ten years later, dumped in the Atlantic.

NEATH . . . the first electric trams in Wales first operated in Neath in 1885.

NEFYN . . . in the 19th century the village of Nefyn was to sea captains as 20th century Prestbury is to Rolls Royce car drivers.

NEILL (A.S.) . . . the anti-authoritarian educationalist (who believed in no discipline in the classroom) brought his model school, Summerhill, to Blaenau Ffestiniog, Gwynedd during WW2.

NELSON, Admiral Horatio . . . the sailor who shot the sniper who had shot Nelson was born in Newborough, Anglesey.

NÊST . . . her heyday was 1100-1120, when she was abducted, thus earning her 'the Helen of Wales' label. She had many lovers including Henry I who would have been father to some of her seventeen children. She was the daughter of Rhys ap Tewdwr, the last king of Deuheubarth.

NEITHIOR . . . The custom associated with the wedding feasts when guests helped the newlyweds with gifts of money which they, in turn, had received from the families of the bride and groom.

NEWBOROUGH WARREN in Anglesey is a vast expanse of over a thousand and a half acres of sand dunes.

NEWPORT . . . recently the New York Times labelled Newport as 'the new Seattle' due to the exciting music scene.

NEWPORT RIOTS . . . The Chartists rioted in November 1839 and troops fired into the mob killing twenty. Some of the leaders of the riots were transported for life. (*FROST [John])

NEWTOWN . . . in Powys was the 'Manchester of Wales' in the 19th Century in that it was a textile centre with weaving sheds, warehouses and factories.

NEW TOWNS . . . were not really 'new towns', but affordable new extra houses for existing workers. Cwmbran was extended in 1949, followed by Newtown in Powys.

NEW SOUTH WALES . . . in Australia is so called because Captain James Cook's chief scientist on his second voyage (1768-71), Joseph Banks, was a friend of Thomas Pennant the Welsh naturalist and antiquarian.

NEW YEAR'S EVE . . . a 1999 survey by the Whitbread brewery revealed that the Welsh are less inclined to organise a New Year's Eve party than the English. The survey did not reveal who were most-likely to gate-crash, however.

NEW YEAR . . . the residents of the beautiful and secluded Gwaun valley in Dyfed peculiarly celebrate New Year in mid-January – they base the year on the pre 1572 calendar.

NEW YORK TIMES . . . The co-founder, in 1851, was George Jones who was of Welsh parentage.

NEWSFILM . . . Britains first ever newsreel film was taken in 1896 when the Prince and Princess of Wales visited the Cardiff Exhibition.

NEWSPAPER BARONS . . . the Berry brothers whose family had Merthyr Tudful origins, became press barons. William Ewart Berry (1879-1954), owner of the Daily Telegraph became Viscount Camrose in 1941. James Gomer Berry (1883-1969) owned the Western Mail and Echo and became Viscount Kemsley in 1945. They were joint owners of the Sunday Times.

NEYLAND . . . in Pembrokeshire became Isambard Kingdom Brunel's port and railway terminus to link South Wales and London with Ireland in 1856, to be replaced by Fishguard as the Irish port in 1908.

NICHOLAS (Dafydd) . . . born Ystradyfodwg, Glam (1705-1774), sometimes regarded as the last of the Welsh family bards. The Rees family of Aberpergwm mansion in Glamorgan were the last patrons.

NICHOLAS (Jemima) . . . almost single-handedly repelled French invaders of Fishguard in 1797, and legend declares she captured twelve men, armed with only a pitchfork. She died in 1832 aged 82 and her tombstone declares her 'the Welsh heroine'.

NICK NAMES . . . the much-vaunted waggish wit of the scousers in issuing nick names is totally eclipsed by the ability of the Welsh. Read on. A few examples will suffice. *Dai Piano* was not the accompanist for the village choir. This mean man had to 'borrow' off his friends as he'd left his fags on the piano again. *Jack Amen* and *Hughie Hallelujah* were the local religious maniacs. *John Scratch* and his brother *Tommy Chwanen* were both lousy. *Tonsils* was the local glamour-puss whom everybody wanted to take out. *Dai Central Eating's* home was not necessarily blessed with a controllable source of heat – he lacked a full set of teeth. *Garibaldi* was actually Christened Gary but had lost his hair. *Maggie Bont* was actually Princess Margaret who married Anthony Armstrong Jones whose parents had a second (or third) home at Bontnewydd near Caernarfon, *Emlyn Kremlin* was a particularly left-wing TUC official. Old Fox was the overconfident English immigrant who maintained he was too much of an old fox to be given a nickname. *Emlyn TV* was obviously the proprietor of the village television shop and his son was naturally *Portable*. *Olympic Torch* was the village policeman who was so bogged down with paperwork that he never went out. *Dai Yankee* doodled all day and the seemingly perpetual learner driver was *John L* because of the ever-present L-plates on his Austin Allegro. The day he passed his test *John L* metamorphasised into *El Paso* until he had an automobile accident when he became *John Crash*. Finally, *Jones The Crust* was the village baker until he was invited to the 1969 Investiture of Prince Charles when he became *Upper Crust*.

NID OES BRADWR YN Y TÝ HWN (There is no traitor in this house) . . . was the sign on the door of those without bread on the table during the record-breaking lock-out at Penrhyn Quarry.

NINIAN PARK . . . home of Cardiff City FC whose only real success came over seventy years ago, and the occasional home of Wales International matches.

NINNAU . . . The North American Welsh Newspaper issued monthly (except in September). It proudly claims to be answering the needs for a stronger link between the many Welsh communities in North America'.

NOBEL PRIZE . . . to date, there have been only two Welsh winners: Brian Josephson and Bertrand Russell.

NON . . . was St David's mother and is commemorated in five Llanons, all near St David's churches in Wales. Non is also remembered in Devon and Cornwall.

NORSE . . . Norsemen in the form of fearsome Viking raiders gave many Welsh coastal parts and islands obvious Nordic Names e.g. Bardsey, Swansey(sic), Great Orme, Little Orme, Skomer, Skokholm Island etc, etc. Contrary to popular belief, they all had Welsh names for centuries before The Vikings applied their names.

NORTH-SOUTH DIVIDE . . . the advent of S4C, the Welsh language TV channel, in 1982 ended the *Mason-Dixon* line of Wales, in that now South Walians are more familiar with the Northern dialect and vice versa.

NOS DA . . . Means 'good night'.

NOSON LAWEN . . . traditionally a Welsh evening spent at home by the fire, but nowadays a concert in a public hall or large barn.

NOSON WAU . . . a sort of noson lawen with a bit of work i.e. knitting thrown in, which kept everyone in stitches.

NOVEL . . . the first Welsh novel in the English language appeared in 1828 with T.J.LL. Prichard's *The Adventures of Twin Shon Catti.*

NOVELLO (Ivor) or properly Ivor Novello *Davies . . .

NUDISM . . . There are countless nudist beaches in Wales – it's not a naked lie and we can't say where they are. Seek and ye may find.

O'SHEA (Tessie) . . . born in Cardiff in 1918. A larger than life popular radio singer who was nicknamed *Two Ton Tessie.*

OATH OF ALLEGIANCE . . . MPs were first allowed to take it in Welsh in 1974.

OCEAN MONARCH . . . the vessel sank off Llandudno in 1884 *en route* to America. One hundred and eighty lives were lost.

OCEANOGRAPHY . . . the department of Oceanography at the University of Wales is unique. *Prince Madoc* was their vessel, moored at Menai Bridge, and newly replaced in May 1999.

OFFA'S DYKE . . . a defensive fortification along the English-Welsh border built under the direction of King Offa of Mercia between the mouths of the rivers Dee and Severn. It was almost one hundred and fifty miles long when constructed in the 8th Century, and over eighty miles still stand. Felons were fully aware that the dire punishment for being on the wrong side of the dyke was to have their right hand severed.

OFF-LICENCE . . . Rhiwbina shop, The Full Moon, became the first off-licence in Wales to be included in the Good Beer Guide when it was featured in the 1997 edition.

OGHAM SCRIPT . . . an alphabet of twenty letters in the form of straight lines and notches carved on stone. There are about forty Ogam stones in Wales and nearly three hundred in Ireland.

OGOF FFYNNON DDU . . . in Powys became Britain's first National Nature Reserve in 1976.

OIL . . . *Morris Evans' Oil* of Ffestiniog was made locally and bottled. It provided an universal cure for all ailments for people and animals.

Production lasted from 1870 to 1970 and the oil was exported to Patagonia and used during the Boer War.

OIREACH TAS FESTIVAL . . . inspired by the National Eisteddfod of Wales, the Irish established their own week-long festival.

OLD CATTLE . . . The Dinefwr Herd from the Llandeilo area in Carmathenshire is Britain's oldest breed of cattle. These rare white cows with black ears, muzzles and hocks, are probably descendants of the the bovine breed that gobsmacked the Roman invaders of 55 BC — 'Holy Cow!' as Robin (of Batman fame) might have exclaimed. (*ANTHRAX ATTACK)

OLD CHURCH . . . St Tanwg's Church near Harlech dates to around 435 AD and is one of the oldest churches in Britain.

OLDEST EWE . . . We won't name her, but the world's oldest ewe ruminated in the Aberystwyth area. She died one week before her twenty-ninth birthday in September 1999. She had given birth just a few months before her demise and left an orphan lamb – which has probably been eaten by now.

OLDEST FONT IN BRITAIN . . . can be found at Llanrhychwyn church near Llanrwst whose roof timbers date back 800 years.

OLDEST POEM . . . Y Gododdin written *circa* 600 AD, it is the oldest poem in Welsh predating its English counterpart by around six centuries.

ON THE BLACK HILL . . . film drama of 1988 (based on the book of the same name, written in 1982) which was fittingly filmed in Wales (fittingly as the writer Bruce Chatwin was Welsh).

ONEDIN LINE . . . the popular TV series was an adaptation of the work of Alun Richards (born 1929), the Pontypridd novelist and playwright who has also written books about Rugby.

ONEIDA . . . a Welsh settlement area in New York state, USA.

OPERATION JULIE . . . in mid-Wales in the 1970s a very long and costly drugs surveillance operation led to many convictions. So called as one of the detectives (female, naturally) was called Julie. Also inspired the album track *Julie's Been Working For The Drug Squad* by punk band The Clash.

ORANGES & LEMONS . . . Thomas Mansel Talbot built an orangery at his Margam Park estate in 1787. The 100 yard (91.4m) long greenhouse had under floor heating and rivalled those at Blenheim Palace and Chatsworth for citrus fruit production.

ORCHID . . . The Welsh marsh orchid (*Dactylorhiza majalis cambrensis*) was discovered on Anglesey in 1959 by amateur botanist Richard Henry Roberts.

ORDINATION OF WOMEN PRIESTS . . . became a reality in the Church in Wales in January 1997 when seventy-four were ordained.

OSCARS . . . Welsh winners are thin on the ground. Since Academy Awards were first awarded in 1929 (70 years x 30 awards per annum = 2,100 to date) Welsh people have won a mere four. Ray Milland won Best Actor in 1945 (*The Lost Weekend*), Anthony Hopkins also won Best Actor (1991 *Silence of the Lambs*), Hugh Griffith was Best Supporting Actor for *Ben Hur* in 1959 and Jack Howells won Best Short Documentary in 1962 (for *Dylan*). Who wants accolades anyway?

OTTER HOUSE . . . there was a home for specially bred otters at Yoke House Farm, Pwllheli, Gwynedd. With a water-filled base, the 'kennel' was a home from home until hunt time, when the luckless creatures were 'evicted', hunted and killed. Otter hunting was banned in the 1980s.

OUTLAWED LANGUAGE . . . English factory-owner Brewer-Spinks, unsympathetic to the Welsh language, outlawed the Welsh tongue in his Tanygrisiau factory in the mid 1960s. Many others have found the practice to be unbeneficial to their businesses.

OVERTON . . . in Flints. Once had twenty-one tall yew trees in its churchyard, which were one of the Seven Wonders of Wales.

OVINE RADAR . . . surprisingly, free-range sheep in Wales ruminate in summer in unfenced mountain pastures. Different flocks (identified by earmarks or coloured paint) have over the years stayed (not strayed) in their own unmarked territory (or *cynefin*).

OWAIN GLYNDŴR . . . born *circa* 1354 in Sycharth Castle near Oswestry. A dispute over land ownership at Glyndyfrdwy brought to a head pressures that had building for many years, and escalated into an attack on Ruthin (Rhuthun) by Owain and his followers in 1400. The English sovereign, Henry

IV, was weak and the rising spread. Owain, a gifted military leader, won control over large parts of Wales and in 1404 held a parliament at Machynlleth and was crowned Prince of Wales. His ambitions for an independent Welsh Church (not answerable to Canterbury) and two Welsh universities all helped to make him an inspiring Welsh national hero.

OWAIN GWYNEDD . . . (died 1182) a prince who sired nineteen sons (including Madog of America fame).

OWAIN TUDUR . . . (c.1400-1461) Not whodunnit, but How Did He Get Away With It? This Welsh adventurer fought with Henry V against France. As a reward, he became Head of the Royal Household and Gentleman of the Bedchamber. Henry V died in 1422 leaving a widow Catherine of Valois, who kept giving birth to Owain Tudur's children (at least three sons and a daughter). One son, Edmund Tudor (Earl of Richmond) was father of Henry Tudor, the founder of the Tudor dynasty of kings and queens.

OWEN (Daniel) . . . of Mold (1836-1895) a novelist who wrote *Rhys Lewis* (1855) *Enoc Huws* (1891) and *Gwen Tomos* (1894).

OWEN (Gerallt Lloyd) . . . born 1944, the poet who established Gwasg Gwynedd publishers and twice won the Chair at the National Eisteddfod (1975 and 1982). He is the man behind the extremely popular *Talwrn y Beirdd*, a bardic tournament on Radio Cymru which has been on the airwaves since 1979.

OWEN (Griffith) of Tryfan . . . a 19th century orthopedic surgeon who published a text book on trusses, artificial limbs and devices for remedying deformities. He also invented a mechanical crutch.

OWEN (Johnny) . . . boxer from Merthyr known as the Matchstick Man. Died after lapsing into a coma after a bout in South America in 1980.

OWEN (Michael) . . . Liverpool and England's free-scoring football striker who was born in Chester, but was brought up in neighbouring Flintshire.

OWEN OWEN . . . the famous department store in Liverpool's London Road was opened by Owen Owen of Machynlleth in 1868. The 20 year old draper became enormously wealthy with business ventures in London and America. Philanthropic by nature, he died in 1910.

OWEN (Robert) . . . (1771-1858) of Newtown, Montgomery. A capitalist who experimented in practical socialism with his model factory at New Lanark in Scotland, where workers enjoyed ideal conditions and social welfare. He was in favour of trade unions, the co-operative movement, and even established his utopian dream in America which he named 'New Harmony'. Alas, this co-operative village failed after two years.

OWEN (Robert) (1885-1962) . . . brought up in Llanfrothen, Mer. And known as 'Bob Owen Croesor.' A renowned genealogist, lecturer and collector of Welsh language books, an authority on the Quaker movement throughout the principality. He was later awarded with an Honorary degree from the University of Wales.

OXFORD BOOK OF WELSH VERSE . . . it was not until 1962 that the Welsh language 'merited' such a voulme – despite a poetic tradition dating back six centuries earlier than its English counterpart.

OXFORD DICTIONARY OF QUOTATIONS . . . with over seventeen thousand inserts from over two thousand five hundred people . . . few of them are Welsh. Dylan Thomas, R.S. Thomas, W.H. Davies and Neil Kinnock feature, but not many others.

PALTROW (Gwyneth) . . . the Oscar winning US actress is not of Welsh descent despite her Welsh first name. Her mother, Blythe Danner, chose the name whilst pregnant and reading a novel with a Welsh heroine called Gwyneth.

PAGET . . . Family name of the Marquesses of Anglesey.

PAPUR PAWB . . . 'Everybody's Paper' a weekly publication by Herald newspapers of Caernarfon which appeared between 1893-1917 and again 1922-1955.

PARACHUTES . . . G.Q. parachutes are sold worldwide and have their HQ in Bridgend.

PARKIN (Molly) . . . the fashion editor and writer was formerly Molly Thomas of Pontycymmer, near Bridgend (*Pen-y-bont ar Ogwr*).

PARRI (Annette Bryn) . . . born Dinorwig. Leading Welsh accompanist, pianist, teacher and musician. One of the leading figures (with Elinor

*Bennett) behind the idea of a music conservatoire in North Wales.

PARRY (Robert Williams) (1884-1956) . . . born Tal-y-sarn, Caernarfon. Despite a relative paucity of poetic output (only two volumes), he is regarded by some as the finest Welsh language poet.

PARRY-WILLIAMS (Thomas Herbert) (1887-1975) . . . born Rhyd Ddu, Gwynedd. Twice won the double of Chair and Crown at the National Eisteddfod. Prolific writer, linguist and renowned scholar. A cousin of Robert Williams Parry.

PATAGONIA NEWSPAPERS . . . early Welsh language newspapers produced at the colony included *Y Brut* and *Y Drafod.*

PATRICK . . . A 6th century saint who was shipwrecked off the Anglesey coast and rescued. As thanksgiving, he built a church at Llanbadrig near Cemaes Bay (one of the oldest in Anglesey), and then left to convert the Irish eventually becoming their patron saint.

PATRIOTS . . . who will do anything for their country, except actually live there.

PAYS de GALLES . . . French for 'Wales' and the name of Richard Burton's villa near Lake Geneva.

PEACE MOVEMENT . . . Gwilym Davies (1879-1955) who was born in Bedlinog, Glamorgan was a peace movement pioneer who became Honorary Director of the League of Nations (1922-45), and the constitution of UNESCO was based on the plan he drafted for international peace. As an additional aside, his message of goodwill to the children of Wales on St David's Day 1923 became the first ever Welsh language radio broadcast.

PEACOCK STORES . . . The Cardiff-based chain of one hundred stores was bought by the management in 1998.

PEATE (Iorwerth) . . . the first curator of St Fagan's Folk Museum.

PEDAGOGUE . . . Wales' best known fictional pedagogue, Robin Soldiwr, appears in Daniel Owen's novel *Rhys Lewis.* The ex-soldier opened a school where he lazily inculcated a little ignorance.

PEEL (John) the famous disc-jockey attended preparatory school in Deganwy, Conwy.

PEMBROKE CASTLE is the second largest in Wales and is noted for its five circular towers. It was the birthplace of Henry V.

PEMBROKE DOCK . . . housed the Royal Naval Dockyard for one hundred and twelve years from 1814 until 1926 when over two hundred and fifty naval ships, including two Royal Yachts, were built.

PEMBROKESHIRE COAST NATIONAL PARK . . . established in 1952, this is 230 miles (370km) of beautiful coastline, unique as it is the only National Park which is only coast-based. Its emblem is the razorbill which represents the bird life that makes it renowned worldwide as the habitat of sea-birds. The Pembrokeshire Coastal path (170 miles, 274km)) is the third longest British footpath, and the route from St Dogmaels to Amroth leads walkers over about five hundred stiles.

PENAL LAWS . . . Henry IV is infamous for his penal laws against Wales and the Welsh *circa* 1400. For example English men were forbidden to marry Welsh women, the Welsh were not allowed to carry arms, hold public office or public assemblies and Welsh bards were 'banned'. These laws remained in force until the rule of Henry VII in 1485.

PENCLAWDD on the Gower provided tons of cockles to feed the workforces of Swansea and Llanelli, and the cockle women with their carts and donkeys are still well known.

PENDERYN (Dic) *LEWIS (Richard), CHARTISTS and MERTHYR RIOTS.

PEKING SACKING . . . In 1860 when the Chinese capital was sacked, a musical watch made by Anglesey clockmaker William Hughes was found.

PENDINE SANDS . . . this stretch of $6^1/2$ miles (7km) of Carmarthenshire beach was the home of British land-speed record attempts in the 1920s. The only Welshman to hold the record was John Godfrey Parry Thomas who hit 170mph+ (over 275kph) in his on-going duel with the famous Donald Campbell. Parry Thomas was killed in 1927 when *Babs* overturned and caught fire at Pendine during another record attempt. The car lay buried in the sands until it was recovered in 1969 and restored.

PENILLION . . . singing to accompaniment of a harp which plays a different tune. Also known as *CERDD DANT.

PENMYNYDD . . . on the Isle of Anglesey is the ancestral home of the Tudor dynasty of Kings and Queens.

PENMAENMAWR . . . since 1889 a full train of railway ballast (stone and granite) has left Penmaenmawr every working day. The quarry was established by the Darbyshire family in 1878.

PENMAENPOOL BRIDGE . . . built in 1879 to replace the ferry across Afon Mawddach (Gerry Marsden take note!). It saved a four mile detour between Barmouth and Fairbourne and is one of only five wooden bridges remaining in Britain. Modern motorists are charged a toll to cross and must not exceed 5 mph.

PENNANT (Thomas) of Downing, Holywell (1729-98) . . . renowned travel writer. Historian Dr Johnson praised him as the best travel writer he knew. Pennant's *Tour In Scotland* drew the country to the attention of English travellers, as did his *Tour In Wales* of 1778.

PENRHYNDEUDRAETH . . . In 1917 Britain's first purpose-built Women's Institute Hall was built in the Gwynedd small town. The very first Women's Institute was founded in Llanfair Pwllgwyngyll in Ynys Môn in 1915.

PENRHYN QUARRY LOCKOUTS . . . renowned workers strikes of 1896-97 and 1900-03. Penrhyn Quarry at Bethesda in Gwynedd was, naturally, owned by Lord Penrhyn, a rich man who employed three thousand poor quarrymen. This led to the celebrated class-struggle variously labelled as 'lock out' and 'strike'. Members of the North Wales Quarryman's Union, for some reason, failed to share the views and attitude of Lord Penrhyn.

PENRY (John) (1563-1593) . . . of Llangamarch, Brecon. A celebrated puritan martyr of the Elizabethan era who bemoaned the lack of a preaching ministry in Wales. He wrote pamphlets against priests and bishops and is credited with writing the well-known *Martin Marprelate Tracts*. These were dangerous times for worshippers who were not Anglicans. As a Puritan, Penry was an anti-establishment figure, was on-the-run and used the alias of John Harrison. Penry was executed in 1593.

PENSIONS . . . were introduced by none other than David Lloyd George in his so called 'People's Budget' of 1909.

PENYBERTH BOMBING SCHOOL . . . War clouds over Europe led to a rapid OK for the establishment on a RAF bombing school at Penyberth, Pwllheli. The government in London refused to discuss the plan and forged ahead, thus causing considerable bitterness because similar agricultural areas in England had been successful in refusing land for the planned school. On September 8, 1936 three prominent Plaid Cymru members set fire to workmen's huts on site and reported their actions to the police at Pwllheli. At the subsequent trial at Caernarfon the jury failed to find a verdict against the three men, Saunders *Lewis, Lewis *Valentine and D.J. *Williams. The retrial was moved – not 'down the road' to Chester or Ruthin, but to the Old Bailey in London where, in January 1937, the three were convicted.

PEN Y FAN . . . in the Brecon Beacons is the highest mountain in southern Wales at 2,907 feet (872m).

PEN-Y-GWRYD HOTEL . . . at the head of the Gwynant Valley and the foot of the Llanberis Pass was first licensed as a hotel in 1847 and became famous as the 'home' of northern Wales mountaineering. *EVEREST

PETROL STATIONS . . . Nantgarw-born Donald Humphries once owned thirty-eight Action filling stations across South Wales and shipped oil directly from the Middle East to compete with the conglomerates. In 1991 he sold out to Gulf. He is often cited as the prime example of 'rags ro riches'. Affectionately known as 'Curly', he is always in the upper part of the lists of 'Welsh and Wealthy'.

PETTICOAT LANE OF WALES . . . is the name enjoyed by the open air market at Pontypridd, birth place of Wales' most famous son, Tom *Jones (the town, not the open air market).

PHILADELPHIA . . . The street layout of this US City was planned by Thomas Wynne of Caerwys.

PHILADELPHIA 2 . . . Jack Jones' novel *Off to Philadelphia in the morning* (1947) was about the Welsh musician and composer Joseph Parry.

PHILIPS (Eluned) . . . was the first woman to win the Crown at the National Eisteddfod – in Bala in 1967.

PHILLIPS (Sian) . . . of Gwauncaegurwen, the actress famous for her roles on stage, film and TV. Once married to Peter O'Toole.

PHONE BOX . . . the busiest public telephone box in Wales is in Ebbw Vale's Market Street and is used for forty-five thousand calls a year.

PI . . . the mathematical sign, Pi, was invented by William Jones (born 1675) at Llanfihangel Tre'r-beirdd, Ynys Mon. As every school pupil knows, this is the ratio of the circumference of a circle to its radius.

PIBGORN . . . musical pipe which came to the Isles with the Celts and was played in Wales until at least the end of the 18th Century. It was made of the upper leg bone of a deer with an animal horn at either end, and it contained a single reed made of rushes. It was one of the three main Welsh instruments, along with the *Crwth and the *Harp.

PIES . . . the offspring of Merthyr Tudful's Stanley Thomas (Stanley Jnr, Peter and sister Mary Case) are amongst the top dozen or so richest people in Wales. The brothers launched Peter's Savoury Products in 1970, and sold out in 1980 for £75million.

PIERS . . . Two of Britian's ten longest piers are at Llanduno and Bangor. Llandudno is fifth at 2,296 feet (700 metres), while Bangor scrapes into the top ten at 1588 feet (472 metres). Some Welsh piers, damaged beyond repair, have been 'lost' e.g. Penarth and Rhyl.

PIGS . . . Drovers ensured pigs' trotters were protected by leather-soled socks during their trot to market before the arrival of the railways in the mid 19th century.

PILGRIM'S PROGRESS . . . John Bunyan's epic was translated into Welsh as *Taith y Pererin* by Carmarthen-born Puritan minister Stephen Hughes (1622-1688), who also translated the Bible into Welsh in 1678.

PILKINGTON (Mark) . . . the young Welsh golfer who is the third longest hitter on the tour (after Tiger Woods and John Daly). Once hit a hole in one when aged only six!

PILLETH . . . This bloody battle was one of Owain Glyndŵr's victories over the English, whose losses numbered about one thousand. Shakespeare immortalised the battle by referring to the dismemberment of the English corpses by the female camp followers.

PINE MARTENS . . . Snowdonia National Park ecologists are so concerned about this rare creature that any reports of sightings would be appreciated.

PIOZZI (Hester Lynch) (1741-1821) *Thrale (Mrs).

PIPS . . . the six pips used by the BBC, which are acknowledged as a reliable indication of standard time, were the invention of Welshman Frank Hope-Jones (died 1950). In 1928 he was awarded a medal by the Horological Society.

PIRATE TREASURE . . . Captain Kidd's treasure – not just trinkets – is believed to be hidden in a cave on Steep Holm Island.

PISTYLL RHAEADR . . . This waterfall, one of the Seven Wonders of Wales, is 240 feet (72m) high and dwarfs the Niagara Falls by 73 feet (21m). Niagara does have a slight edge in width, however.

PIT PONIES . . . After the Mines Act of 1842 prohibited the employment of women and children underground, pit ponies were used for haulage. Stories of cruelty and neglect led to the so-called Pit Ponies Charter of 1911 which governed stabling, a daily work record, and ensured one horseman per fifteen ponies. Also, horses under four years were prohibited from underground work. Figures for 1913 revealed that, of the seventy thousand ponies deployed underground, twenty thousand worked in Wales.

PLAID CYMRU . . . political party formed at the Maesgwyn Temperance Hotel in Pwllheli in 1925. The party has a depth of support in western West Wales and growing numbers of voters all over the country. In September 1998 the party adopted a new bilingual name, *Plaid Cymru – the Party of Wales* whilst the original name was *Plaid Genedlaethol Cymru*.

PLANET OF THE CREPES SHOES . . . are some of the humourous designs of the You Must Create Company of Fraser Moss, the Newport born fashion designer, who is helping to make the world aware that Wales' industrial past was a mere phase.

PLANT (Robert) . . . the rock star front man of *Led Zeppelin* bought a country house near Monmouth.

PLAS MAWR . . . Conwy's Elizabethan town house is the headquarters of the Royal Cambrian Academy of Art and has three hundred and sixty-five windows – you never have to look out of the same window twice in normal year. It also has fifty-two doors and fifty-two steps (one a week?)

PLAY FOR VOICES . . . is how Dylan Thomas describes his best known work, *Under Milk Wood*.

PLOT . . . Chepstow-born William Bedloe (1650-1680) was a Popish Plot informer, thief, swindler and adventurer. The Popish Plot was a fabricated plan to remove Charles II and replace him with a Catholic monarch. The plot was nothing more than a Titus Oates and Israel Tonge spoof, but resulted in the deaths of over thirty supposed conspirators and brought down the government of the day. Bedloe, whom many regarded as an 'equal if not superior' perjurer to Oates, gave evidence against numerous priests and even accused the Queen, Catherine of Braganza, of wishing the downfall of the king.

PLYGAIN . . . is a traditional Welsh religious carol service held very early on Christmas morning. Every area has it's own Plygain carols, which have been forgotten in many places. The tradition has continued though in the area between Dolgellau and Llanfair Caereinion and has been growing in many other places over the last few years.

POBL Y CWM . . . Welsh language TV soap opera that has been broadcasted since 1974.

POETRY . . . Poetry has never lost its traditional importance in Wales – especially so in the Welsh language, where it is still an essence in many social and family gatherings. The sale of poetry books in Welsh consistently soars higher than English language poetry publications – *Barddas*, the main Welsh language poetry magazine, has the second highest circulation for poetry periodicals (in any language) throughout the British isles.

POETRY IN MOTION . . . Percy Bysshe Shelley was kicked out of Tremadog by the locals, who objected to his yobbish behavious e.g. taking pot-shots at sheep and the like.

POINT OF AYR . . . colliery in Fflints. Closed in 1997, it was the last deep pit worked in North Wales. Since 1868 miners had worked the seams which stretched out under Liverpool Bay.

POLAND . . . since 1949 the former RAF airbase at Penrhos on the Llŷn Peninsula has been the home of many Polish people. Managed by the Polish

Housing Association, *Dom Polski* (Polish Home) has around one hundred and sixty residents who enjoy a vast range of activities.

POLLY GARTER . . . 'walked naked past the Sailors Arms' in a well-known bit from Dylan Thomas' *Under Milk Wood*.

PONT . . . (Bridge) As Wales has many rivers, many towns and villages bear the prefix Pont or Bont.

PONTCYSYLLTE AQUEDUCT . . . at Trefor, Denbighshire was another engineering triumph for Thomas Telford. This graceful construction carried the Shropshire Union Canal across the Dee Valley 126 feet below. It cost £47,000 and was completed in 1805. This cast iron trough, 12 feet wide is over 1,000 feet long.

PONTRHYDFENDIGAID . . . the annual Eisteddfod was founded and funded by philanthropist David James and is well known for its big prizes.

PONTYPOOL JAPAN WARE . . . between 1730 and 1830 brightly-coloured household utensils were made of tin plate. Polished and attractive, they are now much sought-after, to coin a phrase.

PONT-yr-AFON-GAM . . . near Ffestiniog was once the site of the highest filling station in Wales.

PONTYPRIDD . . . Birthplace of singing legend and all round good old boyo, Tom Jones. Apart from rugby, the town has one of the longest railway platforms in the UK. When 'Jones The Voice' sang 'The old home town looks the same, as I step down from the train . . .' in (Green Green Grass of Home) was he referring to Ponty's platform?

POOR LAW LEWIS . . . Sir George Cornewell Lewis (1806-1863). Statesman who was responsible for the Poor Law Amendment Act of 1836. Succeeded his father as M.P. for the Radnor Boroughs.

POPE, Mal . . . a writer of songs for Cliff Richard.. so now we know who to blame!

POPE POPPED IN TO WALES . . . in 1982 Pope John Paul II visited Wales – the first time a pontiff had come to the UK since 1531. As Clement VII didn't cross the threshold of the principality then (he was, after all, trying to hold the whole church together in the face of Henry VIII's anti-papal antics and too busy to sight-see) it was the first ever visit by an incumbent head of the Catholic church.

POPULATION . . . only 5% of the population of the UK lives in Wales.

PORCELAIN . . . its production in Wales was short-lived. Nantgarw porcelain was produced 1813-14 and 1818-23; Swansea porcelain 1814-1826.

PORTHCAWL . . . the current home of 'Waverley' the world's last sea-going paddle-steamer.

PORTHDINLLAEN . . . the Llŷn beauty spot village is now owned by the National trust. A single parliamentary vote in the 19th century 'saved it' from becoming the official packet port for Ireland.

PORTHDINLLAEN LIFE-BOAT . . . the picturesque village took delivery of its first life boat in 1864.

PORTHMADOG . . . A 'new town' indeed. But for William Madocks land reclamation project of the late 18th century, this thriving town in Gwynedd would never have seen the light of day.

PORTH MADRYN . . . (Puerto Madryn) the landing place of Welsh settlers arriving in Patagonia on July 28 1865. There is still an annual 'Festival of Landing' commemorated here. The population of Puerto Madryn has grown from nil at the time of the landing to 50,000 by Y2K.

PORTMEIRION . . . the Italianate village in the former Meirionnydd. Haphazard dream and lifework of architect Sir Clough Williams-Ellis. One of Wales' premier tourist attractions. The fairy-tale village was described by its creator as a 'home for fallen buildings'. Williams-Ellis collected the belfries, fountains, colonnades and other features and rebuilt them between 1926 and 1972.

PORT TALBOT . . . Europe's highest sand dunes once graced the shores at Port Talbot.

POST BRENHINOL . . . on the side of red vans in Wales means 'Royal Mail'.

POTATOES . . . the earliest new potatoes to appear in Britain are the Pembrokeshire kind.

POTTER (Beatrix) . . . the original 'Mr McGreggor's Garden' that inspired the writer is in Gwaenynog, near Denbigh, the home of her uncle and aunt.

POVEY (Meic) . . . Porthmadog born writer and actor most famous elsewhere in the UK for playing Det Sgt Jones in the series *Minder* with George Cole and Dennis Waterman.

POWYS . . . county which is the least populated county in Britain.

POWYS CASTLE . . . built by medieval princes, this has been the ancestral home of the Herbert family since 1587 and is still inhabited. In Ireland it would have been a hotel catering for the American trade for at least twenty years.

PREACHING RECORD . . . the longest sermon record of almost thirty-eight hours was, quite naturally, held by a Welshman – Canon Clive Southerton of Prestatyn.

PRESCOTT (John) . . . the former Welsh schoolboy and later deputy PM is known as 'Two Jags' because of his love of ministerial limousines.

PRESS FREEDOM . . . 1907 litigation by Frank Mason, the then proprietor and editor of the Tenby Observer, led directly to the Admission of the Press Act. Mason had been banned from Borough Council meetings but took his grievances to court. He lost, but the government gave the go ahead for legal reform.

PRICE (Dr. Richard) . . . (1723-1791) of Llangeinor, Bridgend, Glam. A radical thinker and political philosopher revered by revolutionaries in France and America. A friend of Benjamin Franklin, his ideas influenced the American Constitution.

PRICE (Richard John Lloyd) . . . RHYS FAWR *SHEEPDOG TRIALS, WHISKY.

PRICE (Thomas) (1852-1909) . . . Welsh born (at Brymbo, Denbighshire) who emigrated to Australia, entered politics and rose to become Prime Minister of South Australia by 1905.

PRINCE OF WALES . . . Charles Windsor, eldest son of Queen Elizabeth ll is the current incumbent (benefitting from a bent income?) and was invested as Prince of Wales at Caernarfon in 1969. There have been twenty-one holders of the title who have endured the investiture ceremonies – ten of these were held in London. A local Urban Myth from 1969 tells of a typical Caernarfon dweller being questioned by BBC Wales and, having being asked what he thought of The Prince of Wales, blinked at the camera and retorted: 'I never drink in there. The beer's awful'.

PRINCE PHILIP . . . spent some time at HMS Glendower training academy near Pwllheli during WW2. The academy later became a Butlin's holiday camp.

PRINTING MONEY . . . Afonwen Mill near Mold is now a craft and antique centre, but it once held a licence to print money. In the late 18th century, one hundred and fifty people were employed making the special paper required for £5 and £10 notes. The mill also printed the paper used as headed House of Commons notepaper.

PRITCHARD (Edward) (1839-1900) . . . Wrexham born civil engineer who was responsible for building tramways, waterworks and sewerage works in around one hundred UK towns. He later travelled the world advising on similar developments, as well as gold-mining in places as diverse as British Columbia, South Africa and Istanbul.

PRITCHARD (Margaret) . . . 'The Face' of 1970s HTV news. Nicknamed 'Pritch' by her devoted public because of a fault in delaying her name during a post-News at Ten bulletin, which resulted in only the first six letter of her surname being displayed on the screen. A long-lost goddess of the good and bad news – no one before or since has been able to convey the news of Wales headlines about Mrs Rosie Parry's lost cat in Abertillery with such aplomb.

PRISONER (The) . . . 60s cult tv series starring Patrick *McGooghan and filmed on location at *Portmeirion near Porthmadog in North Wales.

PROPERTY MAGNATES . . . The legendary King Arthur is the only man to have owned more property in Wales than Merlin The Magician. They had a monopoly of standing stones and, more especially, residential caves, which remain vacant as the owners are due back at any moment.

PROTECTED FLOWER . . . The South Stack fleawort is only found in Anglesey and is now a protected species under the Wildlife and Countryside Act.

PROUD VALLEY . . . film of 1941 set in a Welsh coal town and starring Paul Robeson.

PROVERBS . . . in 1547 William Salesbury wrote 'Oll Synnwyr Pen Kembero Ygyd' (All the senses in a Welshman's head) which was a collection of proverbs and one of the earliest Welsh printed books.

PRYCE (Jonathan) . . . (born 1947) Holywell born. Gifted, RADA educated actor whose leading roles in *Comedian* (1976) and *Miss Saigon* (1990) earned him Tony Awards. He also won Olivier awards, and appeared as the villain in the James Bond film *Tomorrow Never Dies*.

PRYDERI . . . Hero of three of the four tales of the Mabinogion.

PRYDDEST . . . a long poem in free metre. Since 1860 it has been customary to award a crown for the winning pryddest in the National Eisteddfod.

PUFFIN ISLAND . . . off the Anglesey coast was last inhabited by man in 1860. So-called because of its puffin population, which in 1900 was recorded at two thousand. The current puffin count is a mere twenty pairs, which could mean another name change is imminent. Any ideas? Don't upset the Bimarensians but, as the rat population is counted in thousands – why not Rodent Island? By today a more appropriate name would be Shag Island (seventy-seven pairs) or, better, Cormorant Island (seven hundred and seventy six pairs – over 36% of the Welsh population. Other names include Ynys Seiriol (after a saintly hermit inhabitant, and still the Welsh name for the island), Priest Holm (the Viking name) Ynys Lenach and Ynys y Llygod (Island of mice) . . . which brings us back to the rodents, doesn't it?

PUGH (Maldwyn Novello) . . . a character in *Grand Slam*, the TV film of 1977. Maldwyn, as camp as a tented village, was played superbly by the actor Sion Probert.

PUNCH MAGAZINE . . . the founder, Henry Mayhew, was staying at Erwood, Radnors when he had the idea for the satirical magazine (launched 1841) – Wales, land of inspiration!

PUW (Huw) . . . (1663-1743). Of Tal-y-llyn, Gwynedd. An athlete, wrestler and jumper with an Oxford education. He jumped over the head of his mother one Sunday morning on the way to church, and the shock she suffered apparently killed her.

PWLLHELI . . . The old market town benefits from a highly revered yachting marina, which the authorities swore would never become a 'village within the town'. Hafan marina village lies at the end of Pwllheli's North Quay only a £1.20 taxi ride from Pwllheli old town.

PWLL NOFIO . . . means Swimming Pool although who needs a pool with the glorious waters of Cardigan Bay so readily available?

PYG TRACK . . . up Snowdon is named after the Pen-y-Gwryd Hotel. (*EVEREST)

Q . . . the gadget king a.k.a. Desmond Llewelyn, of James Bond fame, was born in Malpas near Newport. He first appeared in the film *From Russia With Love* in the early 60s and subsequently featured in a further fourteen Bond escapades usually uttering *Pay attention 007* in every one. He died in late 1999.

Q SHIPS . . . Lloyd George, during WW1, introduced Q ships which were heavily armed merchant vessels used against the German navy. One example was the *Mary Mitchell* a slate carrier based at Port Dinorwic (Felinheli) on the Menai Strait.

QUAD BIKES . . . Wales' naturally rough terrain (in part) has seen a proliferation of this growth sport.

QUAKERS . . . before the Religious Toleration Act of 1689, two thousand Welsh Quakers emigrated to Pennsylvania, to William Penn's Quaker colony. There are areas in Pennsylvania that carry Welsh placenames such as Meirion, Bryn Mawr, Gwynedd and Montgomery.

QUANGOS . . . Quasi Autonomous Non Governmental Organisations . . . at the last count Wales has about twenty QUANGOS, including the: National Musuem of Wales; the Wales Tourist Board; the Sports Council for Wales; the Arts Council for Wales; Welsh Language Board and the Countryside Council of Wales which is the only one based in North Wales, at Bangor. Cardiff, as capital city, is the home for fourteen quangos. Former quango the Development Board for Rural Wales was once known as the *Last Quango in Powys*.

QUANT (Mary) . . . Renowned fashion designer associated with the Swinging Sixties when she helped popularise the mini-skirt. She opened her first shop in London's Kings Road in 1955, and was awarded the OBE in 1966. London-born (1934) to a father from Merthyr and a mother from Cydweli, she now lives in Surrey.

QUARRYMEN . . . In 1900 there were four thousand employed in Blaenau Ffestiniog (a quarter of all the quarrymen in North Wales). The Blaenau quarries shipped one hundred and forty thousand tons of slate in that year.

QUIZ LEAGUES are proliferating in North Wales – possibly due to superior intellects aided by the Gulf Stream.

QUOITS . . . the ancient sport of throwing horse shoes at a target is making a comeback in mid and south Wales where club teams have different leagues. As in most revivals, a cleric has taken the lead – Revd Howel Mudd.

QUEEN . . . Llandudno considers itself to be 'The Queen of Welsh Resorts'.

QUELLYN . . . Not so long ago Llyn Cwellyn, Afon Cwellyn and, more importantly, the Cwellyn Arms pub in Rhyd-Ddu, were sacrilegiously spelled with the letter 'Q'. Thankfully the rot has stopped and Saint Cwellyn can stop spinning in his (various) graves.

QUILTS . . . Welsh quilts had military origins as padded clothing was worn under armour in medieval times and early Tudor years. Henry VIII's last suit of armour fits a 53 inch (134cm) girth and can be seen in the Tower of London. Henry VIII had six wives and had five bellies.

QUINN (Joanna) . . . is big in animation. Based in Cardiff, she and her partner Les Mills of Beryl Productions were Oscar nominated in 1998 for *Famous Fred* and in 1999 for *Canterbury Tales*.

QUINNELL FAMILY . . . their contribution to Welsh rugby needs no comment.

QUOTATION FROM ANON . . . 'Put two Welshmen together and you are guaranteed three points of view.'

QUOTATIONS . . . In the 1992 fourth edition of the *Oxford Book of Quotations* the word 'Wales' is quoted only three times. Once by R S Thomas, once by Ivor Gurney and once by playwright Robert Bolt who wrote, in *A Man for All Seasons*, 'It profits a man nothing to give his soul for the whole world . . . But for Wales'!

RABBITS . . . Newborough Warren on Anglesey was a useful meat provider in wartime Britain, and eighty thousand Anglesey bunnies made the dinner table a year via markets in Manchester and Liverpool.

RACECOURSE . . . Halkyn mountain, Flints. once had a racecourse managed by the wealthy Grosvenor estate. It was short lived and the last horse passed the post about 1790.

RACECOURSES . . .There are two in Wales, at Chepstow and Bangor on Dee. Chester, which is in terms of Christmas shopping the 'capital' of the north might also qualify for this region. There is also the *Tir Prince* trotting racecourse at Towyn, near Rhyl.

RADIO BROADCAST . . . the first Welsh language radio broadcast was made in 1923. *Davies (Gwilym)

RADIO CYMRU . . . is, you've guessed correctly, the main Welsh language radio station.

RAGLAN (Lord) . . . the current Lord lives at Cefntilla in Gwent and played a big part in the development of Cwmbran as a new town. The First Lord Raglan was the Duke of Wellington's right-hand man at Waterloo . . . until he lost his right arm after being shot. Three days later he wrote a letter (obviously with his left hand which was no mean feat, but then his feet were intact).

RAILWAYS . . . the first major stretch of railway to open in Wales was the line from Llanelli to Pontarddulais, which opened in 1839.

RAILWAY RESORTS . . . Talacre, Abergele and Llandudno seaside resorts mushroomed as the Chester and Holyhead Railway inched its way along the coast, when the London – Ireland connection was made.

RAILWAY CROSSINGS . . . the length of railway between Pwllheli and Machynlleth is believed to have more stops, halts and crossings than any other similar sized length in the UK – no fewer than twenty-five. This might account for the high incedence of accidents on the *Cambrian Coast Railway.

RAINBOW TROUT . . . In June 1999 at Pen-y-Ffrith lake, northern Wales, six year old Ben Wood of Chester caught a record breaking 19lb 14oz (9.016kg) rainbow trout on his first fishing trip!

RARE COIN . . . A silver penny coin bearing Hywel Dda's name was the first Welsh coin. Only one exists, and it is in the British Musuem. Was it currency, or commemorative?

RARE FERN . . . Richard Kayse *polypodium australe* is an extremely rare fern that was discovered in Dinas Powys over three hundred years ago by Mr Kayse, after whom it is named. Soon after the discovery in 1668 the fern was lost until it was rediscovered in the 1970s. It grows on a limestone cliff, the exact location of which is a secret.

REARDON (Ray) . . . Welsh snooker legend known as 'Dracula' because of his widow's peak hairline. The Tredegar born cuesman is an MBE, and dominated World snooker in the 1970s winning six world titles.

REBECCA RIOTS . . . were attacks on toll gates in south-west Wales. The first was at Efail-wen, Carms in 1839. The rioters found a convenient anti-gate text in *Genesis* (the book in the Bible, not the Rock group): 'And they blessed Rebecca and said unto her – let thy seed possess the gate of those which hate them'. Armed with Biblical backing, they enacted a little pantomime with Rebecca, the designated leader, in drag for the gate-crashing. By 1843 the sporadic riots ceased and tolls were reduced.

RECORD RECORDS . . . Bernard Lavery of Llanharry features no fewer than twenty-four times in the Guinness Book of Records for his outsize vegetables. He has grown a marrow to 5' 7' (170.3cm) weighing in at over 108lb (49kg) and a 16' 10^1/$_2$' (5.154m) carrot.

RECORDE (Robert) (died 1558) . . . mathematician and physician. Born at Tenby. Best remembered for inventing the = sign of equality in maths. However he was also at one time court physician to the monarchs Edward VI and Mary I. In 1549 he became controller of the Royal Mint at Bristol and, subsequently, the general surveyor of the mines and money in England (which included Wales in those days) and Ireland. He was also the author of many mathematical books, including *The Pathway To Knowledge* in around 1557. In one book he explained the solar and lunar eclipses of the Copernican system, which he was the first to adopt in England. Died in prison at Southwark, although little is known of why he was gaoled in the first place.

RED BERET . . . In 1953 Trawsfynydd became occupied Europe in WW2 and Alan Ladd helped the Americans to help the British war effort. The film was *The Red Beret*.

RED COATS . . . who rose through the ranks (not the Rank Organisation, the present holding company) at Butlins (Pwllheli) or Barry Island, include Sir Cliff Richard, Des O'Connor, Michael Barrymore and Jimmy Tarbuck, to name but a few. Wales is proud to have assisted.

RED FLAG . . . the first red flag ever raised in Britain was during the Merthyr Rising of 1831.

RED LADY OF PAVILAND . . . in 1823 a Paleolithic skeleton was discovered in Goat's Hole Cave, Pembrokeshire. At first thought to be a woman, but later agreed to be male. The body had been buried around 16,000 BC and is now in Oxford's Natural History Museum.

REDWOOD (John) . . . the 'popular' former Conservative Welsh Secretary was rightly slated for not learning the Welsh National Anthem and positively hammered into the ground for having the audacity to mime to it with all the synchronisation of a one legged can can dancer.

REES (Abraham) (1743-1825) He improved Ephraim Chambers' *Cyclopaedia* by adding four thousand four hundred new topics.

REES (Angharad) . . . Cardiff-born actress who became famous in the 1970s, starring as Demelza in BBC TV's *Poldark*.

REFERENDUM . . . The percentage results of the latest Welsh Assembly referendum speak volumes. 50.3% agreed that Wales should have 'home rule', 49.7% did not want it. The turnout was 51.3%.

RELOCATION . . . Dafydd Wigley, wanting S4C to relocate in Caernarfon, said 'Cardiff is not the centre of gravity'. One might suggest that it is the centre of gravy, as in gravy train.

REPTON (Humphrey) . . . the famous landscape gardener's handiwork can be seen at Plas Newydd on Anglesey where, between 1799 and 1804, he planted a wealth of trees and plants.

RESURGAM . . . the world's first mechanically propelled submarine sank off Rhyl, Fflint. in 1880. Ironically, *resurgam* is Latin for 'I will rise again'.

RHAEADR FAWR . . . the great waterfall at Abergwyngregyn, Gwynedd gushes an estimated 50 million gallons (227.5 million litres) a day during rainy weather.

RHANDIRMWYN . . . the Dyfed valley was once home to the largest lead mine in Europe.

RHEIDOL (Afon) . . . in Aberystwyth is one of Britain's fastest flowing. In 28 miles (45km) it drops 1750 feet (525m).

RHITA FAWR . . . *CLOAK OF BEARDS.

RHODRI MAWR . . . (Rhodri the Great) who died in battle in 868 is regarded as the first ruler to unite all three main Welsh kingdoms.

RHONDDA . . . the only valley in Wales so it seems. Everybody in Wales lives in the Rhondda and works in a coalmine and sings in a choir. Not strictly true because Glamorgan, Monmouth and Carmarthenshire alone have twenty-two valleys between them.

RHOOSE (Rhws) . . . in the Vale of Glamorgan is the home of Cardiff International Airport, formerly Cardiff Wales Airport and formerly Rhoose Airport.

RHOSYDD MINES . . . . the highest slate quarry in Wales.

RHUDDLAN CASTLE . . . the fact that the site was two miles from tidal water was not a problem. Two thousand three hundred *fossatores* or ditchers (medieval navvies) dug a new channel for Afon Clwyd. Master James of St George, the master-builder, ensured that the project was completed by 1280. Building had started in 1277.

RHYL'S SOAP CONNECTIONS . . . Jack and Vera Duckworth of Coronation Street have a grandson, Tommy who is resident in Rhyl. Meanwhile the more snobby Max and Susannah Farnham of Brookside spent weekends (before they split) in the coastal resort.

RHYMING DICTIONARY . . . *Yr Odliadur* published in 1978 is a Welsh rhyming dictionary written by Roy Stephens.

RHYS AP GRUFFUDD . . . (1132-1197) is always referred to as Yr Arglwydd Rhys (The Lord Rhys). He ruled Deheubarth (South-western Wales) and established his court at Aberteifi where he convened what is regarded as the first national eisteddfod in 1176.

RHYS FAWR (of Bala) . . . standard bearer of Henry Tudor at Bosworth in 1485 (the standard was the red dragon of Cadwaladr), is acknowledged as the killer of Richard III, the act which was instrumental in creating the Tudor dynasty and the massive Rhiwlas estate in Bala. The Tudors have long gone, but the Rhiwlas estate is still flourishing under the Price (Ap Rhys) dynasty. * SHEEPDOG TRIALS, WHISKY.

RHYS AP THOMAS . . . 'Kingmaker', one of Henry Tudor's chief supporters in his victory at Bosworth in 1485. He was rewarded with Newcastle Emlyn Castle.

RICE-DAVIES (Mandy) . . . one of the girls involved in the 1960s Profumo scandal was the then 16 year old Welsh model. The other was Christine Keeler who claimed some trivial connection with Abergele.

RICHEST MAN IN WALES . . . Newport businessman Terry Matthews (born 1944). In a 1998 list he was said to be worth around £960 million having sold the electronics firm *Mitel* and floated *Newport Networks* on the stock market. Obviously not the author of a book *What To Do If Your Giro Doesn't Come*. Terry Matthews is a thrice times winner of the Queen's Award for Export Achievement.

RIFT VALLEY . . . Dyffryn Clwyd (The Vale of Clwyd) is a rift valley with an underground artesian lake.

RISMAN (Gus) (1911-1994) . . . Cardiff born rugby league star of the 1930s who scored over three thousand points in his distinguished career which took in seventeen Great Britain tests (he was captain nine times).

RIVERS . . . there are over 15,000 miles (24,000km) of rivers in Wales.

ROAD SIGNS . . . Bilingual signs were approved by the government in 1972 – another step towards giving the Welsh language an official status following over four hundred years of being officially illegal.

ROBERTS (Evan) (1878-1951) . . . an evangelist who led the short-lived Welsh religious revival of 1904-05. Many of his congregation 'saw the light' and were awakened and spiritually converted.

ROBERTS (John) (1576-1610) . . . Benedictine monk and martyr who lived during a time of religious upheaval. He was arrested by the authorities at least four times on suspicion of Catholic subversion. One of these times was in November 1605 when suspects were being rounded up after the discovery of the Gunpowder Plot. Six years later he was arrested again and charged with high treason. He was executed. Born at Trawsfynydd in the old Meirionnydd.

ROBERTS (Kate) (1891-1985) . . . born Rhosgadfan near Caernarfon. Probably the best writer of Welsh prose of the 20th century.

ROBERTS (Rachel) . . . (1927-1989) born Llanelli. Film actress and one time wife of actor Rex Harrison. She appeared in *Our Man in Havana* and *This Sporting Life*.

ROBERTS (Richard) (1789-1864) . . . inventor, born at Llanymynech. Acutely mechanically minded even as a child (aged 10, he designed and built a spinning wheel for his mother). Roberts was not in the least materialistic as he invented items for the pleasure rather than the financial gain. He NEVER took out a patent on any of his vast and varied inventions which included improvements in the textile industry, a steam-powered motor-car, steam engines, ships' gear, lighthouses and clocks. He was also interested in local and national political reform and was at Peterloo in Manchester in 1819 at the time of the Peterloo Massacre, when the armed forces broke up a public-meeting about government reform, which left eleven people dead. He later became a Borough councillor in Manchester.

ROBERTS (Samuel) (1800-1885) . . . a political and social reformer who preached racial equality in the USA between 1857 and 1867. He was an advocate of penny postage, extra franchise and extra temperance. *Tennessee.

ROBESON (Paul) . . . In 1941 the American actor and singer starred in *Proud Valley*, a mining drama based in South Wales.

ROBIN GOCH . . . was the first aircraft that was designed and built in Wales. It is also a very pretty little bird with a red breast.

ROBINSON CRUSOE . . . was the Defoe character actually Welsh? His name sounds and looks remarkably like 'Croeso'? This is, however, rather unlikely since Defoe hardly had a good word to say about Wales on any of his journeys to the country.

RODIN'S MISTRESS . . . Tenby-born artist Gwen John (1876-1938) was the sister of portrait painter Augustus John who modelled for, and became a mistress of the sculptor Rodin.

ROGERS (Ken) . . . of Hull built up the Hypervalue chain of stores by starting very humbly in Barry where his 12 foot x 12 foot (3.7 x 3.7m) lock up was most modest. He later bought Barry Island Pleasure Park.

ROLLS-ROYCE . . . Mr Charles Rolls was born in Monmouth and was more than just a partner in the creation of the most famous motor car in the world – he was also the first flying fatality.

ROMAN SPRING . . . Decantae Mineral Water Ltd produce over six million bottles per year from a spring at Trofarth Farm, Llangernyw. The same spring quenched the thirst of invading Roman soldiers two thousand ago.

ROMAN STEPS . . . the centuries old slabs of stone steps about 1000 feet (900m) above sea level over the Rhinog hills between Cwm Bychan and Bwlch Tyddiad have mystified experts for decades. Where they built by the Romans? Did they lead to gold mines in the hills or to ports on the coast?

RORKE'S DRIFT . . . In this epic British victory, eleven Victoria Crosses were won, a record number in any battle. For more than twelve hours a mere one hundred and fifty soldiers of the 24th Regiment of Foot held out against four thousand Zulus. Two years later the regiment became the South Wales Borderers. *ZULU

ROTHESAY CASTLE . . . a steam packet ship wrecked near Beaumaris in August 1831. Of the one hundred and fourteen people on board, ninety-three died. The ship had been sailing from Liverpool to Menai Bridge.

ROWING . . . the rowing events at the 1958 British Empire and Commonwealth Games were held on Llyn Padarn in Snowdonia.

ROWLAND (Daniel) (1713-1790), a Methodist leader whose powerful preaching saved many souls when they were converted by his sermons. He pioneered hymns in Wales.

ROWLANDS (Goronwy Wyn) . . . of Anglesey became the first Urdd Gobaith Cymru member in January 1922 at Treuddyn.

ROYAL ACADEMY . . . a co-founder of the Royal Academy in London (1768)

was Wales' most celebrated painter, Richard Wilson of Penegoes, Machynlleth. (Not many artists boast Royal Academy membership.)

ROYAL BOROUGHS . . . there are four in the UK. Kensington, Kingston-upon-Thames, Windsor and some place in Wales called Caernarfon.

ROYAL CHARTER . . . October 25, 1859 saw one of the worst storms ever to hit Britain, and over eight hundred mariners died as two hundred sailing vessels sank in treacherous conditions. The Royal Charter was carrying gold miners from Australia to Liverpool when it foundered and sank off Moelfre, Anglesey. The gold bullion and coins provided rich pickings for looters for many decades. Charles Dickens (yes, the Charles Dickens) was *The Times* correspondent who wrote of the sickening sight of the rifling of dead men's pockets.

ROYAL COMPANY OF ARCHERS . . . Founded in 1676 this regiment is the Queen's bodyguard in Scotland, despite all the epic successes of the Welsh longbowmen for the English crown at Crecy, Poitiers and Agincourt , to name but a few 'results'.

ROYAL MINT . . . at Llantrisant. It produces not only Britain's coinage but also coinage for many other countries.

ROYAL NANNY . . . Alexandra 'Tiggy' Legge-Bourke, former nanny to and friend of Princes William and Harry, is the daughter of the Lord Lieutenant of Powys.

ROYAL REGIMENT OF WALES . . . was formed in 1969 when the South Wales Borderers and the Welch Regiment were amalgamated.

ROYAL WELSH FUSILIERS . . . formed in 1689 is Wales' oldest infantry regiment and they parade a goat mascot in all parades.

ROYAL WELSH AGRICULTURAL SHOW . . . was established in 1904 and is now a four day event, which costs over £1 million to stage at Builth Wells.

ROYALIST GHOST . . . an English Civil War phantom is said to haunt Hobgoblin's Lane in Pentraeth, Anglesey.

RUGBY . . . supposedly the national sport of Wales. Known by non-afficionados as 'Chase The Egg.' In reality it is a religion in South Wales, a religion in which regular pilgrimages to the shrine that was Cardiff Arms Park were a sacrament. The golden age of Welsh Rugby Union was between 1900-1911 with no fewer than six Triple Crowns being won. The Welsh enjoyed a second golden age in the 1970s with great players such as Gareth *Edwards, JPR *Williams, Phil *Bennett, Gerald Davies and more. The third golden age will be???

RUPERT THE BEAR . . . . a native of Snowdonia . . . *BESTALL (Alfred).

RUSH (Ian) . . . famous international footballer who started his professional career at Chester, won many medals with Liverpool, had a brief unsuccessful spell in Italy, and then returned to Anfield to carry on where he had left off.

RUSHDIE (Salman) . . . when the author first went into hiding after the Ayatollah's fatwah, he fled to Wales to the Brecon Beacons, to be precise. Incidentally, considering he was supposed to be in hiding he didn't make a good job of it – nobody knew what he looked like until he went into hiding.

RUSSELL (Bertrand) (1872-1970) . . . born in Trelleck near Monmouth, he lived near Penrhyndeudraeth, Gwynedd. Philosopher, mathematician and writer of more than 40 books, he won the Nobel Prize for Literature in 1950. Even in his 90s he was a major campaigner in CND.

RUSSIAN IRONWORKS . . . John Hughes (1814-1889) was an engineer who helped pioneer iron-works in Russia. Born in Merthyr Tudful, he gained his experience in the South Wales iron industry before becoming Manager of docks in London. His expertise earned him a Europe-wide reputation and Russia, tiring of importing iron and steel to establish railways and other industries, approached Hughes with an offer to forward the development of a homegrown iron industry. He set up his bases in a desolate place on the edge of the Russian Steppes and took a great number of experienced Welsh ironworkers with him. By the 1870s he had formed the New Russia Company and the town of Hughesoffka had been established to house the burgeoning workforce, and soon became the centre of the industrial Don Basin. After his death the work was continued by his four sons until the Revolution of 1917, when all industrial companies came under Soviet government control. Hughesoffka was renamed Stalino.

RUTHIN . . . St Peter's Church in the town has an ornate oak paneled roof, comprising of five hundred carved panels. It was presented to the men of Wales by Henry VII, a reward for Welsh support in 1485.

RUTHIN INSULTS . . . an US novellist visited in 1853 and called it 'an exceedingly old-looking place' and then described 'witch-like women very unlike anything feminine in America'.

RYGBI . . . is the Welsh (proper) version of the English Rugby.

S.A.C. . . . of Europe's thirty-seven Special Area of Conservation sites, Wales has two – Cardigan Bay with its bottle nosed dolphins, and parts of Pembrokeshire.

S.W.S. actor Stifyn Parri's society (*Social, Welsh and Sexy*) in London has grown to one thousand members. He opened a branch in New York before the new Millennium.

S4C . . . the Welsh fourth Channel was launched in November 1982 (a day before Channel 4). Before its inception, Welsh language television was sporadic and spread between BBC Wales and HTV Wales. Without a doubt, Welsh broadcasting has been a shot in the arm, for the language and campaigners who lobbied for years for a Welsh channel have been proved right. *EVANS (Gwynfor)

ST ASAPH . . . on Afon Elwy in Denbighshire applied in 1999 for city status, which would have made it the second smallest city in Britain after St David's, Pembs.

ST DAVID'S . . . village in the district of Preseli about 15 miles (24.1km) from Milford Haven. It houses a 12thC cathedral in honour of the patron saint of Wales and is the smallest cathedral seat in the United Kingdom.

ST DAVID'S CLUB . . . Welsh exiles in London.

ST FAGAN . . . originally home of the Welsh Folk Museum, now the Museum of Welsh life. Located outside Cardiff, St Fagans Museum was Britain's first open air museum and occupies a fifty acre site in which many historic Welsh buildings have been reconstructed – except, of course castles.

SAIN . . . Welsh record label with studios at Llandwrog near Caernarfon. Launched in 1969 in Cardiff by *Dafydd Iwan and others. The company has recorded hundreds of artists since then and they have more than five thousand registered songs. Artists who have appeared on the label include Catatonia and classical baritone Bryn *Terfel, not to mention Dafydd Iwan,

Huw Jones, Meic Stevens, Geraint Jarman et al.

SAILING WATERS . . . the best in Britain are off the North Wales coast. Had either of Manchester's bids to host the Olympic Games during the 1990s borne fruit then Pwllheli on the Llŷn Peninsula would have been the base for all the sailing events.

SAIS . . . Affectionate term for an Englishman.

SAINTS . . . Wales has a surfeit of saints, mainly shadowy, from the dark ages.

SALE OF THE CENTURY . . . In 1938 the then Marquess of Bute sold twenty thousand houses, one thousand shops, two hundred and fifty pubs, theatres and land in the biggest property sale in British history.

SALEM . . . a painting, a chapel congregation, by the Devon-born artist Sydney Curnow Vosper which is probably the best known Welsh painting of the 20th century.

SALI MALI . . . the heroine of a children's first reading book in Welsh was created in 1969 by Mary Vaughan Jones, and then became a TV star. Sali Mali was the subject of a 1999 Super Furry Animals pop song.

SALESBURY (William) (c.1520-1584) . . . born Llansannan, Denbs and Oxford educated. Noted scribe of *A Dictionary in Englyshe and Welshe, Oll Synnwyr Pen Kembero Ygyd* and later, *Kynniver Llith a Bann* a Welsh version of the Gospels and Book of Common Prayer. What Bishop William Morgan finished, in terms of setting the Welsh language at that time on the right path, was started by Salesbury who was the most influential Welsh literary figure of the Renaissance age.

SALUSBURY (Thomas) (1564-1586) . . . Denbighshire-born conspirator who was involved in the Babington Plot (a conspiracy which aimed to overthrow and kill Queen Elizabeth 1 and replace her on the throne with the Catholic Mary Queen of Scots). Salusbury and another Welshman, Edward Jones, were subsequently charged with attempting to raise a rebellion in Denbighshire in support of Antony Babington's plot. Salusbury was tried and executed in September 1586.

SARN BADRIG . . . (St Patrick's Causeway) is a 14 mile (22.5km) long rocky reef off Harlech in Cardigan Bay. Legend has it that it was once part of the mainland but was flooded after a girl forgot to replace the lid of a well.

SATURNALIA . . . festivals once enjoyed by the Romans are now events boosting tourism in Llanwrtyd Wells.

SCARLETS . . . nickname of Llanelli RFC.

SCORCH MARKS . . . are still visible on Criccieth Castle six centuries after Owain Glyndŵr captured and burnt it in 1404.

SCOTT OF THE ANTARCTIC . . . the *Terra Nova* set off on her final mission from Cardiff in 1910.

SCRIPTURAL DICTIONARY . . . the *Geiriadur Ysgrythyrawl* (1801-1811) was one of the greatest achievements of Welsh Methodism.

SECOMBE (Sir Harry) (born 1921) . . . of Swansea made his name as one of The Goons alongside Peter Sellers and Spike Milligan. A fine singer, he has latterly presented religious TV programmes *Songs of Praise* and *Highway*. He was knighted in 1981.

SEA EMPRESS . . . in February 1996 the *Sea Empress* oil tanker ran aground at the entrance to Milford Haven harbour and seventy-two thousand tonnes of crude oil leaked into the sea. Around four thousand tonnes was washed up on some of the most beautful shorelines in the UK. It cost around £60 million to clean up and it is estimated that the accident cost the fishing and tourist industries were over £50 million – without mentioning the damage done to wildlife.

SEAHORSES . . . in the late 1990s, two pairs in an Anglesey sea zoo produced two hundred young – a hitherto unheard of event in captivity.

SEALS . . . 30% of the world's grey seal population lives off the Pembrokeshire coast. *SEA EMPRESS!

SEALYHAM TERRIERS . . . these strange dogs were first bred in 1890 near Haverfordwest.

SECOND HOMES . . . Government improvement grants for second homes (or indeed third or fourth homes) were iniquitous in areas where Dai or Blodwen had no hope of even one home, so the local Llŷn council (pre 1974) dug in their heels and refused to award them. Some half a decade later, the fires ignited.

SECONDARY SCHOOL . . . the first purpose built secondary school in Wales was built at Caernarfon in 1894, only five years after the Welsh Intermediate Education Act of 1889.

SECRET . . . The first Masonic lodge in Wales was established at Carmarthen in 1726.

SEGONTIUM . . . a bunch of stones left in Caernarfon by the Romans – was actually the remains of a fort which guarded the Menai Strait crossing to Anglesey. It was built to protect Anglesey's copper.

SEMTECS . . . a Welsh-language thriller novel from the pen of Geraint Vaughan Jones, which featured the SAS officer turned detective Samuel Tecwyn Turner. Winner of the Daniel Owen Prize at the National Eisteddfod in 1998.

SENGHENYDD DISASTER . . . in 1913, four hundred and thirty-nine people died in a coal pit explosion.

SEPTUAGENARIAN CLIMBER . . . In 1966, seventy-two year old Roger Dimension of Beddgelert notched his four thousandth ascent of Snowdon.

SEREN GOMER . . . the first Welsh language newspaper was founded in Swansea in 1814.

SEVEN . . . Queen Victoria's lucky number. During her lengthy reign she spent seven years in Scotland, seven weeks in Ireland and a meagre seven days in Wales. We are not amused.

SEVEN DAYS OF THE WEEK . . . Dydd = Day, and the Welsh have Dyddiau Sul, Llun, Mawrth, Mercher, Iau, Gwener and Sadwrn. Llun (Monday) is also a picture, Mawrth (Tuesday) is also a month while Iau (Thursday) is also your liver.

SEVEN WONDERS OF WALES . . . Pistyll Rhaeadr and Wrexham Steeple, Snowdon Mountain (without its people), Overton's yew trees, St Winifred's Wells, Llangollen Bridge and Gresford Bells. Actually the six wonders of Denbighshire with a token Caernarfonshire hill thrown in. What do you expect from foreigners?

SEVERN . . . river which rises on Mynydd Pumlumon in mid Wales, and flows over 210 miles (336km) through Shrewsbury, Worcester, Gloucester and meets the sea at the Bristol channel. While it is in Wales, it is called Afon Hafren.

SEVERN BRIDGE . . . opened in 1966 the bridge is a very important link between England and the South Wales valleys. It became a Grade 1 listed building in the late 1990s. Harry Webb's witty verse implies the nature of Anglo-Welsh relations pre-devolution:

'Two lands at last united
Across the waters wide
And all the tolls collected
On the English side.'

SEWIN . . . migratory sea-trout that frequents the rivers of West Wales.

SEXY . . . According to a 1998 survey in Men's Health magazine, Welshmen have weekend sex more than any other men in the country. As for Welsh women, the magazine did not elaborate.

SGRIN . . . launched in 1997 at the Welsh International Film Festival. Sgrin is the media agency for Wales and is a unified effort by agencies working in film and TV to capitalise on the rapid rise of film and film-making interests in Wales. Sgrin's members comprise actors, producers and directors.

SHANE . . . the classic western starring Alan Ladd was the first film to be 'dubbed' into Welsh in the 1970s.

SHAKIN' STEVENS . . . South Wales born pop star, whose real name is Michael Barrett. First sprang to prominence playing a young Elvis Presley in the stage musical *Elvis*. His chart-topping hits include *This Ole House* and *Green Door*.

SHEEP . . . 1996 statistics from the Welsh Office revealed there were 11,190,000 sheep and lambs in Wales. In the Snowdonia National Park sheep outnumber humans by 25:1 and on Anglesey it's 4:1

SHEEP AND THE ECONOMY . . . sixteen thousand farm businesses depend on the sheep industry and it is estimated that the humble woolly back is worth around £47 million to the Welsh economy.

SHEEPDOG TRIALS . . . Bala is believed to have been the venue of the first recorded Sheep Dog Trials in October 1873 after R J Lloyd Price and a Scottish friend had argued about whose dog and shepherd were the best. The Scots hound Tweed beat poor Welsh Mot, and evidently, Price and his Scottish pal never spoke again.

SHELL ISLAND . . . when is an island not an island? When it's Shell Island attached to the mainland in former Meirionnydd. It is home to over one hundred and seventy species of wild flower.

SHELL SHOCK . . . in 1955 the National Museum of Wales received a bequest of over a million shells from John Read le Brockton Tomlin who, nine years earlier, also bequeathed his collection of eighty thousand beetles (insects, not German cars).

SHELTA . . . an ancient hybrid code language used by Welsh and Irish tinkers and gypsies, in which Irish and Gaelic words were altered.

SHENKIN . . . why not SIENCYN . . . Lance-Corporal Shenkin is the only goat in the Royal Regiment of Wales and makes formal appearences at major events.

SHERLOCK HOLMES . . . Arthur Conan-Doyle's *The Hound of The Baskervilles* was written at Clyro in the Wye Valley where he was a guest of the Baskerville family of Clyro Court.

SHORTHAND . . . 'Stenographia' , a book by Thomas Roberts published in 1839, showed the Welsh system of shorthand.

SHOULDER OF MUTTON . . . no, not the first choice of a hungry miner on finishing his gruelling shift. It was the original name of the 'Sarah Siddons Inn' in Brecon, where the actress – the most famous of her day – was born.

SIAM . . . The King of Siam and family stayed at the Lake Vyrnwy Hotel in Powys during WW2.

SIDDONS (Sarah) . . . 1755-1831. Brecon born actress. Peerless in her time who excelled in dramatic roles. She was the eldest daughter of theatre impresario Roger Kemble.

SIEGFRIED SASSOON . . . was not Welsh. The 'War Poet' was an officer in the Royal Welch Fusiliers.

SILENT MOVIES . . . twenty-six silent movies were made in Wales between 1920-1928, probably because of the scenic locations available. The first was *'Aylwyn'* directed in 1920 by Henry Edwards, and starring his wife Chrissie White and set in rural Snowdonia. Others included *'The Belle of Betws y Coed'* and *'The Pedlar of Penmaenmawr'*. Most of them sound like operas by *Donizetti.

SINCLAIR C5 . . . the short-lived, much-maligned vehicle, invented by Sir Clive Sinclair in 1985 was an electronic tricycle produced in a Merthyr Tudful vaccuum cleaner factory.

SINGERS . . . The Welsh sing, even if they can't!!

SIÔN CORN . . . the Welsh Father Christmas.

SIÔN CWILT . . . an 18th century smuggler of Cross Hands, Ceredigion. Famous for his patched coat, he sold his swag to the gentry.

SIR GAWAIN & THE GREEN KNIGHT . . . a movie flop which was filmed in Wales.

SKERRIES (Ynysoedd y Moelrhoniaid) . . . two miles off Trwyn y Gadair (Carmel Head) on Anglesey's Holy Island lie these islands, Wales' most northerly part. Home to countless terns and, since 1716, a lighthouse.

SKIN GRAFTING . . . One of the first to graft skin on humans was Dr William Price (1800-1883) of Llantrisant – better known for another 'first' in the field of *cremation.

SKOKHOLM ISLAND . . . at the tip of Penfro where Ronald Lockley established Britain's first bird observatory in 1933. *SEA EMPRESS

SKOMER . . . this island off the Pembrokeshire coast is host to a variety of seabirds, especially one hundred thousand pairs of Manx shearwater. *SEA EMPRESS

SLATE – Probably North Wales' greatest exported product. At one time the Penrhyn slate quarry at Bethesda in Dyffryn Ogwen (valley), supplied slate to almost every school in the country. At the peak of the slate boom in 1898, 93% of British slate was of Welsh origin. Only 10 % of mined or quarried slate was usable, so for every ton of slate produced, there were nine tons of waste, hence the heaps of slate slag. Welsh slate is around six hundred million years old.

SLATES TITLED LADIES . . . Even slates in Wales have a hierarchy. In descending order of size and rank, these titled ladies are empress, duchess, countess and ladies. Other ranks include doubles and singles.

SLUR . . . Lord Aberdare once wrote of the Welsh language: 'I consider it a serious evil, a great obstruction to the moral and intellectual progress of my countrymen'.

SMALLEST CATHEDRAL . . . Whilst St David's is the smallest cathedral city in Britain., the actual smallest cathedral building is that of St Asaph.

SMALLEST CHURCH . . . in Wales is St Trillo's at Rhos-On-Sea and has room for just six worshippers. It measures approximately 15 feet by 9 feet (4.5m x 2.7m) and holds a service every Friday morning.

SMALLEST CITY . . . in Britain is St David's with its population at around twelve hundred.

SMALLEST HOUSE IN BRITAIN . . . stands on the quayside at Conwy. It is only 6 feet (1.8m) wide and 10' 2' (3m 5cm) tall. It has been featured in the Guinness Book of Records since the 1960s.

SMITH (David) (born 1945) . . . of Tonypandy. In collaboration with Gareth Williams, he wrote *Fields of Praise: The Official History of the Welsh Rugby Union 1881-1981*. Written at the right time, after the 1970s golden years.

SMITH (Delia) . . . Half Welsh TV cook and author. Her mother, Hettie, comes from Llwyngwril on the Cardigan Bay coast, near Tywyn.

SMUGGLING . . . Lantern lights, visible only from the sea, indicated that the coast was clear for landing brandy, wine, spices, lace and silks. Stories of wholesale smuggling involving entire coastal communities, led by the local gentry and clergy, are common in 17th and 18th century Wales. Evading duty was a way of life and stories abound about casks hidden in caves, secret passages, houses, inns and even graveyards.

SNOWDON . . . (Yr Wyddfa), the tallest peak of Wales and England at 3,560 feet (1085m).

SNOWDON BEETLE . . . *Chrysolina ceralis* a rainbow coloured beetle found only in the Snowdon area.

SNOWDON LILY . . . *Lloydia serotina* a rare species of arctic-alpine plant unique to Snowdon, as far as Britain is concerned.

SNOWDON (Lord) . . . Anthony Armstrong Jones. Once married to Princess Margaret. Renowned as a photographer and designer of an aviary at London Zoo. Not Welsh as far as we can remember. Became (and remains) Constable of Caernarfon Castle in the early 60s.

SNOWDON MARATHON . . . in 1997 some nine hundred runners completed the 26 miles 385 yard race around the mountain.

SNOWDON MOUNTAIN RACE . . . annual slog by fell runners up the majestic mount. Since 1981 the event has been twinned with the Italian Trofeo Vanoni in which the top three in each race qualifies to compete in the other. The record run up Snowdon was set at 1 hr 2 mins 29 secs in 1985 by Kenny Stuart (for men), and 1 hr 12 minutes 48 second set in 1993 by Carol Greenwood (neè Haig).

SNOWDON MOUNTAIN RAILWAY . . . has been the only rack and pinion railway in the UK since 1896. It has carried 5 million passengers in the last 100 years.

SNOWDONIA . . . the Welsh name is Eryri which translates as 'place of eagles'. There aren't many about nowadays.

SNOWDONIA NATIONAL PARK . . . one of the eleven National Parks in Wales and England which have all been designed to preserve their special features for future enjoyment. The Snowdonia National Park has more national Nature Reserves than the other ten Parks.

SNOWDONIA SOCIETY . . . one of its aims is the removal of electricity pylons which defile the landscape.

SNOWFLAKE PUNCHER The . . . Freddie Welsh (1886-1927). Pontypridd born boxer who was given the nickname by rival fighters who believed Welsh could not punch hard – however he did win many fights with a knockout. He was born Frederick Hall Thomas.

SNUFF BOX . . . Sir Henry Morton *Stanley's discovery of Dr Livingstone in Ujiji in 1871 earned him a knighthood, a gold medal from the Geographical Society and a gold and diamond snuff box from Queen Victoria. Stanley, a journalist, capitalised on overnight fame and wrote *How I Found Livingstone* (1872), *Through The Dark Continent* (1878) and *In Darkest Africa* (1890). Not bad for a workhouse-reared Welsh lad.

SOBERS (Gary) . . . in 1968 the famous West Indian batsman scored a record six sixes in an over of six balls – bowled by Glamorgan's Malcolm Nash.

SOCIAL OUTCASTS . . . in a 1990s survey by society magazine, *Tatler*, only one Welsh person made the top two hundred guest list – Mrs William Hague, the former Ffion Jenkins.

SONY . . . the major Japanese company built its first large factory in Wales in Bridgend.

SOROS (George) . . . allegedly cost Britain £12 billion on *Black Wednesday* in 1992. As a young immigrant, the Hungarian-born billionaire worked as a salesman in Llanduno and Rhyl.

SOS . . . Arthur Moore of Gelligroes near Blackwood, a wireless buff, picked up the *Titanic's* SOS signal from over 1000 miles (1,600km) distance. The official news of the sinking was not cabled to London from New York until two days later. Guglielmo Marconi heard of Arthur's home-made receiver and employed him in the Marconi Wireless Telegraph Co.

SOSPAN FACH . . . the famous song adopted by Llanelli RFC in deference to the tinplate industry.

SOUTH POLE . . . one of the men on Captain Scott's final mission was Edgar Evans (1876-1912). Born in Rhosili in Gower, Petty Officer Evans sailed with Scott to the Antarctic in the Terra Nova in 1910. Evans was one of the five who were involved in the final trek for the South Pole and were mortified when the saw the Norwegian flag of Amundsen and realised they had been pipped at the pole. The five perished as they made their way back to base camp.*TERRA NOVA. Many Cardiff businessmen sponsored Scott's expedition and were at the Cardiff quayside to see the fateful departure.

SOUTH STACK (Ynys Lawd). . . the 200 metre rock off Ynys Cybi (Holy Island) Anglesey, which is home to a lighthouse dating back almost two hundred years, was cut off from the larger island for fourteen years after a rusting suspension bridge was adjudged unsafe in 1983. In 1997 a new aluminium bridge reunited Ynys Cybi and Ynys Lawd.

SOUTH YORKSHIRE . . . between Sheffield and Worksop lies a small town called Wales.

SOUTHALL (Neville) . . . goalkeeper, holder of a record ninety-three soccer international caps for Wales.

SPARKES John . . . Swansea born comedy performer who appeared in the TV programmes *Naked Video* and *The Fame Game*.

SPEAKER . . . George Thomas, Labour MP for Cardiff West and later Lord Tonypandy, was the first speaker of the House of Commons to benefit from parliamentary radio broadcasts – commenced April 1978.

SPEAKING RECORD . . . Canon Clive Southerton of Prestatyn set the record for an after dinner speech in 1998 – 52 hours and 43 minutes. The event helped raise over £50,000 for charity. *PREACHING RECORD

SPECIAL SPECIAL . . . volunteer cop, Roger Smith of Magor was given special dispensation to drive high-powered police cars in the late 1990s – the first special to be allowed to do so.

SPEEDY BLACKSMITH . . . the Powys village of Staylittle got it's name because the local blacksmith was so quick that visitors were not kept hanging around.

SPICE GIRL'S SISTER . . . Sporty Spice Melanie Chisholm's half-sister, Emma Williams lives in Llandudno.

SPOONER (James) (1789-1856) . . . Birmingham born engineer who oversaw the construction of the pioneering narrow gauge Ffestiniog Railway which was built to carry slate from the Blaenau Ffestiniog mines to the new port of Porthmadog, from where it was shipped worldwide. He was succeeded as engineer on the Railway by his son Charles Spooner, who was born at Maentwrog.

SPORTS PERSONALITY OF THE YEAR . . . the annual Welsh awards were founded in 1954 and notable winners since then have included Ivor Allchurch, Gareth Edwards, Terry Griffiths, Ian Woosnam, Colin Jackson and Ryan Giggs.

SPORTSMAN'S ARMS . . . the highest pub in Wales is on the Denbigh moors and stands 1,547 feet (464m) above sea level. It was first licensed in 1829 as Bryn-trillyn Alehouse but changed its name to the Sportsman's Arms in 1870.

SPOTTED ROCK ROSE . . . a rare plant found only in North Wales, in Anglesey and on the Llŷn Peninsula. The plant, with a yellow bloom, flowers in June but only lasts a few hours.

SPRING (Howard) (1889-1965) . . . prolific Cardiff born novelist and one of two civilians in the delegation that accompanied Winston Churchill in his meeting with President Rooseveldt which resulted in the Atlantic Charter. Known in the US as 'The English Writer', he said 'No, I'm not the English Writer, I'm strictly Taffy. I'm a Welsh writer'.

SQUIRES (Dorothy) (1915-1998) . . . born (apparently in a field) at Pontyberem, Rhondda. A singer of no-little renown who famously married toyboy actor Roger Moore (sixteen years her junior), who went on to become James Bond.

SQUIRRELS . . . the fast-disappearing red variety are making a comeback at Newborough, Anglesey. Fittingly, Ynys Môn was also the last stronghold of the ancient druids.

STACKPOLE . . . in Dyfed is Britain's smallest harbour.

STANLEY (Sir Henry Morton) . . . Speaker of the four most memorable words in the history of missionary exploration. 'Dr Livingstone, I presume' . Stanley was born near Denbigh in 1841 under the name of John Rowlands. In his late teens he travelled to America and actually fought on both sides during the Civil War. He worked as a journalist for the New York Herald and was sent to find Livingstone in Africa in 1871. The two explored Lake Tanganyika and traced the course of then River Congo to the sea. They founded the Congo Free State (now called Zaire). Stanley died in 1904. *SNUFF BOX

STATISTICS . . . Only 1% of the British population can speak Welsh.

STATUTE OF RHUDDLAN . . . the declaration of 1284 which signified the end of Welsh independence and the organisation of the occupied territories into governable areas.

STEEL . . . Llanwern steel strip mill employed almost twenty thousand in the

1960s peak – that figure is now down to three thousand. Similar employment statistics fit with the Abbey Works at Port Talbot.

STEELE (Richard) (1672-1729) . . . Irish born writer, publisher and pioneering journalist who founded the *Tatler* (1710), *The Spectator* (1711) and *The Guardian*. He lived in and was buried in Carmarthen – obviously in the 'land of inspiration'.

STEPHENSON (Robert) 1803-1859 . . . Son of the railway engineer George Stephenson. Robert became a civil engineer and is famous in Wales for the construction of the railway bridges over the Conwy estuary and the Menai Strait.

STEEPLE . . . the steeple of St Giles' church in Wrexham is 136 feet (41m) tall and was completed as early as 1520. It is regarded as one of the Seven Wonders of Wales.

STEIN (Jock) . . . The late-great football legend died from a heart-attack close to the end of the Wales v Scotland World Cup Qualifier at Ninian Park in autumn 1985. As a young man he had worked as a steel-worker in South Wales and had captained Llanelli Soccer Club. In 1967 Stein managed Celtic to become the first British club to win the European Cup.

STEREOPHONICS . . . the Award winning trio from Cwmaman (Kelly Jones, Richard Jones and Stuart Cable) who were at the forefront of the record business interest in Welsh bands in the 1990s. The childhood friends formed the band in 1992 as Tragic Love Company, changed their name in 1996, and have not looked back.

STEVENS (Meic) (born 1938) . . . of Treforest, Pontypridd, Glam. A champion of Welsh literature.

STOCKINGS . . . George III in his saner moments (he spent periods in a strait-jacket) recognised the true properties of Bala-made woollen stockings, which greatly eased his rheumatism.

STONE CASTLE . . . in 1067 William Fitzosbern built the first stone castle in Wales, at Chepstow. These Norman castles have been described over the centuries as 'defence against the marauding locals', which is a little rich considering the circumstances.

STONEHENGE . . . the famous *bluestones* of the inner circle are from the Preseli area of Pembrokeshire. Were the Beaker folk long-distance hauliers? Wiltshire is 180 (280km) miles away. Did they use rafts, rollers and sledges, or were the bluestones carried by glacial ice?

STRATA FLORIDA ABBEY . . . in Dyfed is a 12th century Cistercian Abbey, and is said to be haunted by the ghost of a medieval monk.

STRINGER (Howard) . . . the head of the Sony Corporation in America was born in Cardiff in 1940.

SUEZ CANAL . . . the first vessel through the newly opened canal was *Lynx*, a yacht owned by Christopher Rice Mansel Talbot of Margam Park.

SUFFRAGETTES . . . in 1914, vote-hungry women tried to burn Llandudno pier.

SUMMERS (Ann) . . . In July 1998 the first Ann Summers shop in Wales was opened in Queen Street, Cardiff.

SUN . . . Dale in Pembroke is Britain's sunniest place, averaging eighteen hundred hours of sun per annum.

SUNDAY CINEMAS . . . Swansea became the first Welsh town to open its cinemas on Sundays after a referendum in 1950.

SUNDAY SCHOOLS IN THE USA . . . Benjamin William Chidlaw (1811-1892). Born in Bala, Gwynedd, his family emigrated to the USA in 1821. He was to become the first commissioned missionary of the American Sunday School Union. He established Sunday Schools throughout the Central West region. Died at Dolgellau in the summer of 1892, he was buried in Ohio.

SUPER FURRY ANIMALS . . . this North Walian pop group can actually speak and sing in Welsh.

SUPERCOACH Carwyn James (1930-1983) . . . born at Cefneithin in West Wales, he won only two Welsh rugby caps but went on to become probably the greatest coach of his era. Employed by Llanelli in 1969 he was appointed coach for the now famous British Lions tour of New Zealand in 1971 from where the Brits came back victorious. A year later the All Blacks played Llanelli at Stradey Park and, under the tutelage of Carwyn James, the antipodeans were beaten in a now legendary game. James turned town the chance to coach the Welsh national side in 1974 and moved overseas. He died of a heart-attack aged just 53.

SUPERDAD . . . William ap Hywel ap Dafydd ap Iorwerth of Tregaean, Llangefni fathered forty-three children before he died aged 105 in 1581, The thrice married stud had twenty-two children with wife number one, ten with wife number two and a further four with wife number three. He also sired seven who were illegitimate. At the birth of the youngest, the Anglesey stallion was 81 years old. *Longevity.

SUPERTED . . . The cartoon character who was launched on S4C in 1982. His enemies include Skeletor and Texas Sam, whilst his friends include children in the countless countries to which the series has been subsequently sold.

SUPERTRAMP . . . William Henry Davies (1871-1940). Born in Monmouthshire he emigrated to the US where he became a casual labourer, but mostly a tramp, travelling around the country by jumping trains from place to place. Disaster befell him when he lost one leg in a train jumping accident, so he returned to the UK and became a writer. His most famous work is *Autobiography of a Supertramp,* and his most oft-quoted couplet 'What is this life, if full of care We have no time to stop and stare'. He died in Gloucestershire. A statue in his memory stands in Newport.

SURNAMES . . . in descending order the top six most common surnames in Wales are:- Jones, Williams, Davies, Thomas, Evans and Roberts. Surnames that indicate Welsh origin include: Walch, Walsh, Wallace, Walles, Wallis, Walsman, Welch, Wellish, Wellsman and Welsh.

SUTHERLAND (Graham) . . . the artist, a regular visitor to Pembroke, painted many Welsh landscapes which are hung in Picton Castle's Graham Sutherland Gallery. He was the 'Official War Artist'.

SWALLOW FALLS . . . a waterfall tourist attraction outside Betws-y-coed whose English name came about by accident. The Welsh name is *Rhaeadr Ewynnol,* which means something like 'Frothy Falls'. The Welsh word for 'Swallow' however is *Y Wennol.* Can you work out what the accident was?

SWANSEA (Abertawe) . . . it was the first town in Wales to enjoy gas street lighting in 1821.

SWEARING & OBSCENITIES . . . the novel *y.t. and his holiness* by Holywell-based author Jennifer Rhead was taken off supermarket and book shop shelves because of the obscenities and expletives on virtually every page.

SWEET PEAS . . . the first in Britain were grown in Conwy by Queen Eleanor of Castile (wife of Edward I). The only sweet aspect of his dealings with Wales, one might add.

SWIMMING POOL. . . . the first heated pool in Wales was built at RAF St Athan, Cardiff in 1939.

SWORDFIGHT . . . Tony Curtis and Kirk Douglas had a memorable one in the 1950s movie *The Vikings*. The scene was filmed at Caernarfon Castle.

SYCAMORE TREE . . . the tallest in Wales is at Baglan near Port Talbot.

SYRIA . . . a scheme to establish a Welsh settlement in Syria failed in 1825.

TB . . . the Welsh disease. Figures for 1939 show the highest incidence of tuberculosis in Wales and England were led by the Welsh counties.

TABERNACL . . . Morriston Chapel, Swansea built in 1872 is Wales' biggest chapel with a two thousand capacity.

TABLE . . . in 1998 the government commissioned a £50,000 table for politicians attending a European Union summit in Cardiff.

TACITUS . . . in his *Annals* XIV, the Roman writer dubbed Anglesey a 'druid centre'. He was right.

TAFF VALE RAILWAY STRIKE . . . resulted in a change in Trade Union law in the early 20th century.

TAFFY BASHING . . . seemed to be a common practice in the 1990s. It was *de rigeur* to deride Dafydd, the mode to maltreat Maldwyn, all the rage to ridicule Rhodri and to hurl hateful digs at Dewi. Water off a duck's back.

TAID . . . the Welsh word for grandfather.

TAKE THAT . . . the boy band used a Pembrokeshire sheep farm as a bolt hole during the peak of their fame.

TALBOT (Christopher Rice Mansel) . . . a Victorian entrepreneur and captain of industry who was Glamorgan's biggest landowner and MP for nearly sixty consecutive years. He was a renowned penny-pincher who died aged 87 but not after extending Aberafon port to create Port Talbot. *SUEZ CANAL

TALBOT (Thomas Mansel) . . . *ORANGES & LEMONS

TALL SHIPS . . . were able to sail under the Menai Suspension bridge as it was built 100 feet (30m) above the high tide water level.

TALL STORY . . . a Douglas fir in the gardens of Powys Castle is the tallest tree in Britain.

TALLEST . . . Matthew Langmaid of Llanishen, Cardiff is 7' 1^1/$_2$" (2.13m) tall. He has featured in the Guinness Book of Records since 1992 as one of the world's tallest men.

TALLEST BUILDING . . . Cardiff's Capital Tower is the tallest Welsh building at 260 feet (78m) high. It has twenty-four floors and one thousand six hundred windows.

TAL-Y-LLYN RAILWAY . . . the line running from Tywyn to Nant Gwernol, Abergynolwyn opened in 1865 and became the first in the world to be preserved. The line inspired the *Thomas the Tank Books* of Revd Awdry, who whiled away many hours as a volunteer guard on the line.

TAYLOR (Elizabeth) . . . the former wife (twice hitched to him) of Richard Burton has stated publicly on numerous occasions that it is her wish to be buried in Wales.

TEA SELLER . . . William Williams of Pantycelyn – the most prolific hymn writer ever produced in Wales was also a successful tea seller. *Nearer Thy God to Tea* indeed.

TEACHERS UNION . . . Undeb Cenedlaethol Athrawon Cymru (U.C.A.C) is Wales' answer to the N.U.T. (National Union of Teachers).

TEMPERANCE . . . Wales' first Temperance Society was established in Holyhead in 1832.

TEMPORARY TRAFFIC LIGHTS . . . in 1979 Gwynedd Council erected a set of temporary traffic lights at Drws-y-nant on the A494 Bala-Dolgellau trunk road, after a rock slide. They were removed in July 1999!

TELFORD (Thomas) (1757-1834) . . . Scots born engineer who certainly left his mark on Wales with the construction of the A5 and the Menai Suspension Bridge. Southey dubbed him 'the colossus of roads'.

TENBY (Dinbych-y-pysgod) . . . the golden beaches of the town have long attracted visitors. Beatrix Potter and George Eliot were regulars in the 19th century.

TENNESSEE . . . social reformer Samuel Roberts bought 100,000 acres of Tennessee in 1856 and embarked on a Welsh colony venture. As usual (except in Patagonia) the venture failed. Roberts returned to Wales and those who had tried to colonise moved to Ohio.

TENORS . . . from Wales have made tenners (and twenties and fifties etc) from their tonsillar techniques.

TENOVUS . . . the cancer charity was founded in Cardiff.

TEPEE VALLEY . . . Britain's oldest and largest alternative community of tent-dwellers was established at Llanfynydd, Carms. in 1976. 'Carry on Camping' said the High Court in 1999.

TERRA NOVA . . . Captain Scott's 1910 Antarctic Exploration ship sailed from Cardiff.

TERFEL (Bryn) . . . internationally acclaimed Welsh baritone who hails from Pant-glas, Gwynedd. A local legend (from Pwllheli) states that whilst back home on leave from appearing at the Hollywood Bowl or Sydney Opera House or La Scala in Milan, Bryn Terfel went out for a few drinks with old schoolfriends (you never forget you're Welsh!) and twixt pints did a few vocal excercises. The locum licencee heard him and instructed an underling to 'tell that bloke to shut up or get out'.

THETIS HMS . . . ill-fated submarine which sank in July 1939 whilst on sea trials from Liverpool. When the SOS was finally relayed via messenger, all the way to Royal Navy HQ in Southampton, it was too late for many survivors. The sub was located and eventually taken to Moelfre off Anglesey where the grizzly task of identifying the bodies was performed. The oxygen had probably run out . . . and the faces and bodies of the dead would have been hideously bloated and distorted. A plaque commemorating those who died on the Thetis stands near the harbour at Moelfre. Ninety-three out of one hundred and three seamen and dignitaries, who came along to experience this fairly new-fangled form of sea travel, lost their lives in the suffocating tomb of steel. The Thetis itself was refitted, renamed HMS Thunderball and served during WW2. She vanished, this time, without trace in 1943.

THOMAS (David) (1794-1882) . . . iron-industry pioneer in Wales and then the USA. Born near Neath he became manager of the blast furnaces at the Ynyscedwyn Anthracite Iron Works where he oversaw the experimentation of using anthracite as a smelting fuel, and cast the first anthracite smelted fuel in the world. His stature was such that he was invited to the USA where he revolutionised their iron industry and earned the reputation of being one of the greatest ironmasters in the world.

THOMAS (Dylan) . . . Hard living/playing Welsh writer. Born in Swansea in 1914 he began writing poetry while still a schoolboy and later began a career in journalism. He married Caitlin Macnamara in 1937 and they lived for a while at Laugharne near Swansea. His most famous prose works were *Portrait of the Artist as a Young Dog* and *Under Milk Wood*. Thomas had a reputation for hard-drinking, which ultimately led to his premature death in New York in 1953 whilst on a lecture tour. He is the only 20th century Welsh poet commemorated in Poet's Corner in Westminster Abbey.

THOMAS (Eddie) . . . (1925-1997) of Merthyr Tudful. A boxing legend who was British, European and Empire Welterweight boxing champion, manager of two subsequent world champions, and known to the people of Merthyr simply as 'Our Eddie'.

THOMAS (Iwan) . . . speedy Welsh runner.

THOMAS (Jennie) (1898-1979) . . . born in Birkenhead to Welsh parents. Children's author best known as joint-writer (with J.O. Williams) of *Llyfr Mawr Y Plant* featuring the timeless characters of Wil Cwac Cwac and Sion Blewyn Coch.

THOMAS (Leslie) . . . the author of *The Virgin Soldiers* series of novels hails from Newport.

THOMAS (Mickey) . . . A 'legend' in some footballing circles. The former

Welsh international starred for a host of top clubs including Manchester United. He is also remembered for being jailed for his role in a counterfeit money scam. When he later joined Porthmadog in the League of Wales, the players – all down-to-earth lads – were always wary of playing cards with Mickey in case they won and he passed them dodgy cash! A star man who is always selected when magazines pick their 'Soccer's Bad Boys XI'.

THOMAS (Robert) (1765-1841) . . . of Abererch, Pwllheli, Gwynedd. One of the founders of the Cymreigyddion Society in London. A writer and pamphleteer he wrote *An English & Welsh Vocabulary* (1827) and *The Welsh Interpreter* (1831), which he sold to tourists who visited Wales to gawp at Telford's Menai Suspension Bridge.

THOMAS (R.S.) . . . Welsh poet and retired clergyman, regarded as one of the best poets writing in English in the 20th century. He was born in Cardiff in 1913 and was later educated at Bangor University. He was ordained in the Church of Wales in 1936. His first volume of poems was published in 1946. His work is described by the *Oxford Companion to English Literature* thus: 'His poetry is deeply coloured by his experience of working in remote rural communities . . . where life was harsh and the landscape bleak'. R.S. Thomas was vicar of Aberdaron when he retired from the cloth.

THOMAS (Thomas) (1880-1911) . . . the first ever British middle-weight boxing champion was born in the Rhondda and won the Lonsdale belt in 1909. He died as a result of acute rheumatism.

THOMAS THE TANK . . . books written by the Revd Awdry and latterly his son Christopher. They were inspired by their voluntary work on the Tal-y-llyn Railway.

THOMPSON (David) (1770-1857) . . . explorer. Born in London to Welsh parents, David ap Thomas became an explorer who traversed the St Lawrence river to Lake Superior for the North-Western Company, having been apprenticed to the Hudson Bay Company for five years. He later concentrated on creating a map of Canada which was so accurate it was unsurpassed for over a century. Monuments to him were erected in British Columbia and North Dakota, and the Thompson river in British Columbia was named after him. In 1957 he was featured on a set of Canadian postage stamps.

THOROUGHBREDS . . . Lord Penrhyn's stable block at Penrhyn Castle housed three dozen thoroughbreds. Thanks to paltry amounts he paid his quarrymen he was able to keep the horses well shod.

THRALE (Mrs) (1741-1821) . . . born at Plas Bodfel outside Pwllheli. She was proud to be Welsh and corresponded with David Garrick, Oliver Goldsmith, Joshua Reynolds and Samuel Johnson of the so-called 'London elite'. Her first husband was Henry Thrale, a wealthy London brewer. She later married Italian music teacher, Gabriele Piozzi.

THREE DEGREES . . . a recent survey showed that the sea off West Wales is three degrees warmer than at some English resorts.

THREE PEAKS YACHT RACE . . . a gruelling annual event from Barmouth to Fort William in Scotland, first held in 1976. It involves yachting and running up the three highest peaks of Wales, England and Scotland.

TIGER BAY . . . short lived BBC Wales soap opera set in the Cardiff docklands area of the same name. Famous people: Shirley Bassey (docklands area); Nobody really (the TV soap).

TIN PLATE . . . was born in John Hanbury's mill in Pontypool around 1730. Iron was rolled flat instead of being hammered. This meant the end of the German monopoly of iron rolling.

TIN PLATE 2. Worldwide demand for Welsh tinplate meant the opening of the Prince of Wales Dock at Swansea in 1882.

TINTERN ABBEY . . . William Wordsworth wrote his classic *Lines composed a few miles above Tintern Abbey* – that he was a master poet, but there is no doubt his titles left a little to be desired. The abbey was also the source of inspiration for the painter J.M.W. Turner.

TITANIC . . . Harold Lowe, a native of Barmouth in Gwynedd, was the Fifth Officer of the fateful *SS Titanic* and in charge of the (pitifully few) lifeboats on board.

TOBACCO . . . Tomos Prys of Plas Iolyn, Denbs and William Middleton from Chirk (Y Waun) were the first Welshmen to smoke tobacco in public in London.

TOLKIEN (J.R.R.) . . . the South African author of the *Lord of The Rings* found inspiration in the Vale of Clwyd during a short residence there.

TOLL . . . the Skerries Islands (Ynysoedd y Moelrhoniaid) off Anglesey boasted a lighthouse since the 18th century and levied tolls on passing shipping. It was the last lighthouse to be taken over by Trinity House, in 1841.

TOLLGATE . . . the last to charge in Wales was Llanfair Pwllgwyngyll on Anglesey which ceased to charge in 1895.

TONIC SOL-FA . . . the Pwllheli born musician and author, Eleazar Roberts (1825-1912) was a pioneer on tonic sol-fa in Wales. As well as music text books he wrote the novel *Owen Rees* in English, in 1894. Revd Eli Jenkins' words in Dylan Thomas's Under Milk Wood 'Praise God we are a musical nation', and the fact that it is common knowledge that all Welsh people can sing, owes much to tonic sol-fa.

TONYPANDY . . . Viscount Tonypandy was the title bestowed on former Speaker of the House of Commons, George Thomas.

TONYPANDY RIOTS . . . in November 1910 Home Secretary Winston Churchill ordered troops to assist the police when shops were wrecked by striking miners, angry over blackleg labour which affected 12,000 men.

TOSHACK (John) . . . former Welsh footballer who excelled at Liverpool and later dragged Swansea City from the old division four to the top of the then first division. Tosh has been the manager of the mighty Real Madrid on more than one occasion, having earlier spent a single game in charge of his national team

TOUR OPERATOR . . . in 1993 the travel giants Airtours bought the company Aspro for something in the region of £20 million. Aspro had been founded in the back room of a Cardiff docklands grocery shop by Michael Asprou in 1979.

TOURING LITERATURE . . . During the reign of George III (1760-1820) over one hundred books were published about Welsh tours.

TOURIST ATTRACTIONS . . . In the 1970s there were only sixty officially recognised tourist attractions in Wales. Now there are over six hundred.

TOURIST BOARD . . . The Welsh Tourist and Holidays Board (Wales & Monmouth) Ltd was a forerunner of the Wales Tourist Board.

TOWER COLLIERY (Glofa Tŵr) . . . was the last deep mine in Wales. It was so-named because Richard Crawshay erected an observation tower on the land, so that a watchful eye could be kept on the potentially unruly workers at the time of the Chartist unrest, which coincided with the opening of the colliery.

TOY (Humphrey) (died 1575) . . . Carmarthen merchant who paid for the printing of the Welsh translation of the New Testament and Book of Common Prayer.

TRAFFIC LIGHTS . . . a rare species in Wales. Anglesey and Gwynedd have only two permanent sets each. (Note: Pedestrian crossings are not 'traffic' lights.) Indeed, red light districts tend to be features of cities.

TRAINS' GRAVEYARD . . . the metal recyclers Woodhams have an enormous railway siding in Barry – it is a graveyard for steam railway engines.

TRANSPORTER BRIDGE . . . at Newport is one of only three in the world. It was built in 1906 with towers 245 feet (74.5m) high giving a clearance of 177 feet (53m). Middlesbrough and Marseilles boast the other two. It was designed by Arnedin.

TREADMILL . . . Beaumaris Gaol, open to the public as a tourist attraction, has an unique treadmill which provided useful exercise for the prisoners, and presumably helped pump the gaol's water supply to boot.

TREASURE ISLAND . . . Robert Louis Stevenson's book became famous as a direct result of a gushing review in *The Spectator* in 1883 by Welsh born critic Amy Elizabeth Dillwyn (1845-1935). If she had not lauded the yarn, then Long John Silver, The Hispaniola and Captain Flint (and that pesky parrot perpetually pontificating 'pieces of eight') may have been confined to the chum barrel of history.

TRECCO BAY . . . the biggest caravan holiday park in Europe is here, at one of Porthcawl's two beaches.

TRECŴN . . . near Fishguard is 504 acres of fifty-eight underground tunnels in a wooded valley, which were used for bomb storage during WW2.

TREEMENDOUS . . . Thomas Jhones of Hafod Estate near Devil's Bridge, an ambitious landowner (and compulsive tree planter) in the 33 years between 1780 and 1813 planted six million trees as part of his own agrarian revolution.

TREFECCA COLLEGE . . . in Brecon. In 1752 Howel Harris, the Methodist leader, established a self-sufficient relegious community of about one hundred at Trevecca, which became a Methodist college with a printing press.

TREFOR BAND . . . the well-known North Wales brass band took part in the North American Welsh Society's annual singing festival at Wisconsin in 1997.

TREFRIW SPA . . . in the Conwy valley was first used by the Romans.

TRELEW . . . one of the original settlements in Patagonia in 1865; by now it has a population of eighty thousand.

TRE'R CEIRI . . . remains of a prehistoric hill fort on the Rivals mountains (Yr Eifl) on the Llŷn. The name translates as 'the town of giants.'

TRIBES . . . the four main tribes in what is now known as Wales and England at the time of the Roman invasion were the Silures, Ordovices, Deceangli and Demetae.

TRICOLOUR TRIANGULAR BADGE . . . of Urdd Gobaith Cymru was introduced in 1944. The three colours of white, red and green represented Christ, fellow man and Wales in that order, while the motto, which reversed the order, was 'I will be faithful to Wales, to fellow man and to Christ'.

TRIPLE HARP . . . a traditional Welsh instrument that has seen a revival in the country in recent decades. Predating the concert harp, the relatively small sound made by the Triple Harp led to its fall from grace.

TROLLEY BUS . . . the first trolley bus in Wales began running at Aberdare in 1914.

TROLLS . . . contemporary writer A A. *Gill has called the Welsh 'a nation of ugly trolls'. What do you expect from someone who wears a monocle?

TUDORS . . . dynasty of English monarchs including Henrys Vll and Vlll, Queen Mary Tudor and Queen Elizabeth l. The family's ancestors hailed from Penmynydd on the Isle of Anglesey, where they were known as Tudur.

TUDOR (Richard) . . . round-the-world yachtsman from Pwllheli who has twice competed in the Chay Blyth – suggested race, going around the world against the prevailing winds.

TUNNICLIFFE (Charles F) . . . a very accomplished painter who lived at Malltraeth on Anglesey and painted animals and birds. Ynys Môn local authority bought £400,000's worth of his work at auction in 1981 and exhibit them at Oriel Ynys Môn Art Gallery.

TURNPIKE CRASHER . . . David Davies (1812-1874) was a Rebecca Rioter. Known as Dai'r Cantwr. After his trial (for demolishing the turnpike gate at Cydweli in 1843) he was deported to Tasmania. He was involved in skirmishes with the authority on a few occasions, but was pardoned in 1854. There are records of a person known as Dai'r Cantwr selling alms in Wales, which has led to the belief that the convict returned home.

TURPIN (Randolph) . . . the late boxer's wife was from Abergele, where they once owned Gwrych Castle. They later owned a hotel at the summit of Llandudno's Great Orme (Pen y Gogarth). In the 1950s, Turpin was a world class boxer who fought against the great Sugar Ray Robinson.

TV COP . . . Det. Chief Insp. Bain (played by actor Philip Madoc) in the Welsh-based series *A Mind To Kill* has become a universally known sleuth as the series has been sold to sixty or so countries. The original series was also filmed in the Welsh langauge under the title *Yr Heliwr*.

TV WRITER . . . St Tudwal's Island East in Cardigan Bay off Abersoch is owned by comedy scriptwriter Carla Lane who wrote the renowned TV series; *The Liver Birds, Butterflies* and *Bread*.

TWENTY-FIRST CENTURY . . . Wales was one of the last places on earth to welcome the new century. No, not Wales, UK. Wales in Alaska USA. The village is just 55 miles (88km) from Siberia across the Bering Strait, and is home to around two hundred native Inupiat. It was named by Captain Cook, who discovered it in May 1785.

TWIN TOWN . . . acclaimed 1990s film, set and filmed in the Swansea area of south Wales. Regarded by many critics as being the *Welsh Trainspotting*, but only because of the financial input of Andrew MacDonald and Danny Boyle. The *Western Mail* was far from in love with the film. It said; ' . . .a foul mouthed, ill-humoured film which mistakes obnoxious, lawless behaviour for dark humour.'

TWM SIÔN CATI . . . the Welsh equivalent of Robin Hood or a medieval bandit? Discuss.

TWO THOUSAND CLIMBS . . . John Robert climbed Snowdon more than two thousand times and eventually built a hotel (*c.*1887) at the summit.

TŶ – Bingo enthusiasts in Wales don't shout 'Tŷ', they shout 'HOUSE' just like you do. And why is that it is always 'her', who never usually comes to Bingo, who wins the snowball when it crawls over the £100 mark?

TŶ BACH . . . 'the little boys room' in a Welsh abode. Not the bedroom of the youngest progeny but the convenience – if it's convenient or vacant, and not engaged.

TŶ NEWYDD . . . the most popular house name in Wales – the second is Rose Cottage. Did we hear the poetic nature of the Welsh mentioned?

TYLER (Bonnie) . . . Welsh songstress (from Swansea) who first gained fame with the single *Lost in France*. She had a number one in 1983 with *Total Eclispe of the Heart* – one of only a clutch of Welsh artists to achieve the lofty perch at the top of the hit parade.

TŶ UNNOS . . . ancient laws stated that a house built overnight on common land would be considered the legal property of the person who built it. Hastily thrown together shacks would be cobbled together from twilight to dawn, usually built with the help of others. The main consideration was that the *tŷ unnos* (one night house) had to have a functioning chimney. A garden or vegetable plot could be added by measuring the distance of an axe thrown from the centre of the uncompleted dwelling.

TYLWYTH TEG . . . are the fairies.

UGLY . . . Dylan Thomas described his home town (now a city) Swansea as: 'Ugly, lovely town'.

UGLY HOUSE (Tŷ Hyll) . . . on the A5 between Capel Curig and Betws-y-coed is one of the best known surviving examples of the *tai unnos*, shacks built in a single night on common land by a previously landless peasant. *TŶ UNNOS

UKRAINIAN SOCIAL CLUB OF KIEV . . . there is one in Senghenydd.

UNEMPLOYED . . . during the years of depression and slump (1920s and 1930s) Welsh unemployment averaged 27% compared to England's 16% and

Scotland's 18%. However, the hardest hit was Newport (which relied on the steel industry) at the incredibly high rate of 34.7%. This might account for the adage that, when London sneezed, South Wales caught a cold.

UNDERGROUND . . . crippling lung disorders contracted by far too many of our ancestors who worked underground include pneumoconiosis, bronchitis, emphysema and silicosis.

UNDER MILK WOOD . . . radio drama by Dylan Thomas which portrays the lives of the inhabitants of the mythical Welsh seaside town of Llareggub (which when read backwards gives an insight into the mind of the author)!

UNDER SUSPICION . . . powerful dramatic thriller movie of 1992 which was partly filmed at Portmeirion, Gwynedd. The movie starred Liam Neeson.

UNIQUE AWARD . . . Griffith Rhys Jones conducted the five hundred strong South Wales Choral Union (not just a bloody trio, mind you, boyo) which won the chief choral prize at the Crystal Palace (London) in 1872 – a feat which he repeated in 1873. His reward? Not just a medal or gold watch, but a statue in Aberdare – the ultimate accolade!

UNIT OF FREQUENCY . . . most of us know that the SI Unit of frequency is Hertz, named after the German who first transmitted radio waves in the 1880s. However, there is a school of thought that the Unit of frequency should rightly be the Hughes. David Edward Hughes was born in Bala. His family emigrated to the USA when he was seven. He was the first to transmit and receive radio waves in 1879 but failed to get proof. Hughes also invented the teleprinter and became a Professor of Music in Kentucky.

UNITED STATES PRESIDENT . . . in the 1916 US Presidential election, American Welsh Republican candidate, Charles Evans Hughes (from an Anglesey family) was declared the winner on a Times Square electronic sign. It would mean that three of the most important World Leaders at a time of great crisis (WW1) had strong Welsh roots (Lloyd George was PM in the UK and 'Billy' Hughes was running Australia). However, the Times Square sign operators were jumping the gun as the Democrat and incumbent President, Woodrow Wilson, rallied in the run-in and held on to power by polling just over half a million more votes than Evans Hughes.

UNLUCKY FOR SOME . . . the number thirteen? The Sunday Times list of Britain's wealthiest one thousand people shows that only thirteen live (or rather, reside) in Wales.

UPRIGHT BURIAL... in Aberamman, Glamorgan, a certain David Williams was buried upright in 1789 because he wanted to be ready for the Day of Judgement.

URDD GOBAITH CYMRU ... the Welsh youth movement was founded by Ifan ab Owen Edwards (later Sir Ifan) in 1922 as Urdd Gobaith Cymru Fach. It now boasts over sixteen hundred branches and a membership exceeding forty-seven thousand.

URDD NATIONAL EISTEDDFOD . . . Europe's largest youth festival. A seven day event held in May each year, with thirteen thousand finalists including individuals, groups and choirs aged between about 5 – 25. The number of competitors exceeds the competitors of any Olympic games to date.

USK (Afon Wysg) . . . the longest river wholly within Wales at 85 miles (136km) long.

UTGORN CYMRU ... a Merthyr Tudful-based periodical 1840-42.

UTGORN RHYDDID . . . first published in Pwllheli in 1888, it was the brainchild of Lloyd George.

V ... has ceased to be a Welsh letter.

V-SIGN . . . during the Hundred Years War, captured Welsh longbowmen who did so much damage at Crecy, Poitiers and Agincourt, had their first and index fingers – the ones used to draw back the bow – chopped off by their French captors. It became a tradition before a battle that the longbowmen would give the V-sign to show that the deadly digits were in place and ready to wreak havoc amongst the Gallic ranks.

VALE OF RHEIDOL RAILWAY . . . running from Devil's Bridge (Pontarfynach) to Aberystwyth along a 12 mile (19km) track. It opened in 1902 to carry lead and timber from the Rheidol valley to the coast. A narrow gauge line, it became the last steam railway owned by British Rail until privatisation in 1989.

VALENTINE (Lewis) (1893-1986) . . . born Llanddulas, near Colwyn Bay. He was a Baptist Minister who became first President of Plaid Cymru, and in 1929 stood as the party's first parliamentary candidate (standing in

Caernarfonshire he polled only six hundred and nine votes). In 1936 he was one of the 'Penyberth Three' whose symbolic act of arson ended in imprisonment. (*Saunders LEWIS, David John WILLIAMS and PENYBERTH BOMBING SCHOOL)

VALLE CRUCIS (Valley of the Cross) . . . a Cistercian Abbey at the foot of the Horseshoe Pass (Bwlch yr Oernant) near Llangollen. Founded in 1201 by Madog ap Gruffydd Maelor and later taken over by monks from Strata Marcella. In the mid-13th century, fire decimated the building which was lovingly restored.

VALLEY (RAF) . . . the air training base on Anglesey, when in full training mode, sees more landings and take-offs than Heathrow airport.

VALLEYS (The) . . . insulting misassumption of many outsiders who believe that all of Wales consists of slagheaps and valleys, and that we all burst into song at every available opportunity. There are a few of us who don't!

VASECTOMY . . . is one of the possible solutions to the growing goat problem on Llandudno's Great Orme. Unkind as it may seem, it's far pleasanter than shooting the blighters, which is the favourite alternative! The herd is fast approaching 100 in strength – and all are descended form a pair that were presented to Queen Victoria by the Shah of Persia at her coronation in 1837.

VAUGHAN (Henry) . . . the metaphysical poet of Llansantffraid below the Brecon Beacons was known as 'the swan of Usk'.

VAUGHAN (Robert) (1592-1667) . . . collector of the celebrated Hengwrt Manuscripts. Born near Dolgellau.

VAUGHAN-THOMAS (Wynford) (1908-1987) . . . born in Swansea. Immensely popular writer, TV and radio broadcaster, and famous WW2 War Correspondent who was awarded the Croix de Guerre in 1945. In the 1960s he helped launch Harlech Television (later to become HTV).

VAUXHALL . . . David Reilly, who grew up at Trearddur Bay, Anglesey, became managing director and chairman of Vauxhall Motors in 1996.

VEGETARIAN . . . Christine Gwyther, the Welsh National Assembly's Rural Development Secretary (which makes her responsible for the many millions of sheep in the country) prefers paella to prime Welsh lamb as she is is a vegetarian. Her appointment caused considerable consternation, and the only things to be seen actually smiling in the fields of Wales since then are the sheep.

VEHICLE . . . the first motor vehicle to arrive in Wales was a Thorneycroft Steam Van – a 'horseless carriage' weighing two tons. In December 1896 the driver/owner got off in Cardiff to admire his pride and joy, and to give it a little spit and polish. Unfortunately, he had forgotten to apply the brake and the vehicle ran over his foot. His big toe was subsequently amputated.

VELVET UNDERGROUND, The . . . John Cale, one of the 1960s cult rock band 'The Velvet Underground', was born in Garnant in Cwm Aman and grew up in a Welsh-speaking family.

VENTA SILURUM . . . the Roman name for Caerwent.

VICARI (Andrew) . . . while an 11 year old pupil at Neath Grammar school, he won a gold medal for painting at the National Eisteddfod. At 16, he was the youngest ever student at Slade School of Art, London. He was the official artist for the 1999 Rugby World Cup.

VICKERY (Frank) (born 1951) . . . of Blaen-cwm, Rhondda writes popular plays.

VICTORIA (Queen) . . . The longest reigning British monarch only deigned to visit Wales three times in over sixty years. As a princess she visited Llanberis in 1831, she spent one night at Penrhyn Castle, Bangor in 1852, spending the night in a four poster bed made of four tons of Penrhyn Quarry Slate. In 1889 she made a four day visit to the country visiting, among other places, Barmouth.

VICTORIA CROSS . . . Richard Evans, coxswain of the Moelfre Lifeboat in Anglesey was awarded two RNLI Gold Medals (the equivalent of the VC). His exceptional gallantry inspired his crew in rescuing 'Hindlea' in 1959 and Nafisporos in 1966.

VICTORIA CROSS AUCTION . . . The VC awarded to Private Robert Jones for his gallantry in the Anglo-Zulu wars fetched £80,000 at a London auction in 1996.

VICTORIA CROSS WINNERS . . . During WW1, thirty-two VCs of Welsh origin were awarded.

VICTORIAN PIER . . . Colwyn Bay's pier was the last Victorian one of the era to open in Wales, in 1900.

VIKINGS . . . raided Wales to loot churches and monasteries, and to capture slaves to sell at markets in Dublin and Scandinavia.

VINCENT (Tim) . . . the Wrexham-born former presenter of TV's Blue Peter.

VIOLENT CRIMINAL . . . Aberystwyth's Michael Peterson is in his middle forties. He is currently serving life in Wakefield prison. His number is 1314 Bronson. He changed his name by deed-poll to Charles Bronson in 'honour' of the *Deathwish* films featuring the Hollywood actor of the same name. Mr Bronson (the lag) has served over twenty-one years in isolation because of his violent nature.

VIRGIN GLOBAL CHALLENGE . . . the giant hot air balloon used by Richard Branson and co. on their attempt, at non-stop circumnavigation of the world in the 1990s was made with Welsh expertise, at Per Lindstrand's factories in Wrexham and Oswestry.

VISCOUNT RHONDDA . . . David Alfred Thomas (1856-1918) born at Aberdare. An industrialist and politician who became Controller of Food during WW1.

VITRIOL . . . A poet pens twenty-two lines and gets slated. Fair enough. But twenty-two thousand lines of blank verse (which possibly should have been left blank), and all the critic could write was 'there is in the whole barren length of the work scarcely one poetic virtue'. The poem was *Emmanuel* by William Rees (Gwilym Hiraethog) (1802-1883).

VOLCANO . . . Sugar Loaf Mountain above Gilwern is an extinct volcano.

VOMIT (The) . . . a location near Dale, Pembs.

VORDERMAN (Carol) . . . the brainy one on Countdown, and presenter of the National Lottery as well as other TV programmes, was born in Prestatyn. She once worked underground during the building of Electric Mountain in Llanberis (wearing another hat – a safety helmet of course).

VORTIGERN . . . a legendary Celtic king known in Welsh as Gwrtheyrn.

VOTES FOR WOMEN . . . Did not become a reality in the UK until 1929. However, in the Welsh Settlement in Patagonia (Y Wladfa Gymreig), women were granted the right to vote as early as 1865 – first place in the world where equal suffrage was allowed. Hywel Dda's laws respected the rights of women in the 10th century, to be replaced by far less enlightened alien laws.

VOUCHERS . . . Until the Anti Truck Act of 1831 it was not uncommon for industrialists who owned mines or steelworks to pay their workforce in vouchers which they could only use to buy goods from the Truck Shops, which were also owned by the boss. Naturally, the workforce begrudged the inflated price structure in force. The Anti Truck Act was introduced by Sir Benjamin Hall, MP for the Monmouth Boroughs.

VYRNWY . . . the man-made reservoir Llyn Efyrnwy feeds Liverpool with 350 million gallons (1592 million litres) of water a day. Built between 1881-1890, contractors had to drown the village of Llanwddyn. *DROWNED VILLAGES. The dam is 144 feet (43m) high and has a perimeter of around 14 miles (22km). It is Wales' largest artificial lake.

W I . . . the Women's Institute began in Canada in 1897 and the first branch in the UK met at Llanfair Pwllgwyngyll, Anglesey in 1915.

WAENAFON . . . at 1,400 feet (420m) is the highest railway station in Wales and England (if you omit the one at the top of Snowdon).

WAREHOUSE . . . sportswear manufacturer Umbro International has one of Europe's biggest warehouses at Deeside, it measures 330,000 square feet (30,000sq.m) which is about 5 football pitches (which are also, no doubt, filled by Umbro wearing soccer players.)

WAILS . . . the Prince of Wails was 1950s pop star, Johnny Ray.

WALES BRAND IMAGE . . . the stereotypical Welshman has a coal-blackened face, sings in small groups on the return from the pit, calls everyone *boyo* or *butty*, mutters 'indeed to goodness', attends chapel, watches rugby and molests sheep.

WALES TOURIST BOARD . . . Quango whose task is 'moulding the image of Wales as a tourist destination'. In the late 1990s, they appointed a London-based agency to conceive and design their latest campaign. The company, FCA, were handed a £5million budget over a three year period, and used a

London-based photographer (Alan McPhail – an excellent landscape photographer, mind you) to take the snaps. To be fair, the WTB did use weather girl Sian Lloyd's real voice, and not that of a London-based mimic.

WALLACE Alfred Russel (1823-1913) . . . born Usk. Famous naturalist who worked with Charles Darwin. In 1870 he wrote *Contributions to the Theory of Natural Selection*.

WAGS . . . the Welsh American Genealogical Society was formed in 1990 and now has eight hundred members.

WALTER (Lucy) (1630-1658) . . . the west Wales-bred mistress of Charles II, who bore him a son, James, in Rotterdam in 1649. Arrested as a spy in 1656 and sent to the Tower of London. Later released and ordered to be deported, she died in Paris. Meanwhile Charles, who acknowledged paternity of James, had left the child in the care of his mother, Henrietta Maria (widow of Charles 1). James later became Duke of Monmouth. Speculation was rife that Charles II had actually married Lucy Walter, which would have entitled James to succeed to the throne. But Charles II was succeeded by his brother, James II.

WAR DEAD . . . during WW1 and WW2, the town of Caernarfon in Gwynedd suffered greater losses per head of population than any other Welsh town.

WAR TIME COVER UP . . . mystery surrounds the sinking of *The Endeavour* a top-secret landing craft off Milford Haven on Easter Sunday, 1943. There were seventy-nine fatalities and only three survivors. In 100 mph (160kph) winds the St David's lifeboat was not called for six hours. Why?

WATER . . . Welsh Spring Water is now better known than Welsh Spring Lamb.

WATER WHEEL . . . Aberdulais Falls, now managed by the National Trust, is the site of Europe's largest electricity-generating water wheel.

WATERFALLS . . . Wales has a plethora of these – so many in fact that twenty-two are not even marked on the OS Map (1:50,000 series). Pistyll-y-llyn on the old Powys/Dyfed border is a waterfall with a 240 feet (72m) drop. Pistyll Rhaeadr on the old Powys/Clwyd border is slightly smaller with a 235 feet drop.

WATKIN PATH . . . one of four paths up Snowdon, named after the rich industrialist Sir Edward Watkin who once started a tunnel between England and France. One mile (1.6km) was dug at each end before the government put a stop to it by a special act of parliament.

WEATHER . . . the warmer summers and milder winters in Wales are helping our grape growers – thirty different wines are produced in the country.

WEDDINGS . . . in Welsh have been allowed in Anglican churches since 1837.

WELCH PIETY . . . the annual report on the great success of the 18th Circulating Schools of Gruffudd Jones, detailing the number of schools, sessions, pupils, donations and so on. It was read even in Russia by Empress Catherine the Great.

WELCOME . . . in Welsh is *Croeso*.

WELLS . . . water from St Gwenfaen's well near Rhoscolyn on Anglesey reputedly cured mental illness; St Non's well in St Davids cured eye ailments and crippled limbs; the well of St Peris in Snowdonia was a multi-purpose panacea; and water from Ffynnon Fyw near Mynytho on the Llŷn Peninsula cured blindness.

WELSH . . . is one of the oldest languages in Europe. It is called *Cymraeg* in Welsh, and comes from the same group of Celtic languages as Breton and Cornish. All three ultimately came from the ancient *Brythonic* language, and Cymraeg had been formed sufficiently to be recognized as such as early as the 6th century.

WELSH AMERICAN HERITAGE MUSEUM . . . was established at Oakhill, Ohio in 1971.

WELSH BISHOP . . . Joshua Hughes was Welsh. He was a bishop. He was a Welsh speaker. So what? When appointed Bishop of St Asaph in 1870 he became Wales' first Welsh-speaking bishop since 1714. In the face of such appalling neglect, there's little wonder that Methodism flourished in this fertile soil!

WELSH BLACK . . . hardy breed of cattle.

WELSH BOOK . . . the first Welsh book to be published in America was *Annerch i'r Cymru* by Ellis Pugh (1656-1718) in 1721.

WELSH DEVELOPMENT AGENCY . . . was established in 1976, and has been a very successful Quango.

WELSH DRAGON . . . an emblem of Wales along the lines of the Scottish Lion rampant. The dragon appeared in the crest of King Arthur. Owain Glyndŵr had a golden dragon on a white background on his banner of 1401. The Welsh dragon flag received royal recognition in 1959 when the Queen give it official status.

WELSH DICTIONARY . . . William Gambold (1672-1728) worked tirelessly on producing a Welsh dictionary between 1707-1722 but, due to lack of finance, his work was not published. The manuscripts are preserved at the National Library in Aberystwyth.

WELSH ENCYCLOPEDIA . . . Thomas Gee's Welsh encyclopedia *Y Gwyddoniadur Cymreig* was produced in monthly parts of ten volumes over a period of twenty-five years (1854-1879) and was a significant lifebelt in preserving the Welsh language.

WELSH EXILES . . . the first Welsh exiles society in London was founded in 1715. It was called *The Society of Ancient Britons*.

WELSH GRAND COMMITTEE . . . 1960 saw the birth of the the Welsh Grand Committee. With a grand sounding name it comprised Welsh MPs who met, as the name suggests, as a committee to consider specifically Welsh matters. Forty years ago this was a grand step forward.

WELSH GUARDS MARCH MUSIC . . . 'Codiad Yr Ehedydd' (The Rise of the Lark) is the regimental march music of the Welsh Guards and was composed by Dafydd y Garreg Wen (Dafydd Owen 1720-1749) who was a famous harpist, poet and, naturally, composer. He hailed from Morfa Bychan near Porthmadog in Gwynedd.

WELSH JUDGES . . . John James Hughes (1842-1875) was an Anglesey born journalist who campaigned for the appointment of county court judges who had a knowledge of the Welsh language.

WELSH HIGHLAND RAILWAY . . . one of the Little Trains of Wales which originally ran from Porthmadog to Dinas (Caernarfon), a range of 21^1/$_2$ miles (34km), carrying slate. It was the longest narrow gauge railway in Wales and opened in 1922 and closed in 1937. Transport Minister John Prescott controversially gave the go-ahead to plans to restore and re-open the line during 1999.

WELSH LADY . . . the traditional red cloak, tall-black stovepipe hat and shawl etc. This was created by Augusta Waddington Hall (1802-1896) (the wife of Sir Benjamin Hall of 'Big Ben' fame). She arranged for hordes of her servants and others to parade in the uniform at eisteddfodau etc held at Llanofer near Abergavenny (Y Fenni).

WELSH MONEY . . . In 1969 Richard Williams of Llandudno made history when he issued Welsh-language paper money i.e. currency notes in the name of Prif Drysorfa Cymru Ltd. Not amused, the government noted his action and stopped him in mid-print. Notes that beat the ban are collectors' items.

WELSH NIGHTINGALE . . . Edith Wynne (1842-1897) was born at Northop and became the first Welsh singer to win acclaim in America, where they dubbed her *The Welsh Nightingale*.

WELSH NOT . . . in the 19th century, educationalists decided that the Welsh language should be eradicated and the *Welsh Not* sign was implemented. Any pupil overheard speaking his mother tongue would have to wear a slate or wooden sign around his neck. The *Welsh Not* would then be handed on to the next pupil caught 'offending'. At the end of the school day the person left wearing the sign would be treated to a dose of corporal punishment.

WELSH OFFICE . . . Established in 1964 under the Labour government of Harold Wilson. Initially the Welsh Office powers were limited to administering housing, roads and local government but, within ten years, employment, education and industry in the principality came under the Welsh Office umbrella. The Labour government of 1974-79 then added higher education (except the University of Wales), agriculture and fisheries. In May 1999 the newly elected Welsh Assembly assumed responsibility for the budget in Wales.

WELSH OSCAR WINNERS . . . Ray Milland (*Lost Weekend*, 1945 Best Actor), Hugh Griffith (*Ben Hur*, 1959 Best Supporting Actor), Jack Howells who won for Best Short Documentary for the film *Dylan* in 1962, and Sir Anthony Hopkins (*Silence of the Lambs*, 1991 Best Actor) are the only Welsh winners.

WELSH OVERSEAS SOCIETIES . . . are flourishing, especially in America. Four of the best known are the Welsh National Gymanfa Ganu Association,

St David's Welsh Society of Nebraska, Welsh Women's Club of the Milwaukee Area, and the Gulf Coast Welsh Society of Florida.

WELSHPOOL (Y Trallwng) . . . not unlike other border towns, Welshpool's nationality was debated heatedly. Known to many as the 'Gateway to Wales', Lloyd George called the town the 'Gates of paradise'. This was logical as he referred to Wales as the 'Garden of Eden'.

WELSH PREFIXES . . . author Thornton B Edwards wrote *Welsh Nots, Welsh Notes and Welsh Nuts* which lists around fourteen hundred phrases beginning with the word 'Welsh' and gives a definition of the phrase.

WELSH RAREBIT . . . cheese on toast. Why this simple dish should carry the name is a mystery. Does the name stem from a derogatory source?

WELSH SOAP . . . a free print of the painting 'Salem' was offered with every half stone of Sunlight soap to try and boost sales. The original watercolour was owned by Lord Leverhulme.

WELSH SPORTS PERSONALITY OF THE YEAR . . . presented every year since 1954.

WELSH SPRINGER SPANIELS . . . despite its ancient lineage the *Colwyn*, as it was called in early Welsh, had to wait until 1902 for a distinctive classifications from the kennel club.

WELSH TERROR . . . John Jones (1854-1913) was also known as Coch Bach y Bala and Jac Llanfor. He was a petty thief and gaol-breaker and a folk hero. He was known in England as 'the little Welsh terror' or 'the little Turpin'.

WELSH TRACT . . . land to the north-west of Philadelphia. William Penn promised a stretch of land to Welsh Quaker immigrants who hoped for an all Welsh settlement, but Penn, him speak with forked tongue. In 1682 the first Welsh immigrants arrived including Thomas Lloyd of Dolobran (a later Deputy Governor of Pennsylvania), Rowland Ellis of Bryn Mawr, Dolgellau and Ellis Pugh.

WELSH WOMEN . . . in the 1997 *International Who's Who of Women* of the five and a half thousand entries, twenty of them were Welsh. Included in the roll of honour were Shirley Bassey, Jan Morris, Sian Philips and politicians Ann Clwyd and Joan Ruddock.

WESLEYAN MAGAZINE . . . 'Yr Eurgrawn Wesleyaidd' (1809-1983) was the longest running Wesleyan periodical..

WEST CENTRAL BRITAIN . . . if Henry VIII's Act of Union had been completely successful, Wales would have been named something like West Central Britain.

WE'LL KEEP A WELCOME . . . the 1949 song popularised by the Lyrian Singers on radio in 'Welsh Rarebit', and latterly by Harry Secombe.

WHALES . . . are currently being saved by Greenpeace.

WHIPROUND . . . Dr Joseph Parry (1841-1903) born Merthyr Tudful in 1841 and his family emigrated to Pennsylvania when he was thirteen. His compositions for the National Eisteddfod were so well received that his fans collected money to repatriate him to study at the Royal Academy of Music in London. In 1872 he was appointed the first professor of music at the newly opened University of Aberystwyth. He wrote many hymns, songs, an opera and oratorios.

WHISKY . . . Richard John Lloyd Price of Bala began marketing Welsh whisky at the end of the 19th century. His demand for perfection was his downfall and sadly, his still stalled because he refused to blend his grains. After fifteen years the venture failed.

WHISPERING GRASS . . . a 1975 chart topper for Welsh actor Windsor Davies and his side-kick Don Estelle who performed the song 'in character' from the popular TV series, 'It Ain't 'Alf Hot Mum'.

WHISTLER (Rex) . . . (1905-44) this Welsh guardsman was a decorator, painter and stage designer at Covent Garden and Saddler's Wells. A well known mural by him hangs at Plas Newydd on Anglesey. Whistler was killed in Normandy in 1944.

WHITEHOUSE (Paul) . . . the TV star comedian was born in Ferndale. He has appeared in *Harry Enfield & Chums* and *The Fast Show*.

WHITEWATER . . . Afon Tryweryn has a renowned, very challenging, white-water canoe slalom course.

WHITLAND (Hendy-gwyn) . . . in Dyfed was the venue where Hywel Dda held an assembly to establish a unified Code of Laws of Wales in the 10th century.

WHO DARES WINS . . . the 1982 film, starring Lewis Collins as an SAS soldier, was filmed on location in Wales.

WHO'S A PRETTY BOYO? . . . In August 1999, RSPCA officers in Kent captured a talking cockatiel, but were unable to understand a word he said because of his Welsh accent.

WHO'S WHO . . . In the 1997 edition of 'International Who's Who' out of twenty thousand people featured, only twenty-two were Welsh.

WIGLEY (Dafydd) . . . Plaid Cymru MP for Caernarfon who was first elected in February 1974. He has increased his majority with every poll since then.

WIG MAKING . . . in the 18th century, Abergavenny was a renowned centre for making hairpieces.

WIL BOOTS . . . William Williams (1805-1861) a big boot boy at a Llanberis hotel, was a noted guide who came to be called 'the Botanical Guide' as he knew the location of rare and unique species in the Snowdon area.

WILDE (Jimmy) (1894-1970) . . . born in Llanfabon. The flyweight champion of the world who weighed only $6^1/2$ stone is regarded by many as the greatest boxer ever. Known variously as the 'Tylerstown Terror' and 'the ghost with a hammer in his hand'. He fought eight hundred and sixty-four bouts in booths and professional fights.

WILLIAM WEBB ELLIS CUP . . . the solid gold Rugby World Cup trophy is named after the inventor of the game. The current proud holders are Australia.

WILLIAMS (David John) (1885-1970) . . . affectionately known as 'D.J.' throughout Wales, he was born at Rhydcymerau, Carms. and became a writer and founding member of Plaid Cymru. After his role in a symbolic act of arson in 1936 he spent nine months in Wormwood Scrubs prison. (*Saunders LEWIS, PENYBERTH BOMBING SCHOOL and Lewis VALENTINE)

WILLIAMS (Emlyn) . . . born near Fflint, North Wales in 1905. He was a playwright and actor most famous for *The Corn Is Green* and *Night Must Fall*.

One of his early proteges was Richard Burton. Williams died in 1987 and has a theatre named in his honour at Theatr Clwyd in Mold (Yr Wyddrug).

WILLIAMS (Sir John) . . . of Gwynfe, Carms. bought the Peniarth Collection of ancient writings (including the Hengwrt Manuscripts) in 1905. He later donated them to the National Library of Wales on the condition that the library was sited in Aberystwyth and not Cardiff.

WILLIAMS (John Owen) (1892-1973) . . . of Bethesda, Gwynedd. A children's writer who, in collaboration with Jennie Thomas, wrote *Llyfr Mawr Y Plant* in the 1930s, which first appeared at the time of a drought in Welsh literature for children.

WILLIAMS (John Peter Rhys) . . . rugby giant with fifty-five caps who is universally known as JPR. He twice toured with the British Lions in the 1970s 'golden age' of Welsh rugby. Incidentally, he was Welsh junior Tennis Champion and, in 1966, won Junior Wimbledon.

WILLIAMS (Iris) . . . sang the hit song *He Was Beautiful (Cavatina)* in the late 1970s. The song was the theme from the classic movie *The Deerhunter* and was also a hit for John Williams (no relation) and The Shadows.

WILLIAMS (Kyffin) (born 1918) . . . at Llangefni, Ynys Môn. An author and painter of North Wales landscapes. He was the first Welsh painter to receive a knighthood (in 1980).

WILLIAMS (William) (1717-1791) (Pantycelyn) . . . born Llanfair-ar-y-bryn, Carms. Wrote eight hundred hymns, eighty books and pamphlets, was an evangelical preacher and a Methodist leader. One of the three leaders of the Great Awakening (Methodist movement in Wales).

WILLIAMS ELLIS (Sir Clough) . . . the far-sighted creator of the fantasy village of Portmeirion.

WILLOW . . . movie of 1988 which was filmed near Llanberis, Gwynedd. The film was one of the first to star Van Kilmer who went on the play Batman. His co-star was his future wife, British actress Joanne Whalley.

WILLY NILLY . . . was the postman in Dylan Thomas' *Under Milk Wood* whose wife was adept at steaming open interesting looking letters.

WILSON (Richard) 1714-1782 . . . very influential landscape painter born in Montgomeryshire. His work, which he finely honed in Italy, was inspirational for most of the later British landscape painters. He was librarian to the Royal Academy and died at Llanberis, Snowdonia.

WINDMILL . . . Anglesey's last working windmill at Llynon, Llanddeusant ceased to operate in 1918. It had been built in 1779 at a cost of £529-11-0. It was returned to full working order by Ynys Môn Council and opened to the public in May 1984.

WINE . . . vineyards are a growth industry in Wales (having hidden away since their introduction by the Romans 2000 years ago). The kind climate obviously helps.

WINNER (Sir Michael) . . . film-director-cum-food-critic said of recent sojourns in Wales ' . . . the two weekends I spent in Wales were two of the most enjoyable periods of my life . . . and the people were terrific'. After you with the salt, Mike.

WINSTONE (Howard) . . . (born Merthyr Tudful 1939). Angelo Dundee, Muhammed Ali's manager, described Winstone as 'the most brilliant boxer I have seen'. In 1969 he defeated the Mexican, Vincente Salvidar, to become World Featherweight Champion. He remains one of only two people to win the Welsh Sports Personality of the Year award three times.

WLPAN METHOD . . . this type of teaching Welsh to beginners has been described as total immersion and is based on Hebrew courses. Wlpan is Hebrew for 'studio'.

WOLF WHISTLE . . . in 1993 attractive Cardiff receptionist Alexa Hamley gained her fifteen minutes of fame after being wolf whistled at in Cardiff Crown Court. The judge did not take kindly to Paul Powell's emission from the public gallery, and promptly jailed him for a fortnight for contempt of court. Alexa was subsequently signed by a modelling agency and featured in a fashion shoot for *The Sun* newspaper, before her quarter of an hour expired.

WOMEN YACHT CREW . . . in 1989-90 Tracey Edwards (born 1962) of Swansea, and her all-female crew, finished second in the Whitbread round the world race and set the then third fastest Atlantic crossing of all time.

WONDERBRAS . . . these assets to a girl's assets were first produced at the

Gossard factory in Blackwood, Gwent. Perhaps then, in those famous advertising posters, Eva Hertzigova should have been saying 'Hello Boyos'.

WOOD (family of Abram) . . . an 18th Century tribe of Welsh gypsies who produced a line of remarkable harpists. Abram himself (died 1799) was reputed to have been one hundred years old when he died, and was an accomplished player of the fiddler. The parish register of Llwyngwril in Gwynedd records his death thus: 'Abram Woods, a travelling Egyptian.' He is buried in the graveyard of Llangelynnin church, near Llwyngwril, which is as good a place as any to end a long journey.

WOOLER (Wilf) . . . multi-talented all round North Walian sportsman. A Rugby and squash international who was also a gifted tennis player, he also appeared for Cardiff City and captained Glamorgan to the County Championship in cricket. And all this over a twenty year period.

WOOSNAM (Ian) . . . diminutive world class golfer who won the US Masters in August 1991.

WORDSWORTH . . . the wordsmith was let down by the Muse when he referred to Plas Newydd (the home of the *Ladies of Llangollen) as a 'low roof'd cot'. The short poem received short shrift and he was never given the chance to duck across their threshold again.

WORLD WAR 1 . . . two hundred and eighty thousand Welsh people served in the armed forces (1 in 8 of the population). Thirty-five thousand of them died (including those who served with the Merchant Navy).

WW1 SONG . . . 'Pack Up Your Troubles in Your Old Kit Bag' was written by Felix Powell of St Asaph (born 1878).

WW2 PLANE CRASHES . . . The area around Llyn Dulyn in Snowdonia saw twenty plane crashes during the second world war.

WOMAN HANGED . . . Ruth Ellis, the last woman to be hanged in the UK, was born in Colwyn Bay. Charged and found guilty of the murder of her lover, David Blakely, Ruth Ellis went to the gallows in July 1955 at the age of 28.

WORMS' HEAD . . . just off the mainland tip of the Gower Peninsua.

WORMWOOD SCRUBS . . . *Beddau'r Byw* is a series of essays by Lewis Valentine recounting his prison days spent at His Majesty's Prison Wormwood Scrubs in 1936.

WRECKERS . . . Life boats and lighthouses in coastal Wales helped shipping, whilst wreckers did not. Many were hanged for luring ships.

WREXHAM F.C. . . . the journalist father of hell-raising actor Oliver Reed (RIP) was, for some inexplicable reason, a supporter of Wrexham football club, and even left a legacy in his will in the club's favour.

WREXHAM LAGER . . . was sold on ships of the White Star Line. The prestigious supply contract was signed in 1904 and passengers on the Titanic were able to enjoy a pint or two – well, any drink without ice!

WRONGLY CONVICTED . . . Timothy Evans of Merthyr Vale was hanged for the murder of his wife and daughter in 1950. It was later discovered that the murders had been carried out by John Christie, who was himself hanged for these and several other murders. The Evans family had lodged with Christie at 10 Rillington Place, London. Timothy Evans was posthumously pardoned in 1966.

WYTHNOS . . . the Welsh word for week.

XANADU . . . 'The Xanadu of Wales' is one description often applied to the village of Portmeirion.

XMAS . . . Christmas in Welsh is *Nadolig*.

Y LLEWOD . . . the Welsh language equivalent of the English *Famous Five*. Enid Blyton's creations viz. Julian, Dick, Anne, Georgina and Timmy the dog would get into scrapes and have heaps of fun whilst on their hols from boarding school at Kirrin Cottage with Uncle Quentin and Aunt Fanny, foiling smugglers and crooks and kidnappers and their ilk, whilst enjoying cream cakes and lashings of ginger beer. *Y Llewod* – by Dafydd Parri of Rowen, Conwy – are Llinos, Einion, Wyn, Orig and Delyth. Oh, and their dog, Smwt. They live in the fictitious Gwynedd village of Moelfryn and are far more up to date, preferring to listen to CDs than have picnics. *Y Llewod* first appeared in the 1970s.

YACHT CLUB . . . the first in Wales was the Royal Anglesey Yacht Club, founded in 1802 at Beaumaris.

YALE UNIVERSITY . . . one of the famous USA Ivy League Colleges has early Welsh connections in that the college's benefactor was Elihu Yale, who was born in Boston in 1648 to a Wrexham family who had emigrated. A replica of Wrexham Parish Curch tower is incorporated into the structure of the University.

YANKS . . . the 1979 film starring Richard Gere was partly shot in Llandudno, Conwy.

YATES (Jess) . . . Organist on the now-defunct religious TV programme *Stars of Sunday*, once lived near Llandudno.

YATES (Paula) . . . erstwhile wife of Sir Bob Geldof, lover of the late Michael Hutchence, mother of Fifi Trixibelle, Peaches, Pixie and Heavenly Hiraani Tiger Lily, former TV presenter and rock journalist, grew up in the village of Rowen in the Conwy Valley.

YELLOW WHITLOW GRASS (*Draba oides*) is found only in Gower.

YEW TREE . . . in Llangernyw churchyard stands a tree said to date back four thousand one hundred years. It is one of the oldest living things on the planet.

YFORY . . . is tomorrow in Welsh.

YNYSMEUDWY POTTERY . . . as recently as 1998 experts would not have flinched to learn that a single dinner plate carrying the YMP hallmark could fetch as much as £1,000. Named after the village of Ynysmeudwy near Pontardawe, the YMP closed in 1877 after just twenty-eight years in production.

YORATH (Gabby) . . . TV sports presenter and newspaper columnist, daughter of Terry.

YORATH (Terry) . . . Former footballer and ex-manager of the Wales national team. For most of his playing career he was a valued squad member of Don Revie's Leeds United and captained his country. Later management forrays saw him appointed as coach of the Lebanese national side.

YOUNG (Thomas) (1507-1568) . . . archbishop of York. Born in Pembrokeshire. Included here simply because he is alphabetically the last listed member of the cloth in the *Dictionary of Welsh Biography*. Literally hundreds of other Baptist ministers, Congregationalists, Wesleyans, Methodists, Catholics, and Mormons are featured, but it is Thomas Young who brings the whole religious litany to a merciful close.

YOUNGEST MOTHER OF TWINS . . . On April 26, 1998 fifteen year old Nicola Doherty of Blaen Rhondda became the youngest mother of twins in Britain.

YR ETIFEDDIAETH (The Heritage) . . . a renowned film of 1949 telling the story of Freddie Grant, a black Liverpudlian, evacuated to Welsh Wales during WW2.

YUN (Joseph) . . . is the head of the Lucky Goldstar electronics company's European operations.

YSBYTY . . . Welsh for hospital.

YSBYTY IFAN . . . a 12th century hospice created by the Knights of St John of Jerusalem. As a watering hole between England and Bardsey Island (Ynys Enlli) this village enjoyed legal exemption and attracted hordes of outlaws and brigands for about four centuries until it was crushed by the Tudors.

YSGOL – Welsh for school – that's a bit of an education for you.

YSGOL GYMRAEG LLUNDAIN . . . The London Welsh Primary School is where exiled parents can choose to send their issue in order to retain their national identity. Established in 1958, some forty years on the school was attended by fourteen pupils who were taught by one teacher. The pupils are taught through the medium of Welsh until the age of eight when they are then taught bilingually. The cost of sending a child there is around £450 per term.

Y WLADFA (Patagonia) . . . In 1865 *The Mimosa* sailed from Liverpoool to Patagonia in southern Argentina, carrying one hundred and fifty-three Welsh settlers to their new colony. Michael D. Jones of Bala financed the venture. Not quite a howling wilderness, the conditions were far from ideal and the early settlers were provided with food by the Argentinian government while the native Indian tribe, the Tuelche, taught them the art of hunting. Surviving the early hardships, Y Wladfa became a distinctly Welsh settlement where the language flourished alongside Spanish. Schools and chapels, estieddfodau, bank notes, text books and newspapers all in Welsh helped to draw new waves of settlers, who ensured the success of Y Wladfa. The centenary celebrations in 1965 fostered revived intercourse between Wales and Patagonia, and a greater awareness of the strength of spirit of the settlers in their pioneering venture into virgin territory.

ZEPPELIN . . . The only German Zeppelin bomb to land in Wales during WW1 hit Buttington in Powys in 1916.

ZETA-JONES (Catherine) . . . from Mayals, Swansea. The actress rose to fame after appearing as Marietta Larkin in the early 1990s TV series, *Darling Buds of May*. Later in the decade she went to the USA and took Hollywood by storm.

ZINC BATH . . . Before the advent of pit-head baths, no self-respecting coal miner would dash off to choir practice without wallowing in a zinc bath in front of a real coal fire. Most zinc baths were basic, bubble-free, handle-less, non-whirlpool types, and were also plug and tap-free.

ZOOLOGIST . . . Thomas Pennant was much more than a travel writer. Darwin's library on HMS Beagle contained some of Pennant's scientific works. In 1761 he was elected a Fellow of the Royal Society.

ZULU WARS . . . The film *Zulu* starring Sir Stanley Baker has been described as 'the great Welsh western.' In 1999 it was voted the thirty-first best British made film of all time. Baker also co-produced the film about the legendary victory at Rorke's Drift in 1879 when a handful of South Wales Borderers sang *Men of Harlech* in their gallant defence against impossible odds. The few decimated four thousand Zulu warriors and were awarded eleven Victoria Crosses.